ADVANCE PRAISE FOR
SHIRTS & SKIN

"Tim Miller is preeminent as a queer artist onstage. *Shirts & Skin* explains why and how. It's an outstanding book by a performer. He manages to perform in print and with the same sexiness as he does onstage."
—SIR IAN MCKELLEN

"In these beautifully crafted pieces, Miller's self-examination reminds us that the personal is not only political but also fabulous."
—HOLLY HUGHES, AUTHOR OF *CLIT NOTES*

"Tim Miller has been at the heart of things, giving voice to what matters most, for the entirety of his career. *Shirts & Skin* is an extraordinary fusion of history, observation, politics, and a kind of shamanism."
—TONY KUSHNER, AUTHOR OF *ANGELS IN AMERICA*

"*Shirts & Skin* should be stored in a time capsule so that future generations will know the exact taste and feel of queer life in the last quarter of the twentieth century. Tim Miller examines his navel and turns it into art."
—MARTIN SHERMAN, AUTHOR OF *BENT*,
ALIVE & KICKING, AND *A MADHOUSE IN GOA*

"Tim Miller is afraid of neither the sensuality of the moment nor of emotion, laying his chest bare to all that has happened to and around him for the past twenty-odd years, willing to embrace the amazing and to weep for the tragic. He's like some jolly naked Buddhist monk, examining the irony and sadness of life, turning it over and chuckling."
—ERIC BOGOSIAN, AUTHOR OF *TALK RADIO* AND *SUBURBIA*

"*Shirts & Skin* captures the essence of Miller's pioneering performances: his unbridled passion for life and loving, his cosmic ability to convey the deepest of emotions with the lightest touch. All are as powerful and moving on paper as they are in person."
—JILL DOLAN, EXECUTIVE DIRECTOR,
NEW YORK CENTER FOR LESBIAN AND GAY STUDIES

"Like his performance work, Tim Miller's writings are always daring, irreverent, direct, and human. Every time I read him, I understand my time and place a bit more."
—GUILLERMO GOMEZ-PENA, AUT

D0709162

SHIRTS & SKIN
TIM MILLER

alyson
books

LOS ANGELES • NEW YORK

Manufactured in the United States of America.
Printed on acid-free paper.

This trade paperback original is published by Alyson Publications Inc.,
P.O. Box 4371, Los Angeles, California 90078-4371.
Distribution in the United Kingdom by Turnaround Publisher Services Ltd.,
Unit 3 Olympia Trading Estate, Coburg Road, Wood Green,
London N22 6TZ, England.

First edition: October 1997

01 00 99 98 97   10 9 8 7 6 5 4 3

ISBN 1-55583-425-6

Library of Congress Cataloging-in-Publication Data
Miller, Tim (Timothy George), 1958–
   Shirts & skin / by Tim Miller.
   ISBN 1-55583-425-6
   I. Title.
PS3563.I4214545S47 1997
813'.54—dc21   97-26917 CIP

Credits
An earlier version of "Tar Pit Heart" appeared in *His: Brilliant New Fiction by Gay Writers*, edited by Robert Drake and Terry Wolverton (Faber & Faber, 1995)
An earlier version of "How to Grow Fuit" appeared in *Boys Like Us: Gay Writers Tell Their Coming Out Stories*, edited by Patrick Merla (Avon, 1996)
An earlier version of "The Maw of Death" appeared in *Out of Character: Rants, Raves, and Monologues From Today's Top Performance Artists*, edited by Mark Russell (Bantam, 1996)

Photos
Cover (from *Naked Breath* [1994]): Dona Ann McAdams
"I Am Born" (from *Postwar* [1982]): Paula Court
"Fräulein Rodriguez" (family photo [1963]): courtesy the author
"Tar Pit Heart" (from *My Queer Body* [1992]): Chuck Stallard
"How to Grow Fuit" (from *Fruit Cocktail* [1996]): John Ellis
"I Walk Down Hollywood Boulevard" (from *Buddy Systems* [1985]): Dona Ann McAdams
"Spilt Milk" (from *Some Golden States* [1987]): Dona Ann McAdams
"Good With Wood" (author with John Bernd; from *Live Boys* [1981]): Gene Bagnato
"The Maw of Death" (author with John Bernd; from *Live Boys*): Gene Bagnato
"A Buddy System" (author with Doug Sadownick; from *Buddy Systems*): John Warner
"A Stretch Mark" (from ACT UP demonstration [1989]): Chuck Stallard
"Breathing Naked" (author with Steven Craig; from *Naked Breath*): Dona Ann McAdams
"Shirts & Skin" (author with Alistair McCartney; from *Carnal Garage* [1997]): Mary Milelzcik

FOR DOUG SADOWNICK

CONTENTS

ACKNOWLEDGMENTS

I AM GRATEFUL for the encouragement I have received from many quarters in writing *Shirts & Skin*. The life of this story (as well as the story of my life so far) is a collaboration — a collaboration between me and the men I've loved, between me and the audiences in the theaters I've told these tales in, between me and my community, and between me and my memory. In a way, I have written this book in public over the past dozen years. Hundreds of performances, public demonstrations, discussions with editors, and intimate spaces with friends and lovers have left their mark on the telling. I have grown up in a community of writers and performers in Los Angeles and New York. The inspiration I have received from fellow artists has been crucial food for me over the years.

I extend special thanks to Dona Ann McAdams, Linda Burnham, Steve Durland, Holly Hughes, Michael Kearns, Annie Sprinkle, Hae Kyung Lee, Joan Hotchkis, Guillermo Gómez-Peña, Mary Milelzcik, Leo Garcia, David Schweizer, Ian McKellen, Danielle Brazell, Lillian Kiesler, Maryette Charlton, Jane Smith, Andrew Gouldh, Irit Rogoff, Michael Lassell, Chuck Stallard, Paula Court, John Ellis, Sue Dakin, Dan Kwong, Hung Nguyen, and everyone at Highways Performance Space in Santa Monica, California, and at the gay men's performance workshops I have led there since 1990. I also offer a special thanks to my family, who have encouraged all my creative work over the years.

This book would not exist without the support many theaters and arts organizations have given me throughout my career as a performing artist. Without their presentations of my work, I would never have deepened and developed my voice as a writer. I also would not have been able to pay my rent. I want to thank a few that have presented my performance pieces many times over the years, even during the time of the National Endowment for the Arts defundings, when presenting me sometimes got them in trouble with their own local right-wing watchdogs. These presenters welcomed me to their communities many times and are a courageous bunch, often taking large amounts of flak and financing things out of their own checkbooks.

I want to offer my gratitude to Mark Russell at PS 122 in New York; Howie Baggadonutz in Portland, Oregon; Will K. Wilkins of Real Art Ways in Hartford, Connecticut; Wayne Hazard of Dancers' Group in San Francisco; Joan Lipkin of That Uppity Theater Company in St. Louis; Lois Keidan of the Institute of Contemporary Art in London; Billy Ehret in Philadelphia; Legion Arts in Cedar Rapids, Iowa; Jordan Peimer; Donald Montwill at Josie's in San Francisco; Ken Foster at the University of Arizona; Patrick Scully in Minneapolis; John Killacky; Abe Ryebeck at the Theater Offensive in Boston; Vicki Wolf and Lynn Schuette at Sushi in San Diego; Michael Dixon and Jeff Rodgers of Actors Theater in Louisville, Kentucky; Charles Lago; Howard Shalwitz of Woolly Mammoth Theater in Washington, D.C.; Jumpstart Theater and Vortex Theater in Texas; Jeanne Pearlman and Donna Garda of Three Rivers Arts Festival in Pittsburgh; and many others who have shared my performance work with folks in their cities. A special thanks here to the University of California, Los Angeles, Department of Theater and to the California State University, Los Angeles, Department of Theatre and Dance, two inspiring places of learning at which I have been lucky to be teaching these past few years.

I also need to thank the people who have helped the writing of this book through their guidance, editing, brainstorming, and publishing of my theater works, essays, or stories. Huge gratitude goes to Patrick Merla, who helped me discover "How to Grow Fruit" for his anthology *Boys Like Us*. Thanks also to Terry Wolverton, Therese Jones, Robert Drake, Rondo Mieczkowski, and Malcolm Boyd. *Shirts & Skin* was nurtured by the confidence of Charlotte Sheedy and Neeti Madan, who helped me develop the project and put me in touch with the wonderful folks at Alyson. I appreciate the support of Greg Constante and Julie Trevelyan at Alyson. They were consistently a pleasure to communicate with and soothed this writer, nervous with his first book. I thank Alyson editor Gerry Kroll, who gave me the edit from heaven during our many meetings in the Alyson offices above Hollywood Boulevard in Los Angeles. His intuition, generosity, and good humor deepened this book immeasurably.

Finally, I need to thank the three men who, in very different ways, are closest to me in my life. My best friend, David Román, gave me a feeling of unconditional friendship, which I have longed for since first grade. His companionship has been a true gift. I am also fortunate to have in my world my boyfriend Alistair McCartney, who dared to change my life. His courageous heart and loving touch have been a comfort (and a challenge) to me throughout this writing, and for that I am very grateful. Finally, I could not have written this book, or indeed become who I am today, without the emotional and psychic partnership I have received from Doug Sadownick. In our many years together as boyfriends, Doug shared with me much of the experience detailed in this book. He brought that deep sense of our ongoing journey together as soul buddies to his careful and helpful reading of every word as I wrote *Shirts & Skin*. I feel lucky that Doug and I continue to surprise, teach, and tend to each other. This book is dedicated to him.

Tim Miller
Los Angeles
July 1997

I AM BORN

LET'S START at the beginning.
The very beginning of my story, as far as I can tell:
We're in a bed.
My dad is fucking my mom.
If you want to figure out where you've been, you
gotta know where you started, right?
Every story has to have a beginning.
You just gotta find it.
You gotta be ready to dig into your queerest memories.
Turn over your darkest, scariest rocks to see what's
underneath.
Sniff around and figure out how you came to be the
hero of your own particular story.
Here's how it began.
My parents are fucking.
In their bed.
(Where else would they be?
On top of the fridge?
The Zenith console TV?
C'mon, this is suburban WASPtown, USA, Whittier,
California.
Of course my mom and dad are in a bed this winter
night.)
The lights are off.
The radio is on low so the kids won't hear the creaking.
My parents are young and still hot for each other, I
hope.

I'm trying hard to visualize this.
Half of me is inside my father's penis.
The other half is somewhere inside my mom's body.
(My biology gets a little vague here, female anatomy
*   being as mysterious to me as a car engine.)*
These halves of me-to-be are gathering their juices.
Packing up their valises for the big adventure.
Stopping the newspaper while they're gone.
These halves of me put on their galoshes as the
*   countdown continues.*
My folks are breathing fast.
"Shhh, George, the kids'll wake up," my mom whispers.
When the other children are asleep, my parents
*   decide to make a queer child.*
They don't know it, but some part of them decides.
"Honey, let's have this one be a faggot!"
They would always tell me I had been a mistake.
"You were the one we didn't plan," they would say,
"but we love you anyway!"
They got it wrong.
I was the one they had always been waiting for.
I was the time bomb just waiting to paint their world
*   chartreuse.*
My dad is going to come any minute.
He's thrusting madly. Ah, ah, ah!
Suddenly part of me is thrown like a huge sneeze out
*   of my father's dick and into my mom's vagina.*
I am surrounded by thousands of squirming creatures.
I am swimming upstream.
O humble dog paddle!
O efficient crawl!
O stylish backstroke!
I am swimming upstream.
As I would swim upstream throughout this life.

One queer little spermlet.
Fighting the odds.
A hideous sperm that looks like Jesse Helms
tries to catch me in a net.
I elude him!
A bunch of sperm that look like the military Joint Chiefs
of Staff try to kick me out of this Fallopian tube.
I elude them as well!
Then a bunch of hulking, macho, slimebag, straight-
appearing sperm shove and try to elbow me out of
the way.
"Sissy! Pansy! Fag!" they call me. "You'll never find
an egg! Ha, ha, ha!"
(Clearly this is homophobia, my very first experience.)
But using my superior agility, fleetness, and sense of
style,
I calmly jeté from plodding straight sperm head
to straight sperm head.
Follow the bouncing ball and eat my dust!
All this time the me that is an egg is trying to find
the me that is a faggot sperm.
Egg-me looks for the telltale flourish on each spermy
backstroke.
The XX chromosomey part of me that would be
named Melanie Miller if I turn out to be a girl
swirls into view.
Egg-me and sperm-me see each other across the
crowded room.
We see each other as clearly as when my lesbian pal
from tenth-grade drama class recognized me at a
high school reunion!
Sperm-me quickly finds that willing dyke ovum.
She's reading Virginia Woolf!
What a match!

We agree to power-share.
In fact, we reach consensus immediately
(this is a fantasy sequence, okay?)
and we...fertilize!
There is an explosion of creative electricity.
A shifting of queer tectonic plates.
Sperm and egg skitter across the well of loneliness.
We become a new thing!
The electrical charge of identity pours into me!
Like the crazy buzzing coils as the lightning explodes
    in Bride of Frankenstein!
I receive all this into me at that conceptual moment.
I see Gertrude Stein in a tutu.
She is dancing with Vaslav Nijinsky, who is wearing
    his favorite butt plug.
They do a pas de deux on the wings of a fabulous
    flying machine created by Leonardo da Vinci and
    piloted by James Baldwin.
They are all flying over the island of Lesbos, where
    Sappho is starting to put the moves on the cute
    woman carpenter
who had arrived to build her a breakfast nook.
(Sappho's babe-carpenter gives me a quick zap
of genetic programming to be good with wood!)
There is a puff of feathers!
An angry fist!
A surface-to-air witticism!
The off-the-shoulder amazon look!
The faggot on the half shell rises from the mist of the
    newly dawned space age!
Embodying the bridge between woman and man and
    back again.
The sperm is a fish.
The egg is a rocket.

5, 4, 3, 2, 1!
And...ecce homo*!*
Behold the fag.
Now the big cry to the universe.
Time to be born. W-a-a-a!
The doctor spanks my butt. W-a-a-a!
He spanks it again. W-a-a-a!
I look back, and I say,
"Doctor, I won't be into spanking till I'm at least
 twenty-four!"
With that first pre-erotic and nonconsensual spank,
a wave of body-phobia washes over me.
I fight back. I kick the doctor in the balls,
rejecting his authority over my body.
I slip on my ACTION = LIFE Huggies.
I slither into my WE'RE HERE, WE'RE QUEER, GET USED TO
 IT powder-blue jumper.
I see all the other queer babies in the nursery start to
 shimmer and burst from their diapers.
We all grow in fits and starts into our lives.
Some of these queer babies
eventually find their way to these words!
Some of these queer babies one day will go into a
 bookstore, flirt with the cashier, and buy this book!
They will take it home.
Set it next to the dildo on the nightstand.
They will start to read...

FRÄULEIN RODRIGUEZ

I HAVE A SNAPSHOT OF myself taken in front of my aunt and uncle's house in West Covina, California, when I was a little boy. I am festively dressed in a Union Pacific Railroad shirt and trousers. My five-year-old body is covered in the trademark vertical blue and white stripes, the railroad insignia plastering the front of the shirt, a huge red neckerchief around my neck, a jaunty matching cap on my head. My single-minded obsession with trains had demanded the purchase of this uniform as a birthday present. This was the first costume I had ever wanted, the first time I managed to change how I saw myself by putting a shirt on my skin.

I loved my Union Pacific uniform with a maniacal passion. Shrieks of protest would erupt from me if I was told to wear any other clothes to a family event. The only way to restore peace on earth was to let me get into my train suit.

In this old photograph, though, I don't look like I have been whistling "I've Been Working on the Railroad." I look scared and uncomfortable, as if I am being coerced into *performing* the role of the little boy who loves trains. I seem in shock, terrified, numbed-out, as I do in most pictures from this period. Had my father shouted at me? A drunken aunt given me a too-wet kiss? My next elder brother hit me hard somewhere I wouldn't bruise? Whatever had happened, I look like one scared little boy. I look like I want to turn on my heel and run up the poured-cement steps of the cheap subdivision porch and escape from the eye of the camera. Those cheerful blue and white Union Pacific stripes on the shirt slowly start to show their true colors. If I squint at the photo long enough, the stripes begin looking suspiciously like a well-tailored concentration-camp uniform made for a small boy. Suddenly this little kid looks like he's about to begin pleading for mercy, as though he is about to get on a train to Bergen-Belsen, not to Bakersfield.

Uh-oh. We're digging into the past now. The fog machine starts supplying the mood decor, the music shifts to a minor key, and that memory reaches its hands up through the fecund earth and dead leaves like a B-movie monster. I brought my shovel with me. I know how to use its sharp edge to clear the shit away or to knock a hole in my own argument. I need to remember to put on my hard hat so that no jagged piece of yesterday bruises my brain and sends me to the trauma center.

When I start to remember things, I think it's kind of like the Old Mine Ride at Knott's Berry Farm. I pay my money and agree to pile into the rickety prospecting train and go deep into the red and highly unpredictable earth. There is excitement and fear because I know at some point there will probably be a choreographed disaster of some sort. The roof will cave in. The water will overflow. A dynamite explosion will bury everyone. I will discover something that I might wish I had left undisturbed. But I get on the ride anyway.

I'll try to remember the town I was raised in.

I, like Richard Nixon, grew up in Whittier, California. It's a city where white mothers make tacos for their families every Thursday. Taco Night, it was called. Well, at least it was in my family. All of us kids had a designated Taco Night job. This was the Miller family's most cooperative moment. Sibling feuds forgotten, peace treaties signed, anything to fulfill our duties and make the tacos come forth. My brother Brad, scholar and actor, would fry the tortillas. My sister, Betsy, drill-team leader and dancer, would grate the cheese. My brother Greg, scientist and surfer, would cook the meat.

At the age of seven, I had been entrusted with the most crucial challenge. I got to make the taco sauce. I buzzed around the kitchen in my maroon Hang Ten shirt and bright orange Hawaii-inspired and Mom-sewn jams. (I had outgrown my childish railroad uniform and was now going for a surfer look.) I would pour in the ketchup and the hot sauce. Dollops of A.1. A squirt of Kikkoman. I would slather in anything that smelled spicy to create a salsa fit for a WASP family in Whittier. Then, that most mysterious and resilient-as-a-weed of American institutions, the Messed-Up Family, would begin to eat the reformed sacraments of Taco Night.

I'm here to tell some tales that I have kept marinating in my memory, marinating in a sauce worthy of Taco Night.

Whittier occupies an earthquake-frayed corner of the lazy sprawl of Los Angeles. Skulking there like a three-day-old pimple at the edge of the county, Whittier is close enough to downtown L.A. to have air that is a distinct shade of brown — terra-cotta on a bad day — but not near enough to the ocean to be soothed by a sea breeze with nothing better to do.

Considering the 1987 shaking of the earth that wiped out quaint uptown Whittier, it is ironic that this town was founded by Quakers. Whittier is named for the poet John Greenleaf Whittier (just in case you ever make it to *Jeopardy!*, 19TH-CENTURY AMERICAN POETS FOR 500). He was a prominent, socially progressive writer who was also into "barefoot boys with cheeks of tan." I have tried to carry on both of John Greenleaf Whittier's traditions.

The football team at Whittier College, where my dad studied on the GI Bill, was called the Whittier Poets. Go, Poets, go! Nixon, Whittier's most famous son, spoke to my dad's graduating class. The sea of Anglo-Saxon Southern Californian faces beamed up at Congressman Nixon while his histrionic red-baiting gave him an erection that the speaker's podium fortunately concealed.

The people in Whittier that I come from were mostly Euro WASP mutts who had made their way to California from various failed farms in the Midwest. They came to re-create Kansas, only with a beachfront and better weather. Let's do it right this time, shall we?

My family's house was in East Whittier, off Whittier Boulevard at Pounds Avenue, to be precise. To get to Whittier, you go from downtown Los Angeles over the Sixth Street bridge into East L.A. Whizzing over the span's concrete deco majesty, you cross the rainy-day torrents of the Los Angeles River far below. The warm exhalation of the *dulces* of the thousand Mexican bakeries of Boyle Heights hits you with wind-tunnel force as you set rubber on the most mystic street in my universe, Whittier Boulevard, the psychic Champs Élysées of the San Gabriel Valley! You run a red light in Montebello, drive slowly through Pico Rivera, shoot over the San Gabriel River, and arrive in Whittier!

In the glow of that last moment before Watergate in the first year of the '70s, Whittier had not yet been knocked down by its earthquake. As you drove across the city limits, you were greeted by a big sign that read, WELCOME TO WHITTIER, HOMETOWN OF PRESIDENT RICHARD NIXON. The nice city policeman might even wave a friendly hello. Provided you weren't Mexican, of course. This was Whittier, after all, which some people called *White*-ier.

The house I grew up in was located in a neighborhood that real estate assessors would consider midrange middle-class. (The bad news: Not one family had a swimming pool on our street. But on the upside: No one had a rusting station wagon parked on cinder blocks in his front yard.) Our house was a standard three-bedroom affair, a ranch house, as some would misname it. There was enough room on the property for the tall Chinese elms and a lifetime of psychoses to grow. The neat *Stepford Wives* row houses of my hometown occupied what had formerly been acres of orange trees.

In my backyard there was a single special fruit tree, a Valencia orange — the one remaining tree of the groves that used to be there. Somehow, as I grew up, that orange tree slowly became the symbol of my family. (This special hybrid tree was bred to withstand the pressure of even the heaviest metaphor.) Every waking dream and unnamed desire dangled there as heavy as a juicy orange.

When I was little I'd often carefully remove my Union Pacific shirt and pants and lay underneath that tree naked when no one was home. I'd beg those branches to help me grow. I'd prick my finger on its sharp thorns and drip my blood into the dirt. I wanted its roots to wind through me and let me become part of the tree. I wanted to be as juicy and dangerously tart as the fruit of those Valencias — those oranges so sour and sweet and sharp that one bite could make your face sphincter up into an exclamation point.

When I was a little older, I'd jerk off in the light of day when nobody was home and come on the Valencia tree root. I'd ask it for things my parents said no one should ask for. My breath racing, I'd fall onto my back and look up at the oranges above me. I'd try to actually *see* the tree grow. If I watched really closely with my adolescent eye, I was sure I could see it happen. I'd lay there very still and watch a single orange against the sky. I'd see it slowly grow beyond its boundaries as I slowly grew into my fourteenth year.

I had been drawn to fruit for as long as I could remember. In kindergarten they gave each of us kids an apple sapling. We planted them out next to the jungle gym on Whittier Boulevard. The school showed my kindergarten class the Disney *Johnny Appleseed* cartoon on a daily basis.

My first-grade teacher, Mrs. Walters, gave me *two* apple saplings ("Because you're such a special though unusual boy," she said). As those tiny apple trees grew, I saw that magic was possible. It existed as concretely as the fourteen layers of hairspray on Mrs. Walters's hurricane-gale–resistant bouffant. Those saplings grew, and so did I. They are tall trees today.

Years later another teacher in the California public school system continued the exploration of the fruit kingdom with the old "avocado/toothpick/glass of water" trick. We were instructed to strip the avocado seed of its flesh, torture it with toothpicks, then delicately perch the seed over the lure of the shimmering water. My best friend, Ralph Higgs, and I put our succulent twelve-year-old bodies very near each other as we stared at the reflection of our faces in the glass of water. We wanted to see if our avocado seed was going to crack through its shell and send its roots down toward the hot and wet place below in the glass of water.

Ralph was a real boy: He killed things and liked football. My love for Ralph was also breaking through its shell, growing down toward the heat and damp, the roots of that love as deep as the roots of the trees in the avocado groves where Ralph and I walked every day after school, looking for Indian arrowheads that didn't exist.

Checking our avocado, Ralph and I leaned over the first-peach-of-the-season–colored protozoa-pattern formica table. I was drunk with the nearness of his body. I wanted Ralph to be my special friend and hold me near to him. I didn't have a name for what I felt, but I had an inkling that it was going to be trouble. I wanted to reach underneath his untucked mottled green Boy Scout shirt and let my fingers wander over his belly. I wanted to kiss him so much, I became obsessed with his tongue. I wanted it in my mouth. I stood behind Ralph and saw the smooth skin and downy hairs at the back of his neck. I reached forward to touch him, but something stopped me ("Shields up, Lieutenant Worf!"). I tried to fight it, and my hand moved closer. A tiny moan escaped from my lips. Ralph turned around and looked at me funny. He moved away and said, "I think we should go play war now."

I would have to wait until 1972 to finally tongue-kiss another human being. That little boy in the train suit had grown up a little bit and been disciplined to stop crying so much.

Even though I was really in love with Ralph Higgs, my eighth-grade girlfriend, Janet Mauldin, was the first person I ever kissed. We made out on the Monsanto Corporation's Journey to Inner Space ride at Disneyland. This cheesy ride, complete with its frayed styrofoam snowflakes, was an opportunity to get miniaturized and injected into a water molecule. The forgiving darkness of the Journey to Inner Space ride was also the prime setting for a generation of Southern Californians to engage in heavy petting.

As Janet and I waited in line, I stroked her Marcia Brady hair, reached my arm around her slender waist, and held her close. We climbed into the royal blue automated car that would carry us into the microscope, and I kissed her pool-tanned neck as we journeyed through the snowflake field. We put our lips together as oxygen and hydrogen atoms swirled around us. I stuck my tongue in her mouth as we approached a pulsing red nucleus. The atom got bigger and bigger, a huge throbbing nucleus hanging in front of us as our wet, wet, wet tongues danced around each other.

Janet and I walked through Tomorrowland with our arms entwined the rest of that June day. For the first time I felt the full hot cradling breath of nascent heterosexual privilege wash over me. For a moment, as I felt Janet's body next to mine, I had a new image of myself as someone who could perform the part of a typical guy, no longer the weird kid who looked at other boys on the playing field.

Out of the corner of my eye, I spotted Ralph Higgs, who was also at Disneyland that day. Ralph did not have a girlfriend and was sucking on a snow cone in front of the Autopia cars as he watched Janet and me parade past. Holding Janet closer to me, I puffed myself up proudly. I was thirteen, and I had a cute girlfriend (she had won the Joni Mitchell look-alike contest during Prom Week).

I looked over my shoulder, and Ralph's eyes locked on mine for a moment as he licked the snow-cone ice off his fingers. My heterosexual privilege balloon sprang a leak. I knew my tenure as a straight boy would be brief. Very soon (once I got my first pubic hair during freshman year) I was going to turn into a giant fruit.

I had waited such a long time for my first pubic hair. I was a late bloomer. I'd read all of Nietzsche and Schopenhauer twice before my voice began to change in ninth grade. While I was dating Janet Mauldin, I grew tired of being made fun of in the showers in gym class. I tried to *will* my pubic hair to grow. I'd concentrate very hard: *Grow, grow!* Then I would get the flashlight and a mirror and contort myself to see if anything was growing around my groin. When would I get my first pubic hair?

With the ingenuity of youth, I decided to take extreme action. I thought I could maybe help my pubic hair to grow. I would go out in the backyard and lie naked in the sun under the sprinklers when no one was home, the graceful arc of the water drenching me. Maybe my pubic hair had been planted with special pubic-hair seeds, like the little specks on a poppyseed bagel. Perhaps if I watered them, they would start to sprout. The sun might accelerate this process. I sensed, as I looked at my hairless boy belly and crotch, that when these hairs finally came, they would bring some revelation, a new awareness.

I started putting food supplements, house-plant vitamins, and fertilizers on my crotch to make that fucking pubic hair grow. In desperation I even sent away for special miracle hair tonics concocted for male-pattern baldness. I was sure that would help.

Nada!

Finally, as I was rereading Nietzsche's *Also Sprach Zarathustra* for the fifth time, I looked down at my crotch and saw something. Was it a speck of dirt? A bit of lint? No. It was an actual hair. I doubled up on the vitamin E oil and hot towel treatments. That pubic hair grew from an eighth of an inch to a quarter of an inch to half an inch long. I got out my chemistry-set microscope and saw that there was some strange hieroglyphic writing on this first "naturally curly" pubic hair. I slowly deciphered the words on that pube:

Greetings! Things will not be as you think. You are going to have a very different life from the other boys on your water polo team. You will want to hold and be held by other men. You will feel the tide of gender shift around inside of you. Sacred visions may appear. You will have an unusually developed appreciation for female vocalists of all eras. Welcome to your life.

This was my first pubic hair. There soon would be more and more, each with its own tidings and greetings for the life to come, a forest of tales and guideposts for how to live my life.

Who would that queer spermlet turn out to be? Well, I had survived the rigors of grade-school dodgeball without visible scars and had thankfully discovered jerking off sometime after that kiss with Janet Mauldin. Thus, with the blitzkrieg of puberty tramping through my body over the next two years, I had quickly come to occupy a world of romantic-cum-homoerotic forces that were a strange cocktail of *Crime and Punishment* and *The Front Runner,* a dream life where I was the star of the gay romance Fyodor Dostoyevsky never wrote, a place where Raskolnikov would get enlightenment *and* a locker-room blow job. Maybe I was looking for this imaginary scenario instead of keeping my eyes peeled for the messy real life that just might present itself. I was too smart for my own good and yet not smart enough to know my heart's highways.

I was desperate for love and dick. Throughout the forty-years-in-the-sexual-desert of my adolescence, my backyard had been my only dependable sexual partner. In addition to the orange tree, I had also frequently crept behind the succulents and jerked off there on the jade plants' plump leaves. In addition, my backyard was the site of my earliest erotic experiments exploring the possibilities of vegetables. I was powerfully drawn to the zucchini in the garden behind the garage. (I told my mom about this recently, and she was shocked. "Good gosh, Tim!" she exclaimed. "You stuck those zucchinis where? Then you let me put them in the Tuna Helper?") Those squashes' sunlit heat are still inside me somewhere. The backyard was also a minefield of holes in the lawn where I had stuck the rake handle deep in the warm earth to make a tight, hot, wet hole to fuck on dull summer afternoons.

My quest for sex took me anywhere except places where I might actually find it. I searched everywhere. I hung around the Whittier Public Library, leaning suggestively against the stacks in the psychology section, waiting to be picked up by some graduate student. I leaned too far once and almost knocked over an entire row of bookshelves. This scared off a man in a trench coat reading Havelock-Ellis. I left the library, took the bus into L.A., and walked down Hollywood Boulevard.

I lingered outside the Gold Cup, a diner at the corner of Las Palmas where all the teenage boy prostitutes hung out. I wanted the courage they displayed in their open-for-business bodies. This was the Boy Scout troop I wanted to be a part of. Maybe something would rub off on me from these saucy young men. I too could get a merit badge in cock sucking. I just needed somebody to grab me and show me the way.

What did my fourteen-year-old queer self really look like then? Well, my *goyisheh* boy-child cuteness had transformed with the usual teenage growth explosion. It was like those cabbages in Alaska that would suddenly get really huge when exposed to radiation: our friend the atom at work! For me, as I was mugged by the rampage of my hormones, my hair, bones, and ego had all grown in the most unlikely directions. My cheeks and nose often sported several pimples, sometimes in patterns recognizable as certain constellations (Cassiopeia one week, Ursa Major the next). Nothing that would show up in a dermatology textbook but definitely enough to cause panic as I walked down the hallways of Lowell High School on my way to fulfill my foreign-language requirement. I wanted to learn other languages so that I would be prepared when it came time for me to make my escape.

I learned to speak German at Lowell High School from a Chicana believed-to-be lesbian named Fräulein Rodriguez. I'm not sure why I studied German instead of another language. Spanish, for example, would have been much more sensible. Maybe something had been missing from the salsa I made for Taco Night, a crucial ingredient that just wasn't there in the Miller kitchen.

I grew up surrounded by a weird mishmash Spanish spoken by my family in our house. No, we didn't have

Spanish-speaking maids, okay? I grew up in a hard-core middle-class San Gabriel Valley peasant lifestyle. Both my parents worked selling things: my mom, on the floor at May Company department store ("This platinum-plated Scottish terrier charm bracelet would be the ideal sweet-sixteen present"); my dad, a traveling salesman for Pitney Bowes ("Mr. Gutierrez, this collator–envelope sealer would increase the productivity of your dry-cleaning business 200 percent!"). With both parents working long hours, I was the one who had to clean the toilets, and my language skills had to come from public school.

My dad was a student of Spanish, and he truly loved the language. He taught himself from a book he got when he came back from World War II. This book was called *El Español al Día*. My dad and Uncle Murray had fixed up an old ambulance and had traveled around in Mexico practicing their Spanish for weeks until they got dysentery and had to come home.

I grew up hearing these expressions around the house:

"Pass the *mantequilla*, darling."

"Can I have some more *leche, por favor?*"

"Honey, please get me a *cerveza fría!*"

I was called Timoteo by my parents, which is a name I don't think anybody in Latin America really has. My mom had horned in on the bilingual act too. At the end of every day, she would lean down as she tucked me into bed and whisper gently, *"Hasta la mañana, Timoteo."*

In 1972, the very same year I began learning the irregular forms of the verb *to be* in German from Fräulein Rodriguez, I also took a summer-school course about the colorful history of my state called

"California Heritage." I was fourteen. We learned all
about the horrors of the conquistadores; the bravery of
Sir Francis Drake and his doughty sailing ship, the
Golden Hind; and the wet foot of Cabrillo at Point
Loma. We would go on innumerable field trips to all
the missions the friars had built. I would write and
perform plays about Father Junípero Serra. These
plays had titles like *Father Serra Whips Father José* or
*Father Serra Brutally and Unremittingly Scourges the
Recalcitrant Indigenous People.* We visited some bat-
tlefield near San Diego where our teacher, who was
named (I'm not kidding) Mr. West, said, "Okay, kids!
Everybody off the bus! Let's see where we ripped off
California from Mexico!"

During that summer of my life in "California
Heritage" class, I smoked dope for the first time, in
the tannery of Mission La Purisima de Santa Inez in
Lompoc. I stole a big chunk of adobe as a souvenir
from a collapsed wall of Mission San Gabriel. Most
important, I pined away for the adorable Roger
Blainey in the cool mystery of the chapel at Mission
San Juan Capistrano, which is widely known as "The
Queen of the Missions." No wonder those swallows
find their way back there year after year: They hope
to see once again that sacred look on my face as I
caught a glimpse of Roger Blainey's belly as he did
pull-ups from a pipe that was holding up one wall of
the church after the earthquake. The blinding light
emanating from his Tupperware-taut fourteen-year-
old stomach made me fall to my knees in awe. The
eighteenth-century statue of the Virgin in the corner
had to put on her sunglasses. Roger's shirt was tugged
up with each pull-up just high enough for his belly
button to wink at me. Each rise of his shirt was like

the curtain going up on a movie I really wanted to see. I started to reach my hand forward to touch Roger. But just as when I tried to touch Ralph Higgs's neck, I couldn't force my fingers to do the deed. Something, all the assembled armies of society perhaps, stopped my hand cold in midair, my fingers waving there like a Capistrano swallow trying to find a roost on Roger's stomach. Would I ever be able to push through and finally grab another boy? This summer-school course taught me to appreciate a crucial natural resource of California: the beauty of the sons of the Golden State.

In 1972 my sister married Jorge Olmedo, and my whole family life changed. Suddenly Jorge and his extended Cuban family, who had fled from Castro's Havana, had become the center of our world in Whittier. They lived there too, down by the Sears store. Taco Night now seemed old hat. Life with the Olmedos turned Christmas dinner into black beans, fried platanos, and yuca — not turkey, marshmallow-glazed yams, and cranberry sauce. The Millers set a small blowtorch to a millennium's worth of Northern European glacial cool. The permafrost slowly dripped a little, and we started getting huggy with everybody.

Jorge's mom and dad were pretty old and spoke very little English. So my father spoke Spanish with them. My sister spoke Spanish. My surfer brother, fresh from a year of perfect wave chasing in Lima with his Peruvian girlfriend, Jezebel, was speaking Spanish really well. It was at this point in my life that I began my study of German with Fräulein Rodriguez.

I don't know why I picked German. It didn't really make sense. It had no relation to my reality. I was, after all, living a two-hour drive from Mexico. Picking German over Spanish just meant I couldn't talk to

Jorge's parents on Sundays. It was like refusing to be
where I was, in Whittier with all these Cuban relatives
in the San Gabriel Valley. Why would I be drawn to
this particular foreign tongue? Maybe it had to do
with this strange feeling that was growing inside me
when I looked at Dirk, my school's German exchange
student, in gym class. Of course, I am also of German
heritage. If you have any doubts, just check out my
family photo album and see the gray, dour German
faces in front of my great-great-great-grandfather's
sod house in Kansas in 1868.

Spanish felt too much like the reality of my family,
the lingua franca of excruciating family reunions.
Spanish was Sundays in Whittier. German, as Dirk,
the brooding exchange student, had taught me, was
exotic and gloweringly other. German conjured up for
me all kinds of dark, dangerous, and sexy visions. My
parents had taken me to see *Cabaret* at the La Mirada
movie theater a few months before. I don't think they
knew what they were getting into as we carefully
walked into the already dark theater. I ran ahead of
my folks to sit by myself in the third row with my Pro-
Keds up on the seat in front of me. The movie unfolded a world of homosexuality, performing, and extreme
politics. It was full of sexy German words that I wanted to get in my mouth.

Let's just say I got *very* into my German study.

As I began my studies with Fräulein Rodriguez, I
quickly became obsessed with our subject. I would
read Schiller in the original as I ate my bacon and
eggs. I loved going to Alpine Village, a curious German
cultural theme park in Torrance. Every Oktoberfest I
would go to Alpine Village and spy on the right-wing
Orange County born-again burghers as they salivated

over the forbidden World War II Wehrmacht daggers underneath the glass cases. I subscribed to and religiously read the Los Angeles German-language newspaper, the *California Staats Zeitung.* At a certain point I got a little *too* into my German stuff. After seeing the movie *A Clockwork Orange* at the Egyptian Theater on Hollywood Boulevard, a bunch of my friends and I gathered around a piano in our proto-punk attire and sang "Deutschland über Alles." We'd choose "The Internationale" the next year for even higher snob and shock value, but still! It was hard for us white kids to know who we actually were as we dog-paddled desperately through the blankness of a suburban childhood. You just tried to grab on to *something,* lasso a kind of identity life preserver, and hope you didn't drown. This is probably why I studied German.

Fräulein Rodriguez was a widely feared teacher, her wrath as scary as a six-armed Hindu deity. She was short and solid, her honest face right from the mountains of Michoacán. With her sharp edges and no-bullshit manner, Fräulein Rodriguez ran the German Club (we were only following orders). Fräulein Rodriguez was also the adviser for the MECHA group at my high school, the Chicano students' cultural and political club. I could have been taking Spanish with Fräulein Rodriguez too, but I didn't, which is too bad because though she was a very good German teacher, I'll bet she was an ace at Spanish.

Fräulein Rodriguez mostly spent time with another believed-to-be-lesbian teacher at our high school, Miss Schneider. Miss Schneider was a tyrannical biology instructor who looked just like Ernest Borgnine in *McHale's Navy* as she invited us to plunge our scalpels deep into the frog's formaldehyde-soaked chest. Fräulein Rodriguez and Miss Schneider would walk down the hallways together, lost in conversation. We kids, being complete creeps, made fun of them a lot. "Look out! Here comes the faculty gay parade!" we would furtively shout behind their backs.

I participated in this nastiness once or twice, which was quite a joke since I was just about to bloom into the biggest fag at my high school.

Fräulein Rodriguez and I had a complicated relationship. She was a demanding authoritarian and would drill us ruthlessly in our conjugations, declensions, and adjective endings. She and I would fight a lot in class about realpolitik, but we had to get along: I was the best German student at school. In fact, in my senior year I was the only German 4 student on independent study. This is when I really began to learn the irregular forms of the verb *to be*.

Ich bin. Ich war. Ich werde sein!

In 1975, at the beginning of my senior year, I finally completely figured out that I liked boys. I was the last one on the block to realize this, but better late than never. The understanding finally hit me with all the subtlety of a sixteen-wheel tractor trailer. One afternoon during physical education, my USMC-trained gym teacher divided us into two teams for touch football. The coach used two time-honored techniques to create these teams. First he had us endure the excruciating process of choosing the teams. This served the purpose of ritually humiliating the scrawny, the sensitive, and the clumsy. I would usually be picked third or fourth from last. I made sure I could play these games well enough so that I could avoid the total obliteration of being picked last. The coach watched the torture of this selection process with a Dr. Mengele–like demeanor. The last boy chosen, Ross-who-only-had-one-kidney, slunk off under the barrage of taunts from his teammates.

Then came the second part of this ordeal: The coach divided us up into two teams, Shirts and Skins. The Shirts got to keep their Lowell High School T-shirts on. The Skins had to peel down to our skinny chests. This system allowed the two teams to identify their opponents without the fuss of colored jerseys.

I would always pray that I would be a Shirt. I was afraid all my secrets would be exposed if I stripped down to bare skin with eight other boys. Of course this particular day, as it always seemed to happen, I ended up on the Skins team. This time it seemed that I had been chosen for something more than a team for football. I felt that somehow that single flip of the coin had exposed me, had marked me for what I was, a young gay man. Reluctantly I peeled out of my T-shirt, folded it neatly, and placed it on the bleachers. My skin smarting from the gaze of the other boys, I ran out to the football field, hoping no one called me a fag.

With the first huddle of the Skins, I felt the other boys' heat and smooth bodies against my sides. At that moment I *knew*. No more time-outs. No more inchoate groping toward the Ralph Higgses and Roger Blaineys of the world. I was always going to be on the team where the boys took their clothes off and got close to each other. It felt like the die was cast. I was on the Skins team for life. I could cover up and slip into different shirts and disguises, but underneath it all I would always be there with the other boys who were stripped bare. We would always be recognizable as a different team.

As we broke the huddle with a grunt and a slap of one another's butts, the game had begun. In an hour we would be stripped even more bare when we went naked, except for our desires, into the showers to scrub the mud and grass from our growing bodies.

Now that I knew which team I was on, I began a long process of coming out to myself. At first, because the Bible tells me so, the thought of having sex with these boys in the showers grossed me out. Then I slowly created deals with myself about what I would do with them if I ever got the chance. I decided I could kiss boys, and that wouldn't be disgusting. Then I changed my standards and decided that they could put their mouths on my dick, and that would be okay. As I jerked off three times a day to that fantasy, I figured it might not be too bad if they put their cocks in my mouth from time to time in a kind of "do unto others" gesture. Eventually it occurred to me that I might want to put my dick inside their butts. This thought created a wet dream that exploded like Krakatoa one night as I dreamed (in quite accurate detail, it would turn out) exactly what a boy's asshole wrapped around my dick would feel like. I submitted to my fate with all the gusto of a condemned man.

Fortunately, at my high school, a certain currency could be squeezed out of any kind of "alternative" activity. I was lucky enough to be at a school where the biggest club on campus was the Great Books Club. This was the collecting point for all the artists, homosexuals, drug dealers, and cross-dressing glitter-rock believers who went to *The Rocky Horror Picture Show* at the Roxy on the Sunset Strip every week. The Great Books Club had a glorious teacher-führer, who would

carpool us into Hollywood several times a week to go
see Sergey Eisenstein films and hang out with the
demimonde.

This structure helped me to define myself. It
allowed me to manifest my newly discovered sexual
identity in various behaviors. I wore black nail polish,
black lipstick, and a black cape to school most days. I
insisted on dressing like Oscar Wilde for our Great
Books Club field trips. My friend Lori, a year older
and already in college, began to introduce me to
prospective boyfriends. I encouraged the most extreme
rumors, all fabricated, about my sexual adventures in
Hollywood. My friend Kim Bertola was impressed
with my stories and became my PR agent. Kim wrote
on every available surface at my high school TIM GIVES
GOOD HEAD. I would just smile knowingly.

Of course, Fräulein Rodriguez noticed this. As she
and Miss Schneider strolled the hallways, she gazed at
that graffiti on my locker but didn't say anything.

For my independent study course with Fräulein
Rodriguez, I was translating Thomas Mann's *Death in
Venice* from German to English. This was not easy.
Often Fräulein Rodriguez and I would sit together late
after school, the two of us leaning over the page, an
Anglo-German homo and a Latina lesbian exploring
the pleasures of the subjunctive case *auf Deutsch.*

I shared my progress on a tricky part of my translation with Fräulein Rodriguez one afternoon. I got to
the point in *Death in Venice* where Gustave von
Aschenbach, an uptight-closet-case-writer-from-
Munich-in-need-of-a-dye-job, realizes something
important about himself. Gustave goes to fabulous
Venice for a vacation and then finally understands
that he loves the beautiful boy Tadzio. Gustave falls in

a heap onto the plague-strewn piazza and whispers "I love you" before he dies on the beach at the Lido.

Though only seventeen, I could relate to Gustave von Aschenbach a lot. Two years earlier I had fallen in love with a boy in my driver's education class named Todd. Weaving a rich fantasy life for myself, I believed that Todd, fiercely alternative in his Emerson, Lake, and Palmer T-shirt, actually *was* Tadzio. He was ready to lure me with his beauty to my dissolute fate and keep me from learning how to drive with a stick shift. I would fail my driver's test and be exposed to public humiliation. I followed Todd out of the classroom every day hoping we would get to do our driving lessons together. Maybe he would lean against me as we made a sharp turn to avoid a milk truck on Whittier Boulevard, his hand slipping to my knee.

I went to Venice Beach in Los Angeles, hoping I would find Todd there. I walked along the strand in my dark glasses and wind-blown cape. I saw Todd come out of the bright winter glare of Venice Beach, walk right up to me, and place his hand on my skinny chest as his lips moved toward mine. (Turn up the Mahler real loud here, okay?) Tadzio, I mean Todd, would look bravely into my eyes and whisper, "I love you, Gustave. I have always loved you."

When I got to that point, as I read my freely adapted and contemporized translation of Thomas Mann to Fräulein Rodriguez, I sort of flipped out. I didn't cry hysterically or anything. I am, after all, a WASP. But my lower lip did quiver noticeably as one tear squeezed from my left eye. Who did I think I was? Gustave von Aschenbach or a teenage queer boy with smeared black lipstick and a tear trailing eyeliner down his cheek? I wasn't anywhere near as cool as I thought I was. Not anywhere as sophisticated either. And let's face it, I didn't give good head. The truth be told, I'd never given anyone head! I wasn't even exactly sure what people even meant by *head!*

Fräulein Rodriguez looked at me quietly and shut her copy of *Death in Venice*. She said, pointing at my midnight-black nail polish, "*Das ist nicht nötig.* (That isn't necessary.) *Sei stolz!* (Be proud of yourself.) *Alles stimmt.* (It's okay.)"

Fräulein Rodriguez placed her hand on my shoulder and looked me in the eye for a moment. She was a Chicana lesbian of few words. Then she quickly opened up *Death in Venice* again, and we went back to our translation.

As we began our work, the Lowell High School varsity water polo team walked loudly past the open classroom door after their practice. I could smell the chlorine on their skin from a mile away, chlorine from the pool full of men I was about to dive into.

I was getting ready to move on. I was going to get out of high school soon. I looked forward to the moment when my graduating class would go to Disneyland, and this time maybe I would get it right. Maybe I'd be there with a new boyfriend. Maybe that guy Lori said she was going to introduce me to. I would get older, a tiny bit wiser. Eventually I might even learn how to give good head. Who knows? One day I might even reach the rich old age of thirty. Then I would think of Fräulein Rodriguez and how she helped me learn the irregular forms of the verb *to be.*

I am. I was. I will be.

Danke schön, Fräulein Rodriguez.

TAR PIT HEART

IT HIT ME IN THE HEART, just a little bit to the left of my sternum. Only later would it hit me in the head. Well, a lot of events in my life have hit me in those two places: the election of Ronald Reagan. AIDS. The first time a man put his dick in my ass. All the nights I've lain down with a man next to me.

There is one bed that looms very large in my life. It has an old pine headboard painted Pic-'N'-Save-antique–green. The toxic Vitalis hair tonic on my father's head has rubbed a hole right through the seven layers of paint to the bare maple wood underneath. My mom's sacred jar of Noxzema is still on the nightstand. As a teenager I often was obliged to use that Noxzema to jerk off with, but the sticky cream never seemed to get up a good slide. Plus it can make your penis sting at the tip. (I will never endorse that product for beating off no matter how much money they try to give me.) This is the bed inside my body, the bed I was conceived on, the bed where I would be born once again. I offer my memory of the creak and bounce of this bed in tribute to the first time this meat and bones got close to other flesh and blood. It's the story of the only date I went on with a boy in high school.

I met Robert in 1975. I was seventeen years old. He was seventeen too, and we were both seniors in high school. As I write these words, I'm at the point in my life where I am finally old enough to be my own father in this story. It's a stretch, I know, but it would be possible. I think just maybe I need to be my own father in this story so that I can try to give birth to my queer self.

I want to conjure my queer body at seventeen, when my entire being was a hard-on. From morning till night I was a walking and talking boner. It was necessary for me to have a book constantly riveted over my crotch, hiding my tumescence as I walked down the halls on my way to German class. Almost anything could give me a boner. I would get excited when I felt the sunshine on my neck between my collar and hairline. I'd get a hard-on reading about Admiral Nelson or hearing a song by Patti Smith. Ever since I peeled my shirt off after we picked teams, I often had one throbbing for many of the boys in my gym class. It was lucky I met Robert when I did, or the dangerous temperatures in my body might have caused me to spontaneously combust.

Robert went to a different high school than I did. It was in Anaheim, right near Disneyland. Robert had grown up in the shadow of the Matterhorn Bobsled Ride. My friend Lori had hooked up with him at one of those bohemian hangouts in Fullerton, the Left Bank of (hyperconservative) Orange County. She fell in love with him instantly. But then she discovered that he was a big fag, so she graciously decided to pass him on to her friend Tim.

"I've met a fag for you!" Lori exclaimed, as excited as if she had just seen Jesus walk down Whittier Boulevard. "We have to go to Anaheim today and meet him. His name is Robert, and he's the lead singer in a punk-rock band. They only do songs taken from texts of the Marquis de Sade. Let's go hear them rehearse!"

"Lori, I can't," I protested. "I've never done this before. What would I say to him?"

"I already told him you're gay," she said, pushing me toward the door. "He'll do the rest. Get your coat, *Liebling!*" This affectionate name for me was one of Lori's borrowings from Liza Minnelli. She had memorized the script from *Cabaret* (and often recycled some of its German expressions), but she had decided to study Russian so she could more thoroughly annoy her anticommunist father.

Lori and I went to a white-trash trailer park in Anaheim, about three blocks from the It's a Small World ride. She wanted me to see Robert in action with his punk-rock band, called Sade or Me. We recognized the correct trailer, which belonged to the drummer in the band, by the punk-decorator plastic chickens hung upside down with safety pins over the doorway. The moment I pushed the flimsy aluminum door open, a blast of three-chord electric-guitar shrapnel hit us hard: Robert's band had just jumped into a song. I felt the music in the space inside my balls and between my front teeth. The power of the sound gave me the same tingling sensation I would feel when my dad would drive the car fast over a dip in the road. I wasn't sure if I was about to ejaculate or throw up. I felt like I had come a long way from guitar class, where we had learned our simple version of "Yesterday."

Robert had the microphone cable wrapped around his neck as he screamed out the words to his song based on de Sade's *Justine*. The only word I could understand was "Justine." Robert rubbed himself up and down the flanks of his bass player, who happened to be blind; threw his writhing body on top of the piano; then leaped across the room and landed right in front of me.

"Justine!" He sang/screamed right to my face. "I love you, Justine!"

A painful screech of feedback filled the small living room of the '50s Airstream trailer as the number finished. I blinked and held my hand out toward the sweating singer.

"Hi, Robert. Lori has told me so much about you. I'm Tim."

Robert was skinny as an eel. The slashed-out holes on his black T-shirt showed his Casper-the-Friendly-Ghost–white skin underneath. He wore small Revolutionary War eyeglasses underneath an explosion of bright-as-noon curls that tumbled down his forehead. He had a brooding spirit unbecoming a blond.

We all sat down and drank some cold marijuana tea steeped from cast-off seeds, the best high we could find that night.

"You guys are really intense," I offered, a standard assessment emphasized by a persistent nod. "De Sade would be proud."

"Tim, you and Robert have *so* much in common!" Lori said in her mostly charming ham-fisted way. "You guys should get to know each other."

She left us to our devices.

"I enjoyed your song," I said, groping for the proper language. "I think de Sade is so excellent."

"Thanks. He's my inspiration for the band. I call up his spirit every time I perform," Robert explained, his back jammed into a doorway of the tiny trailer.

I took the plunge as Lori urged me on behind Robert's back. "Would you like to go to the beach with me tomorrow, and then we could go into L.A. to the

'Shakespeare on Film' retrospective at the county museum of art?"

"Sure," he replied, sliding through the door around me and back into the main room. "I'm not too big on the sun, though. I like to be pale. Could we go to the beach late in the day?"

"Oh, yeah," I said, tugging my sleeves down to cover my naked-in-the-backyard tan. "I feel exactly the same way."

Lori and I made our retreat out of the trailer so the rehearsal could continue. As we walked back to the car, she gave me a high five and a hug.

"Excellent!" she said, preening at her matchmaking skills. "At least *you're* on your way to getting laid." Lori sniffled a little bit as she opened the car door.

"I thought the blind bass player was cute." I improvised madly to make Lori feel better. "I think he liked you. Maybe we should mention this to Robert."

"Thanks a lot. The blind guy liked me."

We drove home silently. Had I said something wrong? I looked at Lori with a feeling I had never had before, a mixture of compassion and competition. She had, after all, had been drawn to Robert too. I had always been afraid of this triangle stuff when I was a kid playing with two friends. Would my two pals run off and play by themselves without me? Would they ditch me? I felt pulled in two directions by my we-two-weird-kids-together-clinging friendship with Lori and my I've-gotta-have-him desire for Robert. But this was too much for me to think about right then. I made an unconscious mental note to talk about it with my therapist when I had time — say, in my late thirties.

I went to pick up Robert up the next day driving my beat-up 1965 Volkswagen Bug. This car was the most important symbol in my life, my initiation into adult-hood. My Bug was the source of my freedom. This car allowed me to escape suburbia and drive the streets of Hollywood. When I would start the rumble of the lit-tle engine, I could feel the future grow inside my body. Taking the turns too fast, I would cruise down the Hollywood Freeway listening to David Bowie songs on a sweaty transistor radio pressed into my ear.

When I drove up to his house, in a nice neighbor-hood of Anaheim, Robert was already sitting out at the curb, trying to disassociate himself from his fami-ly life. It looked like Robert was embarrassed by the *Father Knows Best* quality of the split-level house. He had his version of beachwear on: some threadbare ripped-up jeans and a too-small Hang Ten shirt with the words SURF PUNKS SUCK spray-painted on. He jumped in the car and looked straight ahead as his mom waved from the front door.

"Have a nice time, boys!" She seemed to be used to talking to Robert's unresponsive back. "Robert, you forgot the sandwiches I made for you!"

"Drive," he said, slumping low in the bucket seat.

"Okay," I said as I shifted into first, pleased that I hadn't ground the gears. "Do you want to listen to some music? I have the new Patti Smith song."

"Sure. Let's just get out of here."

Robert and I went to Laguna Beach. At the time I had no idea this was a hopping Orange County gay beach. I had been to Laguna Beach many times before, mostly with my Congregational Church Youth Group. We would swim and bodysurf and then hear about the Good News from an earnest Campus Crusade type as we ate warm tuna fish sandwiches. Here I was at the same beach, but it felt totally different from when I was here with the youth group. On my date with Robert, the Laguna Beach sand was epic, like in *Lawrence of Arabia*. My body was new and grown-up. Each word of conversation we shared seemed golden and hung crystalline and perfect in the cool fall air before it was blown by a gentle breeze toward the minimalls of Costa Mesa.

We found a secluded nook. Though we were sheltered in a scooped-out area of the cliffs, I saw that at any moment a boulder could fall from above and crush us. I decided to take the risk. We spread our towels and sat down next to each other. As we talked I noticed that Robert was building a barrier of sand between us with his doodling fingers.

While he built this wall of sand, Robert told me, "I feel like I have always built walls between myself and other people. It makes me feel so alone." The sand was reaching shoulder height at this point.

I listened, feeling like I was having the first adult conversation in my life. Every molecule in my body wanted to hold him and comfort his loneliness.

"This is so intense," I said. "It's such a coincidence. I know exactly what you mean. I feel like I do that. I put up walls between myself and other people too. But maybe we have to find the way to break through those walls."

Robert looked up at me suddenly. He slowly crept one finger through the base of the sand wall. It poked out on my side like a lima-bean sprout. I reached my finger down and touched his. Our eyes locked, and there was this *Star Trek* laser beam of awareness and perfect love. Our lips astrally projected eight feet in front of our bodies, and at last we kissed, the Big Bang.

That kiss was the belated triumph over the times Ralph Higgs had pulled away from me. That kiss held the memory of the tears that ran down my face when my cousin would knock me down in my train suit and hit me in the face, calling me "Half Man! Half Man! Half Man!" That kiss began the process of balancing the emotional checkbook from all the times my sister dressed me as a girl — I looked like Jackie Kennedy in my pillbox hat and bouffant wig — and introduced me to our neighbors as her distant cousin Melinda from Kansas. That kiss soothed that confusing ping-pong of desires I had always felt when I watched David Cassidy on *The Partridge Family*.

Our lips parted; we kissed. Just like you're supposed to — we stuck our tongues in each other's mouths. It was great. His mouth was like a whole cosmos to me. It tasted like so many things: the roof, like the cigarette he had smoked on the curb of his parents' house; his gums, like a child's on Easter Sunday after eating a chocolate rabbit; his tongue, like my own did when I was nervous. We kissed like this for a long time. I didn't care if anybody saw us. I didn't care what my parents or my gym teacher or the California Highway Patrolman up on Pacific Coast Highway thought as he glared down on us.

Robert took his lips from mine and looked at me. He pulled his high school ring off his finger and held it in his palm. This ring, garish with its bright blue stone and growling panther, had the words VALENCIA HIGH SCHOOL carved into its silver-plate crest, where they glinted in the afternoon light.

"I know it's a little corny," Robert whispered sheepishly as he held my hand, "but I'd like you to have my class ring."

Wow! Things were moving pretty fast. I wasn't sure what to say in this situation. Did I need to give him something in return? I kicked myself that I hadn't ordered a class ring of my own that I could give to him. I thought they were only for moronic jocks, and now I was left in the lurch at this important moment.

"I would love to wear your ring," I told him, and Robert slipped it onto my finger. Ever since, I have worn this ring around my neck. I treasure it as a symbol of perfect queer love, of course, but also because I really think this will be the only high school ring a seventeen-year-old boy is likely to give me in this particular lifetime.

A wave crashed on a California beach, and a page in life had turned.

Robert and I drove blissfully back through traffic on the Santa Ana Freeway, past the array of theme amusement parks, with our hands intertwined. We talked about school and art. I was in love, and he was in a punk-rock band, and the world was new in 1975. We drove by Disneyland, the Movieland Wax Museum, and King Arthur's Knights of the Round Table Dinner Theater Joust.

A cloud started to hover over the Bug when we got off the freeway on Beach Boulevard and drove by Knott's Berry Farm. Robert withdrew his hand from mine.

"I need to tell you a secret," he said, speaking quietly while looking out the window at a billboard advertising Ricky Nelson's rock band, currently playing at Knott's Berry Farm. Ricky Nelson had fallen from his *Ozzie and Harriet* sitcom glory and was reduced now to playing nostalgia gigs at theme parks with his retro rock-and-roll band. "There's something you need to know about me," Robert continued as he not-so-gently beat his forehead against the window of my Volkswagen. "I've been having a sex affair with

Ricky Nelson. It has been pretty heavy with Ricky —
I mean Rick — lately. There's been a lot of drugs, and
not long ago we had a very bad sex scene backstage.
All I can say about it is that there was an enormous
summer squash involved."

My circuits were completely fried by this information. Had Robert also been hanging around the vegetable patch doing the squash thing? What about this
Ricky Nelson business? Did I believe him? Was he
making this up? I wasn't sure. What was he telling
me? That he's scared of sex? Scared of me? I could
relate. I was afraid of everything. We were young gay
boys in love, and we were sacred shitless. Some things
don't change.

"It's okay," I said, trying to play the role I was supposed to as I turned onto Whittier Boulevard. "Don't
think about all that. Forget about Ricky Nelson. It's
just you and me now."

We picked up Lori at her house in Whittier. After the
attack of guilt from the previous night, I had invited her
to go to the movies with us. Now, it might seem strange
that I would bring Lori along on a romantic date with
Robert. But let's face it: Although Lori wasn't a dyke,
she was definitely the queerest of the queer kids at my
high school. And throughout this strange life we're all
in, the queer kids, whether they're straight or gay,
should always stick together.

We were going to see the Franco Zeffirelli film of
Romeo and Juliet at the county museum of art. I had
seen this movie as a nine-year-old, when it first came
out. I went with my sister and her best girlfriend, who
had the unfortunate name of Kay Hickey. We all
walked down to the mall and saw it at the Whittwood
Cinema. This was my first grown-up movie. I was ner-

vous about seeing all the kissing, cleavage, and heavy breathing, so I mostly kept my eyes covered.

But there was one shot in this movie where I had to open my eyes. The beautiful Leonard Whiting, who played Romeo, was facedown and naked in a bed, his butt hovering there, lunarlike, in the soft Verona light. The camera slowly pulled away in a crane shot, revealing every possible angle on his ass in all its supple fabulousness. Instinctively my fingers opened over my eyes. I was pulled by some unseen power at the center of the earth up to my feet. I shoved my way past people in my row, knocking over their soda and popcorn. One angry patron poked me in the back with his Big Hunk candy bar as I walked down the aisle, blocking his view. My hands reached over my head, casting hundred-foot-tall Panavision shadows of searching fingers onto Romeo's perfect butt. I grabbed the movie screen and shook it. The image of Romeo cascaded above me as a tidal wave of ideal ass flesh soaked me.

And right then, at that moment, I enlisted. I signed up. I instantly became a career homo officer because I knew someday I would get to see Romeo's butt again. But the next time I encountered this sacred thing, I would be seventeen years old, I would finally have pubic hair, and I would be holding the hand of my new boyfriend from Anaheim.

Robert, Lori, and I got to the museum and found a *free* parking place on Sixth Street. (It was a magical night, okay?) We had a romantic walk (just the three of us) past the adjacent La Brea Tar Pits. Now, for those of you that don't know, the La Brea Tar Pits are primordial pits of petroleum sludge. They have been there since the dawn of time — or at least since our field trip in fifth grade in Mrs. Bush's class. For tens of thousands of years, prehistoric animals, cavemen, and Folger's coffee cans have fallen into these pits and been sucked to the center of the earth.

The feeling of eternity was there in my heart and in my head as I walked, brushing shoulders with Robert past the tar pits. All of those beasts and cavepeople had gotten pulled into this tar thousands of years ago. Those beings were just like me. They only wanted to feed and to fuck, and then they got sucked to a tarry death! I indulged myself in a massive, maudlin awareness of the ways that life can truly suck.

This sentiment put me in the proper mood for the movie.

We continued walking down Wilshire Boulevard toward the museum. This was the building where I had first encountered the idea of art as a thing that could change how I saw the world. In Mrs. Bush's class we had been studying cubism. Mrs. Bush piled us students into a bus and dragged us to the museum to look at the paintings of Braque and Picasso. As I strolled down Wilshire Boulevard with Robert and Lori, I was walking into a space where I had opened my eyes to the fact that human beings might actually have twelve eyes in the backs of our heads.

I knew where the movie theater was and led my friends inside. I grandly bought all of us tickets with the money I had earned mowing lawns. We sat down in the very first row just as the lights began to dim for the movie to begin. I sank down in my seat and slowly reached over to grab Robert's hand. I had never watched a movie while holding someone's hand before. It was so nice! I saw instantly why people liked it so much. Robert's hand in mine gave me a feeling of connection. It was like a lifeline that told me I wasn't

alone as I watched *Romeo and Juliet*. Holding hands
with Robert, I probably would have been just as excited to watch *Soylent Green* at a local multiplex. On the
other hand, *Romeo and Juliet* offered some particular
pleasures. This movie had a lot of what I needed that
night in my life: Big feelings. Fabulous swordplay.
Michael York at his cutest!

Now, what was happening that night when two fag
teenage boys held hands and watched *Romeo and
Juliet* at the County Museum of Art? What were we
doing with these images? There was a survival tech-
nique at play that allows a gay person to see what he
needs to see. Sure, Robert and I enjoyed the cute
Italian boys stuffed in their tights with bulging cod-
pieces. But get real: Watching the big throbbing heterosexual love document of Western civilization
requires some fancy footwork for a young queer person. Part of me was angry that I couldn't see a movie
in which a cute Montague boy loves a sweet Capulet
fellow. I had to figure out how to project myself into
the film and use the images for my own purposes. As
I watched, sometimes I was Romeo/Tim, hanging out
with his friends. The next moment I was Juliet/Tim,
throwing herself on Romeo/Robert's chest. Later I was
Mercutio/Tim, so obviously in love with
Romeo/Robert, if you do a careful textual analysis.
Finally — this was my favorite one — I was
Romeo/Tim and was going to run away with
Mercutio/Robert. Already codependent, I wanted to
save him from his pain. We would run off to some-
place safe and fine — like the Renaissance Pleasure
Faire in the San Fernando Valley. We would make a
life together there: We'd get a little duplex over a tal-
low maker's shop. There would be a big fluffy bed

with feather comforters. Robert and I would take our clothes off and slip our bodies between the cool sheets. We'd swim around like dolphins in the soft bedclothes. It would be just like when I was a little boy and I came home from church: I would throw my clothes off the second I got home, the plaid suit, the clip-on tie, the red velvet vest, and the tight shoes flung to the four directions in a blink. I would then slip my naked little boy's body between the polyester sheets. I loved getting back into bed in the middle of the day. It felt exciting and sinful. I would rub myself all over against the fabric, loving the feelings, making them mine, reclaiming my body from church and state.

Robert squeezed my hand as we watched the film reach its sorrowful climax. The shit happened. The sword was pulled. The poison was drunk to its lees. Everyone was torn from the person he or she loved. There was a plague on both our houses.

The movie ended, and all were punished.

The lights came up slowly in the theater. Nobody in the audience knew what to say. It was very quiet. We left the auditorium and walked quietly out past the tar pits. I went off by myself through the trees down to the chain-link fence surrounding the pits. Hypnotized by the moonlight sheen of water hovering over this fate-filled tar pit, I gazed at the giant plastic sculptures of the woolly mammoth family on the other side of the tar pit lake. They'd been there as long as I could remember, forty-foot-tall statues of a mom and dad and baby woolly mammoth stuck there across the pit. The dad is trapped in the tar and sinks toward death as his son bawls. I looked at the sculptures of the mammoth family, feeling the cool metal of the fence beneath my fingers.

I was about to return to my friends when I saw something move in the water. The woolly mammoth dad started to move. He opened his eyes, and his long trunk snaked out into the night. He lifted one massive woolly mammoth leg, tar dripping from each woolly mammoth toenail. Then a rapier pierced through the tar. There were these shapes by the mammoth. Tybalt and Mercutio and Romeo and Juliet rose out of the tar, hovered a bit, and whispered to me...

"Live these days.
"Love well.
"Value every kiss.
"And savor your body's blink between being born and dying."

The apparitions waved at me sadly, nodded to each other, and sank slowly back into the unforgiving tar pit. Only the woolly mammoths were left. I was sure I saw the woolly mammoth dad wink at me before he threw his tusks back in a permanent plastic death trumpet. My eyes as big as pizzas, I shook my head, and the vision disappeared.

I ran back to Lori and Robert. I wanted to explain to them what I had seen, to share the Good News of the woolly mammoth's message, but I just couldn't find the words. Instead I danced like a lunatic, leading them down the path in the park through the dinosaur sculpture garden. I leapfrogged over the bronze saber-toothed tiger. Climbing up on top of a bronze mastodon, I crowed to the night:

"And yet I wish but for the thing I have:
My bounty is as boundless as the sea,
My love as deep; the more I give to thee,

The more I have, for both are infinite."

(I knew these lines by heart because I had the sound track to the movie.) I fell off the tiger and was caught in Robert and Lori's arms. We raced each other through the park past all the other dinosaur statues toward my VW. I wrapped my arms around the ugly metal bust of a three-toed sloth and gave it a big kiss on its dew-covered metal lips. Robert spun me around and stuck his tongue down my throat, pinning me against the staring eyes of the sloth. Lori stood by my car and called to us. Holding hands tight, Robert and I ran like dive-bombers toward her.

I opened the passenger door, and Robert got in the back and Lori in the front. We laughed and screamed and joked about our night together. We were just so glad to be together in a car in Los Angeles in 1975 and not in Verona in 1303! I drove a little bit too fast down Sixth Street toward La Brea Avenue. I kept trying to catch Robert's eye in the backseat. I just wanted to keep kissing him, splayed out on that three-toed-sloth sculpture. I had to keep the connection going.

Robert looked as if he were about to say something important. He stammered, "I..."

"What?" I asked, looking way over my shoulder, eyes *not* on the road. Our eyes met, and we smiled at each other. Silently Robert mouthed the words "I love you."

Then it happened.

The car was snapped up in the jaws of a merciless *Tyrannosaurus rex.* I heard the crunch of metal, the breaking of glass. Rubber burned. We were thrown into a wild, panic-filled slow-motion tumble. Our bodies flew forward, and I was hit in the heart as the steering wheel knocked the wind out of me. My head snapped forward, and the windshield cracked as my forehead banged against the glass. I saw Lori hit the windshield with her cheekbone as Robert was thrown between the front seats, cutting his face on the rearview mirror. The horn was stuck blowing. Gas leaked from the tank. The woolly mammoth in the tar pit heard it and struggled to escape and come save me, but he just sank deeper toward death.

Why? Why, God? I thought to myself. *Why on my only date with a boy in high school did I have to rear-end a hopped-up maroon El Camino at forty-five miles per hour, thus totaling my beloved Bug?*

As if I had just been shoved off the top of Mount Everest, I fell kicking and screaming through the icy Himalayan air while questions careened through me: *How could this happen to me now, at the pinnacle of my young life? Can I get the car home somehow? Was anybody killed? How will I explain this? Did I look like I had been kissing a boy all night long?*

We got out of the crunched Bug. "Are you okay?" I said, stroking Robert's face to see if he had been scarred for life.

"Wow. That was intense," he said, grinning weakly. "I think I'm all in one piece. I'm going to have to put this in a song."

Lori had a small cut on her face but was also fine. I checked my body for contusions and hemorrhages just like my oldest brother's Boy Scout manual advised. Then I moved back to Robert, my touch lingering a long time — his belly felt so nice under my hand — as I checked for signs of hernia.

It seemed we were all basically in one piece. Onlookers, many of whom had been at *Romeo and Juliet*, began ghoulishly to gather, hoping for blood. My car was dead, the front end smashed in. The woolly mammoth could not help. Who will save me now? With a soul-sucking dread, I realized all I could do was call my father.

I felt about two inches tall as I made my way to a phone booth on Fairfax Avenue. My hands were shaking as I pulled out a dime, slipped it into the slot, and dialed. My dad picked up.

"Hi, Dad," I started cheerfully. There was no easy way to do this. "Have you been having a nice evening at home? Is Mom back from work? By the way, I totaled my car. Please don't kill me."

There was a long sigh on the other end of the phone. It was full of my dad's resignation about many things in his life that had not panned out as he had hoped. Like most of his fellow seventeen-year-old friends from Alhambra High School who had enlisted early in World War II to fight the Japanese, he seemed to feel as if everything that came after the war was a bit of a letdown. I knew that in a few minutes this stew of disappointment about his life would transform itself, inevitably becoming an icy rage. This phenomenon would *not* be something to look forward to.

"Where are you?" my dad asked, settling for a practical mode. "I'll come and bring you guys home."

Twenty minutes later he arrived, followed shortly thereafter by a tow truck. He hauled his large frame out of the small Japanese car, another indignity for this Pearl Harbor avenger. I saw my father's body moving toward me, as lumbering as those dinosaurs in the park. As often happened, I was shocked that this large, aging man had once been a cute, skinny Navy boy. Had he ever actually fit into those South Pacific–blue woolen sailor pants that were hanging up in the front closet? I would hide in that closet and sniff the thirteen-button front flap. Often I wore my dad's sailor suit to costume parties or to private masturbation dates in my bedroom.

Without saying a word, my dad surveyed the situation. I don't think he dumped a big shame trip on me, but I definitely could be repressing that. The tow truck took my VW away, and we piled into Dad's Datsun for the grim drive back to Whittier.

There I was, sitting in my dad's car, looking over my shoulder again at Robert. Mere minutes before, I had been flying down the streets of Los Angeles, full of hope for the future. This was unacceptable. My mind raced as I plotted to myself. How could I salvage this evening? I looked at Robert. All I wanted to do was lie down with him and kiss him. My sense of justice was aghast at the unfairness of these circumstances. I started to improvise plans and strategies. Finally I had the solution.

"You know, Dad," I offered smoothly, "it's very late, isn't it? It really doesn't make sense to drive Robert all the way back to Anaheim. Maybe he should stay at our house tonight, and then we can drive him home in the morning."

This was a pretty creative approach, considering the limitations of my options.

My dad raised one bushy eyebrow: Seventeen-year-old boys do not generally do sleep-overs, but he was beat, and it was almost midnight. He made a grunting sound, which I quickly translated from angry-father language as meaning "okay" in English.

We got to Whittier and dropped Lori off at her house. She gave me a crossed-fingers sign as the car pulled out of her driveway.

My dad drove the few blocks to our house; he was silent as a somnambulist as he parked the car. We climbed out of the Datsun. While my dad struggled to open the front door of our house with his key (my mom kept locking it on the other side!), I decided this was the last chance for the second part of my plan.

"Gee, Dad," I began casually, "Robert and I are both pretty upset about what has happened tonight — traumatized, really, from the shock of the accident. I think it would be best, and I know you'll agree, if Robert and I slept in the same room tonight to provide each other moral support, just like you did with your buddies during the war when you were pinned down at Guadalcanal."

My dad stopped fiddling with his keys at this point, and he now raised *both* bushy eyebrows. An unformed inkling floated above his head that whispered to him there was something not quite right here with his eager-faced son and his friend Robert, who sported a safety pin in his ear. It would take too much energy to consider it, though. He shoved the thought away, gave me a funny look, but then just sighed and grunted out a single word: "Whatever."

Now, I know I had said "same room" to my dad, but I really should have said "same bed," because there was only one bed in my room. This was *the* bed, the bed I had been conceived on. My parents had recently bought a brand-new giant double king, and I, ever the drama queen, decided I wanted to have my folks' marriage bed so that I could sleep on The Bed I Was Conceived On.

Robert and I went into my room. I put a chair underneath the doorknob so nobody could get in. We both stood next to my plaster-of-paris bust of Wagner. Shifting nervously from foot to foot, I patted Wagner on the head for luck and then put my hand on Robert's shoulder.

"What a night!" I said, stating the obvious. Robert looked into my eyes and nodded. I felt our bodies open toward each other, like big doors testing their hinges to see if they work. We started to hug and kiss. Robert's body felt like an alien life-form, hard in some places and soft in others, as he shifted in my embrace. His eyes were closed as he opened his mouth to mine. I saw his eyelashes up close. Those delicate blond lashes seemed like the most beautiful thing I had ever seen.

Feeling his warmth, I suddenly understood that this closeness is what everyone had been talking about. This was the best thing we get while we're in this life. It was what I had been looking for on Roger Blainey's belly — not just the quest for sex but the inside-my-heart desire to hold and be held by another boy revealed itself to me that moment in all its most tender and fierce colors.

Robert and I took off all our clothes except for our cheap, once-they-had-been-white underwear and got into the cold bed. As my skin hit those sheets and I naturally moved to hold his body, I felt like I had started to become a man. That hug just might have been the moment. At that instant I had become a man, and I now had a man's ways: I could comfort my boyfriend as we lay down at the end of a hard day. Kissing Robert's face, I felt that I could soothe Mercutio, who in this story does not die from his wide and deep wound. Tracing the long slide of his spine against the bedclothes, I remembered that little boy I once was who had the good sense to wiggle his body naked between the sheets after church.

Robert and I were silent as we touched each other, our hands moving over one another's bodies, mapping them as our own. I felt the smooth skin on his slender punk-rock stomach. I felt the small child in him still lurking there as his belly button rose and fell with his breath. I stroked his stomach. It felt like a place I wanted to plant a dependable crop, to make a life. I slowly moved my hand farther down to try to feel his cock inside his underwear. As my fingers began to creep under the elastic band, Robert grabbed my hand and stopped me.

"Tim," he said tentatively, looking me in the eye, "you know I'm still pretty fucked-up from that bad sex scene with Ricky Nelson at Knott's Berry Farm. Would it be okay if we just held each other and didn't do a big sex thing tonight?"

My own unreasonable hard-on had taken over my body for a moment, and my first impulse was to kick up a fuss. I could see that Robert was a little scared at how quickly all this was moving. But my heart — and my dick — softened a little, and I realized that just holding each other was more than enough of a miracle for one night. The woolly mammoth had at least taught me that. Something very excellent had happened that night that told me I was so lucky to be there in that bed at the end of a hard day with a scared and (except for his JCPenney underwear) naked punk-rock boy.

Robert looked me in the eye, and we sighed, then settled into our embrace. We kissed. And kissed. And kissed again. His high school senior ring was on my finger. His body was next to mine. His hand was on my heart.

I slept with him on *the* bed, and I was conceived once again.

HOW TO GROW FRUIT

PBS MADE ME GAY. Ultimately we can't give Thomas Mann or Franco Zeffirelli all the credit. PBS finally tipped the scales. This was every right-wing nut's 3 A.M. nightmare come true. They broadcast that homo beam right into my family's Republican suburban living room in the mid '70s and saved my life. It was a *Theater in America* production about Oscar Wilde. Thank you, PBS! From you, public television, I received my first dose of queer images and a sense of historical place and lineage! (I also got a PBS mug and an attractive tote bag, but that's another story.)

Well, maybe I can't give PBS *all* the credit. It could also have been the Los Angeles Civic Light Opera. Their revival of *A Funny Thing Happened on the Way to the Forum,* perhaps? The hopeful downbeat of the tuba at the climax of "Comedy Tonight" may have been the much-needed magic wand to make me queer. That showstopper, replete with the cute chorus-boy queens in their buttock-revealing tunics, of course. Or while we're indulging a Greco-Roman mood, maybe it was those delicious Mary Renault novels with all the buffed Athenian ephebes kneeling at Socrates' feet as they searched for truth, beauty, and biceps? A little dab'll do ya!

No, wait, I know. It had to be George Frideric Handel. His music helped tell me who I was and sent me zooming out of the closet accompanied by those tacky sparklers he wrote music about. Yes, there is absolutely no question: Handel's *Messiah* made me into a faggot!

Allow me to explain. It was 1976. I need to sniff the crotch of my maroon double-thick corduroy bell bottoms to help me remember 1976! The capacious toothy grin of soon-to-be-president Jimmy Carter spread like smooth peanut butter across the land. I can take a whiff of that Jif and then sniff my way back to that tremulous year. Let me rub those bell bottoms through my ass crack, reach inside the pockets of those pants, past the pocket-size tube of Clearasil acne ointment, and grab my dripping teenage wienie.

On September 21, 1976, the day before my eighteenth birthday, I arrived for my first day at California State University, Fullerton, a proto–punk-rock wanna-be and a reluctant virgin. My brief college career began with Modern Dance 101A. Sneaking into the men's dressing room, I molted my clothes and slipped into my slinky dance belt, as dignified as a drag queen.

I had escaped from the S/M rigors of high school PE and had been taking dance classes instead throughout my senior year. No more shirts-and-skins football teams for me! This recruiting of gay boys for dance class was part of an ambitious program during the first term of Governor Jerry Brown called Homosexual Vocational Training. Participating faculty were encouraged to locate likely queer students for inclusion in this employment-development initiative. I get down on my knees and thank my drama and dance teacher, Mr. Bucalstein, for recommending me for the program.

Mr. Bucalstein was not queer but knew a gay student when he saw one. Starting in eleventh grade, he scoured drama, chorus, and band classes to find boys to become part of Governor Brown's vision. He made us all take dance class — and thus helped me escape from the degrading experience of phys ed.

My life really began once I stopped getting hit in the head with various hard balls without my shirt on and started learning how to move my body. One Saturday Mr. Bucalstein piled the gay boys in a school van and drove us to the nearest Danskin shop to buy that special item for our dick and balls, the dance belt. (A dance belt is similar to our friend the jockstrap but is made with a heavy-duty elastic fabric that smashes your meat and potatoes flat into a seamless bulge.) This was the clearest initiation I ever publicly received in acknowledgment of my gay boy's body: my teacher taking his queer male students in a school van to buy their dance belts. Governor Brown was so impressed with the good work Mr. Bucalstein had done that he flew down from Sacramento to present each of us Future Fags of America with a special commemorative dance belt emblazoned with the California state seal.

"Young men," Governor Brown said to us somberly that day after the presentation of the dance belts, "you are the future of homosexual America. Wear these dance belts with pride!" The vocational training program for gay boys had convinced me that the life of the performer was the one for me.

In the changing rooms for the dance studios at Cal State Fullerton this first day of college, I struggled to tuck my dick and balls into a comfortable arrangement in the polyester pouch of the dance belt. This presented me with a challenge as difficult as making an origami porcupine. Balls tucked up above or smooshed below? Should the dick point boldly upward or be

folded under? I opted for the "pointed toward God"
arrangement, and I slipped my tights on over my
dance-belted mound. I completed my ensemble with
my cutoff Patti Smith T-shirt. I reentered the dance
studio and was about to start my warm-up when my
eyes were pulled out of my head by the sight of a sleek
fellow stretching in the corner by the ballet bar.

He was a dark-haired vision doing some deep bending pliés as he faced the mirror. His tights were cut off
below his knees and showed off a pair of powerful
calves. His leotard plunged low on his chest, suggest-
ing a whole new set of possibilities for upper-body
wear. As I watched him warm up, I saw his arm wind-
mill over his leg, where it seemed effortlessly to circle
his ear. The room mysteriously tilted in his direction,
and I began to slip and slide toward his embrace.
Another cute dancer boy, with an obvious perm and
wearing an unfortunate metallic silver unitard,
touched him on the arm and said, "Hi, David."

His name was David! That name means "king," I
thought. *Or if it doesn't, it fucking well should.*

He was totally beautiful. He looked like...David
Bowie. (I'm talking about the hyperstylish *Station to
Station* Bowie, not the saliva-dripping *Diamond Dogs*
Bowie, okay?) The dancer David, like Mr. Bowie, had
long legs and fine black-brown hair courtesy of a
henna highlight rinse. He boasted a tight, hard body,
skinny and thickly sinewy at the same time. In those
days there was more than one possible attractive body
type available to gay men, unlike today's steroid-pro-
voked fantasy ideal sold to us by closeted fashion
designers. David's arms were as long and vital as a
giraffe's legs, his face set off by a delicate strand of
off-white puka shells around his neck. He, without

question, represented one version of the homo physical ideal of 1976, at least as far as my eyes could see.

David was the best dancer in the class, and the big queen dance teacher obviously favored him. David dived into each arabesque, devouring the space as he flung himself through the dance combination, scraping the acoustic-tile ceiling every time he leaped. When my turn came to do the movement sequence in front of the class, I tried to match David's power as I danced only for his eyes.

Who was he? Who was this man who would be so much to me? The fuel he gave me still fires lots of kisses. The taste of the food we ate together is somewhere on the plate at every table where I sit with a man at my side. The touch David taught me is on the tips of my fingers each time they've danced over another man's body ever since. The back of David's neck is suddenly there on another man in a bed fifteen years later. To this day I think I still strive to nuzzle that neck, to sniff my way back to a moment that seems a long time ago. I don't mean this as an obvious Rosebud kind of explanation for everything that would come afterward. It's more like the vulnerability and vitality of the back of David's neck held a few of the answers to the mysteries that I would spend the rest of my life trying to unravel. Of course, I didn't know how David would change my life that first day I saw him in dance class. I just knew I wanted to hold this man with the black-brown hair very close to me.

As I finished the combination, I caught a glimpse of myself in the dance studio mirror wearing the thick wire-rimmed aviator-style eyeglasses that often made people mistake me for a lesbian separatist from Ann Arbor.

I stood near David at one end of the studio, and I got so anxious that hives started to appear on my upper left arm. I began fiddling with my fingers in the new "natural" Afro hairstyle that my barber, Big Al Stumpo, had given me. (Big Al Stumpo had tried for years to tame my relentless curls. All during high school he had forced me to brush through my bristles and comb all those curls to one side. They'd pile up like an electrocuted poodle over my left ear; then, one by one, the curls would spring back with an audible twang. In 1976 Big Al Stumpo finally gave up. He threw his enormous nicotine-stained hands in the air and said, "*Basta!* Have it your own way. A curl's gotta do what a curl's gotta do!")

Forcing my fingers to leave my hair, I danced my way a little clumsily through the next part of the teacher's combination, a really hard turn and jump, watching David the whole time. The dance belt under my tights was strained to its polyester limits by my suddenly growing boner. The word EUREKA on the California state seal was getting bigger by the second. Somehow I managed to get through every contraction and release without anyone noticing.

Now, watching David demonstrate the final set of movements, I felt my head full of frizzy curls pulled toward his dancing form. I wanted time to stop, to walk up to David and begin our pas de deux then and there. I had that scared-excited feeling I had only read about in big books by Flaubert: Everything in my life was about to change.

At the end of the class, my eyes connected with David's for one wide-screen moment in the mirror of the rehearsal studio. My dance belt had crawled up my asshole; there was a big wet spot on the front of my tights. I turned quickly away, trembling.

Out of the corner of my eye, I saw David walk with clipped dignity toward his belongings. He knelt down and wrote something on a piece of paper, glancing at me once over his shoulder. Then he hoisted his dance bag to shoulder height and walked to the door. At the last moment he crisply reached down by my backpack and slipped a folded piece of orange paper inside. He shot me a nervous look, then quickly left.

I took a breath, counted to three, then raced over to my bag. There it was, right next to my Carter-Mondale campaign literature: a flyer for the lesbian and gay student group on which he had written, "Call me later. I'll be home around 9:30. David."

I looked at my watch every three seconds for the next eleven hours. *Why do I have to wait so long to call him? Tomorrow is my eighteenth birthday. I need to have sex before then and stop being a virgin. My homosexual biological clock is ticking!*

For those interminable few hours, I sat in a litter-strewn McDonald's, writing desperate poetry in my journal. Finally, my heart playing the bongos, I called David. No answer. I waited a few minutes and called again. He picked up.

I didn't know what to say. "I got your note," I stammered.

"Good."

I could hear a tiny creak in David's voice too. I listened to his anxious breath flow in and out against my sweaty ear at the receiver.

"Um...thanks for the note," I said. An uncomfortable long pause followed. "It was a nice note."

"Do you want to come over?" David asked.

"Oh, gosh, I don't know. It's late." I tried to play it a little cool. My face was crushed against the phone

booth glass, fogging its surface with my breath. I had
written TIM + DAVID in its residue. "Oh. Sure. I'll be
right there. Where do you live?"

After scrawling the directions on the back of my
class registration form, I sped to David's sprawling
stucco apartment complex off Yorba Linda Boulevard,
just spitting distance from the little house where Nixon
was born (and buried). I parked on a side street by
David's building. I entered the sprawl of the complex,
which was named, in a bold gesture to bilingualism,
Vista de los Muchachos del Mar. I walked past the hot
tub, overflowing with soapsuds. I sniffed in the tart
whoosh of the swooning marigolds in the hot breath of
the September Santa Ana breeze: Sharp chlorine, Mr.
Bubble, and the desert wind are what that night in my
life smelled like. I climbed up three flights of stairs,
found David's unit, and knocked softly.

David opened the door slowly, glowing in his '50s
red rayon bowling shirt. The smell of herb tea and
something baking drifted through behind him.

"Come in," he said, opening the door wide.

I had never before visited a friend who had his own
place. He showed me around. Even today I remember
David's apartment so vividly, I can draw the floor plan
as accurately as any architect. I could diagram the
deep-shag living room, piled high with books and
musical scores. I could draft the military organization
of the kitchen. Every single utensil hanging expec-
tantly there on the pegboard was outlined meticulous-
ly in red paint to mark its proper position. The obses-
siveness of this seemed a warning signal that David
had some pretty serious control issues lurking here.
My feet could still find their way in the dark down the
skinny hallway past the bamboo balcony overlooking

the Mervyn's department store parking lot. I could peek into the red-lightbulb–lit bedroom with the auto repair shop sign over the bed which read, ALL DELIVERIES MADE IN THE REAR. This was David's house; it reflected his independence and his point of view. Someday I hoped I would be just like him.

We sat down on the small couch in the living room and began to talk. David brewed me some highly bohemian herbal tea he had created himself from peppermint, strawberry, and *lavender* flower leaves.

I was awed by the extreme adultness of the situation. I could not believe that I was in a suspected homosexual's house, sipping tea other than Lipton. It made me so jittery that I kept using big words in absurd sentences.

"You know, David," I said, "I think postmodern dance creates an existential opportunity in which the artist must be a kind of Nietzschean *Übermensch* in defiance of stultifying normative bourgeois values."

David smiled mysteriously and changed the subject, telling a story about his family instead. He had been a military brat and had gone to high school in Japan. David let fall a hint that he had graduated from high school in 1970. I quickly did my simple math and was shocked. This meant David was at least *twenty-four* years old. I had never hung out with anyone quite so old before.

David, like all of us, had his scars from those twenty-four years. He told me that he had been queer-bashed in front of a gay bar in nearby blue-collar Garden Grove. The attackers stabbed him nine times in the neck with an ice pick. He showed me the denim shirt he'd been wearing that night. The shirt was still caked with brick-red dried blood. I could see the thin tear lines on the fabric where the ice pick skated along until the sharp point found its way into his flesh. Two months later David would give me the shirt he had almost been killed in. I still keep it safe on a shelf to remind me of where I come from.

These last bits of information were a bit *too* adult and scary. I finally shut up and stared broodingly into my brewing tea.

At last we got to the main subject. I could see David had something he wanted to tell me. I cradled my warm mug of tea in my palm and gave him my rapt attention. This could be it.

"There's something I have to tell you about myself," David said shyly, drawing infinity signs on the floor with his argyle-socked toes as he struggled to say what was on his mind. "I hope what I tell you now won't make you think less of me. I wouldn't feel right if I went even one more second without letting you know this most important part of who I am. I hope that we can still be friends after I share this. Tim, I'm…"

I was so eager for David to spill the beans that my grip on the mug was bending the handle to the snapping point. Why can't he just spit it out?

"Tim, I'm…a musician." David quickly looked away toward the gleaming headlights pouring down Yorba Linda Boulevard. "In addition to my dance classes at Cal State, I am also taking music theory and orchestra conducting. Whew, I feel so relieved to have gotten that out."

Things were not proceeding as I had hoped. I thought David was about to tell me he was a big faggot and that he wanted my body. David was the older man here. I needed *him* to help get this show on the road.

"Now there is something I need to know about you," David continued with a new urgency in his voice. "I must ask you a very personal question. Your answer may really affect how close you and I will be able to become. Tim, what kind of music do you like?"

Oh, no. David was asking me the music question. I'm lost! I knew I had to come up with the right answer. I peeked over his shoulder and scanned his record collection, displayed on the shelf behind the couch.

"I like many kinds of music." While I spoke my eyes danced along the spines of the records, trying to find a hint of the right answer. I locked on target as I saw three shelves piled with Purcell, Handel, and Monteverdi. "I would say, though, that I am primarily obsessed with classical eighteenth-century vocal music." I lied, omitting the Patti Smith and the show tunes.

I had won the daily double! David lit up at this and jumped to his feet and spoke excitedly. "This is such an amazing coincidence. That's my area of study! I have a huge record collection of this period." David swung his arm wide, gesturing to the record shelves two feet behind the couch. "You know, in my conducting class we're working on something right now that will really interest you. We're studying the 'Amen' from Handel's *Messiah*!"

David was so thrilled by the miracle of our shared interest that he jumped up and walked toward his sound system, his butt shifting lazily beneath his thrift-shop tuxedo pants with each step. He approached his Radio Shack combo record player–radio tuner–eight-track–cassette deck. He pulled a record (remember them?) from its sleeve and placed it on the turntable. The phono needle found its scratchy groove and clicked into the final section of *The Messiah.* David listened and then slowly began to talk about the music as the stately voices vaulted through the cheap speakers.

"Listen," he whispered, his eyes pressed tightly closed. "I love this part of the composition. How simply it begins. The voices make a community. People gathering. Did you ever see *How the Grinch Stole Christmas* on TV? Well, it's like when all the Whos down in Whoville sing that sweet song. Everybody holding hands. Greeting each of the voices. Blessings. Honor. Glory. Power."

David moved slowly nearer and nearer to me on the couch as he spoke. I smelled the steeping peppermint on his skin. I put down my tea and turned my body toward him, my center of gravity slowly shifting into his orbit as the record player twirled.

"Handel does something great here!" he exclaimed as the voices leaped up to a new rhythm. "It's like the baritones are flirting with the tenors. The bull-dyke altos are trying to pick up the girlish sopranos. They're all going to go out tonight to the opening of some fabulous club, and they're inviting you and me along. They just might find a way of understanding this weird world. A way of understanding who *we* are."

David moved his leg up and down against mine as he slowly rocked with the music. I stretched my arms wide as I pantomimed a yawn and maneuvered my hand to rest behind his head on the couch. He grabbed my knee — hard.

"And right when it seems it can't get more intense," he continued, letting his hand fall to the inside of my thigh, "at that moment all the voices come together and zap it up one more notch. They remind us to be who we *should* be. Remind us to listen to ourselves. To know ourselves. Loving our bodies. Trusting each other. This is how we should be!"

David gently pulled my hand into his. I worried that my palms were too sweaty.

"It's like they're building a doorway for us," he whispered with the music. "The string continuo kicks in and joins the celebration. These voices are making a place for you and me. It's a way out of a place we have been trapped inside of for so long and never knew it. Finally, Tim, we walk outside together, hand in hand, into this new world!"

The energy of the chorus built. At last David stopped with the music lesson and put his arms around me. He looked into my eyes as his lips moved slowly closer. I felt his breath on my face. Very gently his lips landed on my expectant mouth. Then — so softly, softly, softly — my new friend David, who looked like Bowie, kissed me!

For an instant I thought my brain would explode. I saw shooting lights and every picture in my photo album race in front of my eyes, a crazily shuffled deck. Then David broke away from our kiss, grabbed the phono needle, and noisily scratched it across side B of Handel's *Messiah*.

"I think we've had enough...Handel...for one evening," he said, hiding a little panic.

David made a beeline to the kitchen and boiled some water. He shifted us from the yangy (anything could happen) peppermint to soothing (I'm so sleepy) chamomile. Then we held hands some more, listened to the Bach Mass in B Minor, and called it a night.

As I drove down La Habra Boulevard past Richard Nixon's first law office, I felt David's tongue on my lips, his taste as fresh as a bite of an apple. The skin of that red fruit was so shiny that I could see reflected in it who I was about to become. I pulled my 1965 blue Volkswagen Bug in front of Nixon's office and remembered my fourth-grade crush on Nixon's third cousin Scott Milhous, a schoolmate of mine who'd once walked me home.

I knew that when I got back to Whittier, it would be time to have a very serious talk with my mom and dad. In my adolescence I had always subscribed to the slash-and-burn school of relations with parents: fits of outrage, extreme ideological transformations, a knee-jerk willingness to pass judgment on my parents' meaningless lives. The usual. I insisted on wearing my full Chairman Mao uniform to Christmas Eve midnight mass. When the chorus came in singing, "Oh, come, all ye faithful," I would stand up in the last pew, turn my back, and wave my little red book in protest.

I didn't do these things for *me*. I did these things for *them*. I needed to keep my parents on their toes. I was their last kid, and they needed to keep their parental reflexes up. This scorched-earth policy would now be put to the test. It seemed like a perfectly good time to come out to them.

It was late, really late, when I got back home. My parents were still up. I walked into their bedroom, where they lay in bed reading. Bettie and George looked at me, my dad over his *Time* magazine, my mom over her cleavage-festooned romance novel. My mom had her nightly facial of Noxzema slathered thick on her face; the Noxzema had started to harden around the edges and was turning a graham-cracker brown.

"I think we need to talk," I said, nervously cracking my already cracked knuckles. "I need to tell you something very important. I know you've been worrying about me ever since I first did that summer musical theater intensive before eighth grade. I wish I could tell you those worries were not founded. But I can't. Mom, Dad, I'm gay."

The tense pause lasted a millennium. My dad rolled his eyes heavenward. My mom's book fell to her chin and got smeared with Noxzema as she started making great heaving sobs, like a dying sea lion struggling for breath.

"I just hope you're not going to blame me," she said. "I know they always try to blame the mother."

My dad looked like I had just served him a delicious meal of live baby rattlesnakes. He struggled with his first impulse to fly into a Zeus-like rage. He dug deep into his psyche to locate a patrimony, a special gift for me, his only queer son. My dad went way back.

"Son, I want you to be careful," he offered. "I was in the Navy, in the big one, South Pacific, World War II. I know something about this stuff. Don't wear dresses on shore leave, and you probably won't get beat up."

Clearly this brought up a nervous subject for my mom. "George!" she shouted, rapping him on the thigh. "We said we would never talk about that!" Mom cleverly shifted gears, getting me in her sights once again. Struggling not to telegraph her distaste, she asked, "Do you have a boyfriend?"

"Yes, I do," I answered, squaring my shoulders in an approximation of fierce resolve. "His name is David. He looks like David Bowie. I love him. He lives by Cal State Fullerton. If I'm not home at night, you'll know where I am. I'll bring him over so you can meet him."

As my father so often did in moments of great stress, he lifted up one hip and let out a huge fart that shook the pictures on the wall. This signaled his desire to escape this topic for the time being. "Well, whatever. It's garbage night. Don't forget to put out the trash cans," he reminded me.

My mom's focus was being pulled back to the sex scene in the hayloft of her romance novel. "Honey, we still love you in spite of this soul-killing news," she tossed my way, licking her finger and turning the page in her book. *"Hasta la mañana."*

They went back to their reading. At that moment, like Miss Peggy Lee, I had to wonder: *Is that all there is?* I slipped out into the kitchen and grabbed the one telephone in our house, strategically placed right next to my parents' bedroom so they could monitor my phone calls. I stretched the cable far around the corner, through the service porch, out into the backyard, and back into the kitchen through the patio sliding-glass door. Far from my parents' prying ears, I could now talk in private and called David.

"Hi, David? It's Tim."

"Hi, hon."

Hon! He called me "hon." Have any two people ever been more intimate? We whispered to each other as I twirled the lazy Susan on the kitchen table around and around. I laid the side of my head on the formica and watched it circle. The salt began to blur with the A.1. from Taco Night, which got mixed up with the ketchup, a swirling and twirling of our lives that was as lazy as that Susan.

"I told my parents," I said. "I had the big conversation with them. I was so nervous beforehand. My dad was so uptight, he farted really loud."

"You're kidding!" David said, cracking up. I noticed that he had the most beautiful laugh I had ever heard. "Your dad sounds like Archie Bunker."

"He's actually okay. I need you to meet both of them sometime soon," I said, hoping we wouldn't have to talk about my parents much longer.

"I want to see you tomorrow," David said. "I want us to make love on your eighteenth birthday."

"!"

"Tim, I want it to be special."

"Oh."

"Meet me in the second-floor dance studio at Cal State at 9 P.M. I have the key. I'll be waiting for you."

"I'll see you there, David. Um, should I bring anything?"

"Well, don't bring any Noxzema, whatever you do!" he said, laughing. "Why don't you get some Vaseline Intensive Care Lotion, aloe vera scent, and bring that?"

"Okay. I'll see you tomorrow night."

For the first time in my life, I blew a smacking air kiss into the telephone receiver just to see what it felt like. On cue David returned an equally wet smack. I was in heaven.

The next day was my eighteenth birthday. I got up very early so I wouldn't have to talk to my parents right away. I filled a large salad bowl with Captain Crunch cereal and ate it in my car so my getaway was assured. Burning rubber, I raced through the streets of Whittier and went directly to the Thrifty's drugstore. There I bought the largest bottle of Vaseline Intensive Care Lotion available in the industrialized world. It was so heavy, I made sure to lift it with my legs, not my back. Hauling it to the front of the store, I heaved it up onto the one open checkout counter.

The elderly woman at the cash register could not resist some early-morning Thrifty's humor. Snickering through her Lee press-on nails as she stared at the huge vat of skin lotion, she said, "Young man, you must have *really* dry skin!" An orgy of self-congratulatory laughter ensued. I proceeded to melt into the floor with embarrassment. I felt like I had a huge sign over my head that read, BUTT FUCKER.

"Um...it's not what you think," I stammered, unprepared for her sarcasm. "It's a birthday present...for a friend with a bad case of rug burn." I threw my money down on the rotating rubber mat and fled.

Then I drove up to my special place in the hills of La Habra, where I vigorously wrote for a long time in my journal. As I lay there surrounded by the yellow crackle of the dry grass, I reread the dog-eared sexy bits from Mary Renault's *The Persian Boy*.

As night arrived, I went home, bathed, and then drove to Cal State Fullerton. I parked my car by the gymnasium and went toward the arts building. I paused at the door, inhaling the night's blooming jasmine. Up to that point my life felt like it had been written by somebody else in a big weird dusty book on a top shelf, just out of my reach. That was about to change. I walked up the stairs into the building as if I were going up to accept an Academy Award.

I climbed to the second floor and slowly opened the heavy metal door. The dance studio was dark except for a single white candle. I tried to see where David was.

"David," I whispered. "Psst, David. It's me."

I heard a loud scratch on a record: The "Amen" from Handel's *Messiah* began to play on the dance studio's phonograph. I closed my eyes and fell into the music.

David's arms enfold me, and we begin to kiss, the kiss I had been waiting my whole life for. Our lips hunger for each other, make a dance together. David bites the corner of my upper lip gently. This is the touch I have trying to find ever since I learned to tie my shoes — this brother, this son, this friend, this father in my arms as the sun rises inside me at last. He bites my neck. Yes.

David's hands run over my body. Each rolling feeling lets me know myself even as my hands run down his back, feeling his chest, his heart beating within. I want to climb inside his mouth and swim around inside him, find every hidden wet place, which I know belongs to me now. I come out by pushing one finger into his mouth, even as he teaches me the turn of our bone and muscle.

His hair slips through my fingers. I reach under his shirt and feel his skin, stroking the scars where the bashers' ice pick almost killed him. He peels my clothes from me, uncovering a new life underneath.

Handel's voices waver around each other in great oceany swells, like all the angels in heaven around Dante in that famous Doré engraving or, at least, like the June Taylor dancers on The Jackie Gleason Show. There's a swirling kaleidoscope of kicking legs in high heels. I know more than I've ever known anything in my whole life that this is what God wants me to do. This is what's right for me.

David reaches down and grabs my dick; the touch blows my thoughts to some scattered galaxy I forgot I knew. My eyes look to the back of my brain: Stars shoot inside me, through me, his hand moving on me. His lips surround me. Comets whiz by my eyes. A shower of meteors streaks inside my heart.

David and I spin around each other to the music, leaning far back in each other's arms as we twirl. He falls to his knees, and my cock is in his mouth. Wow! All the voices in my head get really loud. Now. Here. Finally. To find this place inside myself with another man. I am eighteen fucking years old. I know the touch I want on my skin. We jump through each other, blessing each other with our touch. Blessing our lives as we live them. One big fucking Amen to guide us through them. The trumpets pull us higher. All the voices reach a peak. David's mouth is so wet, my body so alive. I can see everything that I ever hoped I'd be. Everything is right and makes perfect sense in that moment of complete and absolute rest!

The music climaxes.

And so do we.

Amen.

My breath rushed in and out, deeper than I had ever felt it before. The oxygen was getting to every last cell in my body. I felt breath race through my blood into my heart, filling my belly, caressing the place where I once broke my right leg, right down to my littlest toenails. I slowly returned from whatever distant part of the universe I had just traveled to. I heard the elegant dance of the record-player needle raising itself, arcing across the now finished music, and placing itself back home.

David nestled down with me on the cool floorboards and rubbed our come onto my chest. I had always focused so much on what it would be like the first time I had sex that I had never imagined what happened afterward. In movies people looked like they had had a chance to comb their hair and have a cigarette. I had never imagined how messy and full of smells sex would actually be. My hair was wet and hanging in my eyes. A thin trickle of sweat meandered down my flank from my armpit. Filling my nostrils, the charged smell of come was as strong as adding a gallon of chlorine to the hot tub. My body felt wet and bloody, like I had been in a battle or just given birth.

David doodled in the come on my body, drawing little pictures, then erasing them with a swipe of his hand. I closed my eyes and tried to sense what he was drawing: a treble clef and some music notes, a house with smoke coming out of the chimney, then a few words that I couldn't make out. Covered in come, I was like an Etch-A-Sketch — my favorite toy as a kid because you could draw and erase it and then draw something new.

I looked at David and got really scared at all this closeness. His face seemed too big, like he might eat me up and swallow me. The fingernail he was drawing with suddenly felt really sharp, like it might cut me right to my heart. I noticed a wrinkle around the corner of his gentle eyes that was a little more human than I was used to. Appearing from nowhere, a tsunami-size wave of shame at being covered in come leaped up in me for a fleeting torturous moment. I quickly suppressed an impulse to run for the hills.

Finally getting the message, I felt the words DAVID LOVES TIM being drawn in come on my body as David lightly kissed my eyelids. I reached down and wrote TIM LOVES DAVID. My body was a surface to be drawn upon. A place to receive messages. A language that I needed to learn to speak.

I WALK DOWN HOLLYWOOD BOULEVARD

"YOU DON'T LOVE ME!"

"I can't be what you want me to be!"

"Just wait until *you* walk the streets of Hollywood!"

"Stop acting like my mother!"

"You don't know what you're losing!"

"I gotta get out of here!"

David and I had just broken up for the fourteenth time since that perfect night at Cal State Fullerton. Our relationship had been a several-month–long passionate roller-coaster ride full of learning, emotional skill building, and sex. At this point I was fluent in the repertoire of eighteenth-century vocal music. However, major stress fractures between us had revealed themselves almost immediately. David wanted to marry me, and I wasn't ready for that. I hadn't even yet escaped from my biological family; I certainly didn't know what to do with David's needs to play mom, dad, husband, and wife with me.

"You'll see what it's like out at the bars," David ominously warned me, drinking tea at a café as we cut our losses. "I hope you don't get hurt."

"I have to explore these things for myself," I replied, more than a little exasperated with him. I hit the table hard, and the teaspoon slid to the floor. "Maybe I *need* to get hurt. I can't have you live my life for me."

"I can't take this, Tim." David sighed. "I know what

I want from a boyfriend. I'm twenty-four years old, I've tricked the list, and I'm sick of it. You won't know what you've lost for a long time. I may need to leave for a while. It's too hard to be around you. I'm thinking of moving to New York to study with the Alwin Nikolais Dance Company."

The waitress slipped our check between us, almost said something, then thought she'd better not. I waited for her to walk away.

"I wish things were different," I said numbly, staring at my hands pressed against the linoleum table. "I might never meet someone like you again." Holding hands in silence for a long time, we mourned where things had ended up as our tea became cold beyond redemption.

I left David there on the rain-slicked street in front of the small café in Fullerton as we parted. The tears that usually refused to come finally made a deal with me when no one would see them. As I watched David climb into his huge sedan and drive away, those tears began to slip down my cheek and around my lips (just a taste) and then drip-drip from my chin.

The last time David and I had had one of these knock-down-drag-outs, I had driven my restored Volkswagen hysterically up into the hills so I could shout into the wind and rain. But I had slipped the clutch and drove my Bug off the dirt road and down into a ravine. It took the combined efforts of three tow trucks to pull it out. This time I would take public transportation.

And I left. Where can you go when you are eighteen and your heart is breaking for the first time? Where else can you go when everything seems doomy and gloomy and all you can see is the "less than" sign...

<

...making everything small and wizened and miser-
ly and suitable only for recycling?

I took a bus to Hollywood.

Many people, especially my pals in New York, get
the wrong idea when I try to explain what Hollywood
meant to me at moments like this. They think I'm
referring to the great industrial Hollywood machine of
celluloid dream and despair. The triumph of pop-cul-
ture banality in Southern California — *that's* what
they think I'm talking about!

No.

For me, growing up in Whittier, just a few miles
east of the glamour capital, Hollywood was a place to
go and have adventures. When you were feeling
wiped out, you could travel to a strange world and
meet people and get in trouble and take drugs and
twist and shout! Hollywood was where the fags were.
Now, maybe if I had been participating with greater
gusto in the prevailing boy-girl routine, I would not
have found it necessary to go into Hollywood. But
since I was clearly and quite happily more interested
in the boy part of the equation, I often found myself
on the Hollywood Freeway going north, a young
homo boy in search of true love, wisdom, and worldly experience.

Leaving David in Fullerton, I had made the long
trek on three buses into Hollywood. I wanted to go
and get messed up by life. I wanted to rub my face in
the mud that David was always telling me about. I
wanted to live the wild experiences David had already
been roughed up by. I pored over my ripped-up copy
of Kerouac's *On the Road* as the bus wheezed through
its endless stops. Finally I got off on Santa Monica
Boulevard in front of the Oki-Dog fast-food joint.

As I stepped down by the plastic bus bench that advertised the services of a nearby Hollywood mortuary, I noticed this guy who looked like John Travolta on *Welcome Back, Kotter* eyeing me as he ate his lewd Oki-Dog chili sausage dripping with relish. His lips made a wide O as they engulfed each bite of the wiener. Chewing the hot dog sensually, he kept eye contact till he swallowed. He was wearing a tight T-shirt advertising the San Gennaro street fair on Mulberry Street in New York City. Dark and compact, the Travolta look-alike seemed as dangerous as a convict in a convent when he popped the last morsel of the wiener into his mouth. He stood up and stretched, offering me a quick glimpse of his hairy, muscled belly, then loped in my direction.

"Hey, John-Boy Walton," he teased, pulling on the strap of my *faux naïf* overalls as he sidled up to me. "You want to come back to my place and smoke a joint?"

"Uh, I don't really know you." I tried to remember the behavior-modification tips the "Goofus and Gallant" comic in *Highlights* magazine had offered for such situations. This eponymous cartoon strip showed us two boys: Goofus was always selfish and belligerent; Gallant, however, constantly shined as a polite and obedient example for the boys of America. I loved reading Goofus and Gallant's binary deportment possibilities as I sat waiting to see the dentist. If there were a cartoon for my current situation, it might go something like: "Goofus goes to strange dark men's apartments and gets his butt fucked. Gallant sensibly ignores such offers and goes home to mow the lawn." It seemed to me like Gallant never had any adventures. I voted for Goofus.

"Sure, let's go," I chirped. "Do you live nearby?"

"I sure do," he smiled and extended his hand. "I'm Vinnie."

We hopped in his car, a Pacer full of old fast-food wrappers, and drove a few blocks. Vinnie parked just below Hollywood Boulevard, and we slowly walked up the block on Highland to his place. It was important to Vinnie that I know he was an Italian-American guy from New York.

"New York! Gosh, what is it like?" I gushed as I waited, like Gallant for a moment, to cross Hollywood Boulevard with the signal.

"It's everything you want it to be," Vinnie replied, waxing poetic as he cruised a stringy-haired boy with a skateboard in front of Danielle's, a drag bar near the corner. "You can fulfill all your dreams and all your nightmares there."

"New York is also the center of postmodern dance and experimental performance art," I added primly, ever the good student. "I plan to go there soon." This was an idea that had popped into my head just at that moment.

My companion arched an eyebrow. "Oh, yeah?" Vinnie purred, knowing he had hit pay dirt. "Well, I know lots of people in off-off-Broadway theater in the Village. I might be able to help you."

"Really? That'd be great," I enthused, my new plan becoming more real by the moment. "Do you know Merce Cunningham and John Cage? I plan to study with them."

We quickly covered the two blocks up Highland to Vinnie's place, a dilapidated little bungalow from the '30s. His front door was charred, as if it had been set on fire by a molotov cocktail.

"What happened to your door?" I asked, my middle-class hackles intuitively rising.

"Oh, someone was trying to scare me," Vinnie shrugged. "They thought I had fucked with them, so they sprayed the door with lighter fluid and torched it. No big deal. I put it out with the hose."

He shoved the door open and invited me in. It was dark inside, like someone was asleep there in the middle of the afternoon. My eyes slowly adjusted. As the room came into focus, I saw there were glossy magazines spread everywhere. Under my feet something crunched, a broken bong in sharp pieces all over the floor. A disturbing smell emanated from the kitchen, where a skyscraper of dirty dishes was stacked precariously in the sink.

I looked for his records. There weren't any. The door shut behind me.

"What are you into, Timbo?" Vinnie said as he began to pinch my left nipple really hard.

Why would anyone want to do that? I thought.

"Feminist politics," I pleaded, backing away from the tit torture.

"Oh, yeah?" Vinnie whispered with hot breath into my ear. "You wanna be my woman? I'm gonna make you my bitch right now."

Kissing me roughly, Vinnie knocked me down on his unmade bed, pulled my pants down over my butt, made the sign of the cross, and rammed his dick up me. (FYI: I had never been fucked before. David had been trying valiantly for months with no results. "It hurts!" I had always whined.)

Vinnie hissed in my ear with each thrust: "Bitch...pussy...cunt...take my big dick!" (This was like the most ridiculous thing I had ever heard. Vinnie, fortunately for my virgin hole, had this really eensy-weensy dick.)

"Bitch...pussy...cunt...take my man-prick, slave. You love it!" Vinnie chanted repeatedly as he plowed his full four and a half inches into me.

In today's phone-sex–obsessed times, Vinnie's monologue might sound tame, perhaps even a little homespun on the scale of dirty talk. But for a neophyte queer teen, I felt like I was in bed with Attila the Hun.

The bare mattress squeaked loudly in protest with each humping, nasty-mouthed bounce. I probably could have fought him off, but I thought to myself, *Why bother?* Maybe this was just the experience I was looking for — a way to show David I could go get hurt by the world too.

I let Vinnie use my ass and waited patiently for him to finish. Allowing myself an out-of-body experience, I began to observe his room. There were dozens of pictures of John Travolta on the walls, a collage cut out from the magazines on the floor of images from the soon-to-be-released *Saturday Night Fever* right there on the fridge. My face was hanging off the end of the mattress, so I could see what was underneath his bed. There were several dildos, reflecting various levels of ambition; an open jar of Vaseline decorated with a mustache of carbon-dated pubic hairs; and a copy of *After Dark* magazine with Rudolf Nureyev on the cover. I thought to myself, *Please, God, make him hurry. I just want to get out of here!*

His thrusts and groans continued a long time. For the first time in my life, I felt the power my asshole had to draw excitement and pleasure from another man. Under more pleasant circumstances, this just might grow on me.

"Oh, yeah, I'm close. Take my load, bitch!" Vinnie shouted as he came with a huge bellow and rolled off me. Suddenly I didn't feel so great. My muscles were sore, as if I had been stuck spinning in a dryer for a long time. The sweat on my back evaporated and left my skin cold and clammy. I pulled the sheet around me and held myself. Rubbing my pummeled butt, I asked myself, *How did I get here?*

"Whoa," Vinnie preened in triumph. "That was hot."

Immediately I knew what I had to do. With every ounce of concentrated decision, I knew I had to get out of there *now*. I quickly got up and threw on my clothes.

"Wait — can I see you again?" Vinnie called after me as the door slammed.

"Fuck you! I hate John Travolta, and disco sucks!" I shouted — it was the best I could do at the moment — then I kicked the charcoal-black front door as hard as I could.

I fled that crummy apartment, my clothes barely hanging on me. Breathing fast, I ran down Highland Avenue. This had all been a little too much for me. I had wanted a taste of real life so I could show David I wasn't just a high school kid, but this was definitely more than the love doctor had ordered. I wanted some adventure. Some romance. A nice dinner. A stuffed bell pepper. Maybe a blow job. Fuck Goofus and Gallant; they both get screwed in the end. *I'll show everyone*, I decided. *I'm going to leave town, hitchhike across the country just like Jack Kerouac. I'm going to find a better world if it kills me.*

I walked down Hollywood Boulevard past the Chinese Theater along the Walk of Fame, the several blocks of sidewalk where the names of film and television and radio stars were immortalized (until the next sewer project tears up the street). Vinnie's come was dripping out of my asshole as I stepped over the stars on the pavement beneath my feet: Billy Graham. Beniamano Gigli. Wayne Newton. Buster Crabbe. Broderick Crawford. Dinah Shore. In a little while they would put John Travolta here, smack dab between Buster and Broderick. There is no justice.

I waited a long time for a bus back to Whittier.

SPILT MILK

I WAS HITCHHIKING TO SAN FRANCISCO. I had started out from Bakersfield first thing that California springtime morning, hitch hopping with several short rides up Highway 99. My thumb, which had been up David's butt the night before in another of our final breakup scenes followed by sorrowful sex, was now out. My thumb had been out on the on-ramps of San Fernando, on the on-ramps of Delano, on the on-ramps of Fresno, and a long time on the on-ramps of dreary Merced too.

And now my thumb was out on a postnuclear-looking stretch of Modesto. I walked backward along the freeway on-ramp, smiling in my best "I'm not a serial killer, and I hope you aren't either" manner. A hot dry wind blew a Taco Bell burrito wrapper into my highway-sunburned face as a Toyota driver raced past, avoiding the commitment of even a whiff of eye contact.

The high octane, emotionally chaotic scenes with David, complete with the big-time challenges of being in a love-and-sex relationship for the first time in my teenage life, had left me on the ropes. Faced with such an array of new emotions that each encounter demanded, I had to choose: fight or feel. (I mean, fight or flee.) I ended up submitting to all the male programming that had been crammed down my throat in a big testosterone cocktail. I listened to the signals that told me that when the feelings get tough, the tough

should get as far away as possible. I decided to leave
David. Vamoose. Get the hell out of Dodge.

It was time to realize my newly discovered Jack
Kerouac–induced poetic aspirations and go out on *my*
road. Adding to my already sagging shelf of beat lit, I
had bought an LP of Allen Ginsberg reading "Howl"
in San Francisco in the gloom of the mid '50s. Even
though I hadn't been born yet, I wished I had been
there, swilling the cheap red wine as Allen saw the
best minds of his generation destroyed by madness
(and cheap red wine). I bet Allen got a date after the
reading too. I slurped up this compelling queer vision
of anarchic, literary, and politicized sex. Sign me up.
I'm heading for San Francisco.

I stretched my arms wide to the Zen indifference of
Highway 99. I looked up at the sky, blue as my
Volkswagen Bug. I opened my chest to the arid-desert
zap of consciousness that each breath could bring me.
In and out, just like the *Zen in Ten Easy Steps* guidebook had said. Focusing (by *not* focusing!) on pure
presence, my entire being listening to each breath,
sensing every subtle shift of my meat and skin, I slowly raised my right arm with thumb pointed up to heav-
en. The mountains sizzled in the mirage offered by the
San Joaquin Valley heat. My thumb was out. My body
was young. My heart was pure. I was emotionally completely fucked up, and I needed a ride pronto.

I was going to San Francisco for a few days. I was
nineteen. As a late-'70s punk Southern California kid,
I had missed out on the hippie/antiwar/cultural revolution by about ten years. I felt the weight of the previous generation's nostalgia heavy as a truckload of
Woodstock albums on my skinny chest. I had even
been cheated out of the juiciest period of socially

transgressive gay political action. I wished *I* had gotten to be arrested in those early Gay Liberation Front actions. Now, in 1978, it felt like all that was left were the table scraps of disco, Izod shirts, and the dreary assimilationist mix of lobbying and partying.

But important things seemed to be happening up in San Francisco. There was this new mayor named Moscone. He was someone less hideous than the usual Democratic Party mainstream sleaze. Also, this gay guy named Harvey Milk had gotten elected a few months before to citywide office. Score one for the good guys in a time when homophobia was becoming a national sport. The previous year's Anita Bryant jihad against gays in Dade County, Florida, had gotten all these right-wing nuts on the march all over the country. In the spring of 1978, St. Paul fell to the dark side of the force in an antigay initiative; Wichita came soon after.

These events, mixed up with Anita Bryant's orange-juice–soaked bigotry, had even unleashed the creeps in California. John Briggs, the state senator from Fullerton, the city where I first had sex with another man, had put forth Proposition 6, a statewide initiative that would ban gay people from being teachers.

It felt like we were at war. I wanted to go help Harvey Milk fight these slime. It was a revolution, a better world trying to be born. El Dorado. The Grail. The perfectible social order. Allen Ginsberg psychically levitating the Pentagon! So I was on my way to check it out and offer my assistance. I had an address of a friend of a friend of a friend — and twelve dollars in my pocket. I was not nearly as smart as I thought I was, but at least (if I recall correctly, and I don't always do) I was starting to realize that.

My thumb was out. Three cars whooshed past without slowing down, not even bothering to glance in their rearview mirror.

Maybe this '74 Vega will stop? Whoosh. Fuck!

Perhaps this '72 Ford Capri? Whoosh. Fucking shit!

This hitchhiking business was harder than I thought it would be. I opened up my copy of Kerouac's *The Dharma Bums* to see if I could glean some tips. As if dead Jack had waved a magical bottle of scotch over my head, I heard the crackle of rubber on gravel as a canary-yellow Pinto eased its way onto the shoulder.

"Hi," I said, tossing a greeting casually to the youthful driver as he wound down the dusty passenger window. It was important not to seem desperate.

"Hey, dude," the driver drawled in a classic San Fernando Valley accent. "Where ya heading?"

"Toward the future," I replied. I had noticed that the car had a NO NUKES IS GOOD NUKES bumper sticker in the back window. I figured this fanciful sentiment would fly.

"Radical. So am I!" He nodded his Restoration England shoulder-length hair. "My name is Meadow. Hop in, and let's make it happen."

I threw my backpack in the cluttered backseat and slipped into the Pinto. While Meadow zoomed toward tomorrow, I suppressed a shriek as the hot Naugahyde bucket seat burned the skin on the backs of my thighs left exposed by my cutoff army fatigue pants.

"So where is the future, do you think?" Meadow hummed as he spoke.

"I'm going to look in San Francisco."

"Excellent. My girlfriend lives in the Haight, so I can drop you off on Market Street." Meadow talked fast as he kept changing lanes without using his turn signal. "What are you going to do in S.F.?"

A Rubicon moment presented itself to me. Should I or shouldn't I? The QUESTION AUTHORITY button on his dashboard tipped the scales. I stated my case this way: "I'm going to San Francisco to commit myself to the struggle for gay political freedom…as it relates to defeating the nuclear power industry, of course."

Unfazed, Meadow ignited with antinuke fervor. "Good point," he said enthusiastically. "If we don't shut down all the nuclear power plants, sexuality will become a thing of the past anyhow. It's good you see the connection. You should join the Clamshell Alliance. We meet every Monday…"

I tuned out on Meadow's outreach effort for a moment. The rolling newborn green of the Alameda County hills filled me up.

"…and just look around you at creation, the trees, the beauty of the Bay Area. We have to fight nuclear power so we can preserve this for our children. I mean, my children." Meadow had hit a pothole in his campaign speech. "Don't get me wrong. It's cool that you're gay and all. What do you guys do in bed anyway?"

After receiving forty minutes of gay sex education, Meadow pulled the Pinto over on a busy San Francisco street. As an afterthought he gave me a patchouli-laced hug.

"Take care of yourself," he said. Meadow was, in fact, quite a sweet straight hippie dude. "Let me know if you find the future."

I found *myself* at the corner of Powell and Market streets. A little sad to see him go, I watched Meadow drive his Pinto away into a nuke-free world. I had a few hours to kill before I could call my friend Neal, a bisexual guy I had met at statewide Gay Student Union Conference during my first semester at Cal State Fullerton.

I nosed around this tourist vortex by the cable-car turnaround. This corner reminded me of so many *cheap* family vacations to the Bay Area. Every year we would come up and visit Aunt Dorlene and Uncle Bill (he was a football coach at UC Berkeley). Then, in a mad rush, the assembled families would do the bridges, do the cable cars, do the wharf, and do Mount Diablo. We were propelled by the primal need to hurry or we might actually realize we weren't having a good time. Mission accomplished, my family could head back south, quick as a wink, secure in the exhausting illusion that we had gone on vacation.

I am not that kid with my family anymore. I repeated to myself this mantra as I hoisted my backpack to my shoulders. *I am a self-motivated young gay man who has escaped from his family. I am on a hero's journey to find immediately a cute boy or the ideal political system. I am a self-motivated young gay man...*

As I walked down the financial-district end of Market Street in the fading evening light, I looked at the sights of San Francisco with a face that was as unsuspecting as an open wallet. I drank up the mixed-up images of the dregs of the hippie era and the black-leathered panhandling punk kids. All of this was surrounded by the shag hair, platform heels, and big lapels of Carter-era America.

I bought a lukewarm lemonade and watched the tourists climb onto the cable cars. Sucking noisily on the sweet drink through a straw, I noticed a clean-cut young man and equally young woman approaching other people under thirty who all seemed to be carrying backpacks. This couple were just a little older than I, and their Donny and Marie good looks seemed to be winning some pedestrians over. Working their way around the cable cars, they finally got to me. I watched them purposefully plant their feet as they extended a small white card toward me.

"Hello," the girl said. "We're from the Creative Community Project, a progressive, forward-looking communal organization working toward a new world order. Please join us for a delicious free meal on our bus as we travel to our utopian farm. My name is Jennie. What's yours?"

"Tim," I said coolly, examining the card as I slurped up the last bit of lemonade. She seemed nice, but I kept trying to catch the eye of the Donny Osmond look-alike. His focus, however, had shifted to a teenage girl in wide bell bottoms and a happy-face sweatshirt.

"Is this farm really a commune?" I asked Jennie, but I craned to see Donny extend a small white card to the bell-bottomed girl.

"Oh, yes. We're very communal," she responded, a quick study as she recycled my language. "We are so communal, we all share our money. We have a great teacher who shows us that humans can love one another. You can come to our farm for only ten dollars for an entire week!"

I checked my watch. It was still too early too call Neal. I could have just waited around, but her offer did *sound* pretty good to me. At first I had actually thought Jennie and her colleague were Stalinists. *C*reative *C*ommunity *P*roject! CCP! It had seemed pretty clear. There was something about their highly rehearsed encyclopedia-salesman presentation that smelled a little like spoiled yogurt cultures, though. Where was Meadow when I needed him? He could tell me what to do.

Jennie saw me wavering. She extended a potent double martini of New Age jive. "Tim," she said, "I look in your eyes and I see that you have always been searching. You have been searching for a place where people love one another. You have been searching for a world that is motivated by charity and kindness, not greed and hatred. Help us create that world now!"

"Um…" I stalled for time. I wasn't sure I could even connect with Neal tonight. Where would I sleep if I didn't? Now, I had been hitchhiking for sixteen hours and had only twelve dollars in my pocket. My careful reading of *On the Road* hadn't prepared me for just how lonely the world could actually be. The offer from these seemingly friendly folk of a ride on a bus with free food was pretty tempting. Also, wasn't this the kind of thing that's supposed to happen your first ten minutes in San Francisco?

I made a decision. "Sure. I'll come with you. Let's make that future happen." I got on the bus with this group of odd smiling people.

"All aboard for utopia!" the bus driver cackled, pounding the clutch as he forced the beat-up gears to mesh. The doors hissed closed as we drove down Market Street. There were eleven other young people, mostly boys with backpacks, on the bus. There was a buzz saw of tension between us, as if we were all embarrassed at the predicament we were in. For a moment I remembered what had happened to all the bad boys in *Pinocchio* as they were tricked and taken away. While we stopped for a red light at Castro and Market, I saw dozens of gay men heading into their new neighborhood, laughing and holding hands with each other as they crossed in front of the bus. They looked so bright and life-filled walking past me, almost a commercial for homosexuality. Pressing my face against the window, I worried that I had made an enormous mistake.

There was a buffet spread out at the back of the bus with some very strange food. The dishes all seemed to be made with broccoli as the main ingredient. In fact, everything was made with wilted broccoli, the kind that you might find tossed in a Dumpster at the back of a supermarket. The million little nubs on the broccoli were all droopy and yellow. There were wilted broccoli muffins. Wilted broccoli sandwiches. Wilted broccoli casserole. Wilted broccoli Danish! What did all this wilted broccoli mean?

As the lights of San Francisco faded behind us, I grew skeptical. I found a new mantra: *This is a progressive, forward-looking communal organization working toward a new world order! This is a progressive, forward...*

So, as the mantra took effect, I loaded up my plate and sat cross-legged by myself at the back of the bus. Nothing like this ever happened to Jack Kerouac. Stuffing my fears down with the wilted broccoli, I ate myself silly and fell into the deep-as-the-Grand Canyon sleep of a nineteen-year-old who has hitchhiked all day.

Three hours later the bus creaked and ground over a dirt road to what my hosts referred to as their "utopian farm." Rubbing a bad dream from my eyes, I staggered off the bus and found myself in a new nightmare. I had a flash for a panicked moment of barking dogs and German accents in the floodlight-illuminated parking area. Emergency mantra: *This is not Dachau. This is not Dachau. This is not...*

Our motley bunch of half-asleep initiates were greeted by a shadowy backlit male figure. "We welcome you with love to the Creative Community Project," he said. "We are all brothers and sisters here."

His two cronies quickly divided the men and the women into separate groups, and then the guys were led silently to a converted chicken coop, now serving as the men's dormitory. My anxiety whistled like a boiling teakettle.

"Excuse me," I said as I approached Jennie. She held a flashlight as she guided the women across a small stream. "I think there must be some kind of mistake. This is not what I had imagined."

Without breaking lockstep, Jennie held my arm firmly and spoke breathlessly into my ear. "It's time to sleep now, Tim. Everything will be fine in the morning. Here is a gift for you. I offer this to you in love." She slipped a silver bracelet on my arm that had a Peruvian llama embossed on it.

"Jennie," I whispered as she departed, "where are we, anyway?"

"You're in Boonville," she replied, a little irritated with me. "You are surrounded by love. Good night."

We were each given a bunk in the cramped former chicken coop. I threw my sleeping bag down, glanced at the already sleeping shapes around me, and zipped myself all the way in. I heard the unmistakable sounds of a boy jerking off under his sleeping bag three bodies down. The repetitive scraping of his hand against the polyester mixed with the almost electrical hum of the crickets. I was too beat to investigate, though. Somehow I slept, holding Jennie's bracelet over my heart.

The sun rose early on our chicken coop. I was awakened by the sound of less-than-spontaneous cheerful singing beyond the trees. The motley group of two dozen young men in my dormitory began to stir. I tried to make eye contact with Jerk-off Boy, but he would have none of it. It seemed we had been scrounged from various parts of San Francisco. Half of the fellows in the chicken coop were Australians, the world's best travelers and ever susceptible to such adventures. A grim breakfast of porridge with a side dish of wilted broccoli was arranged on crude redwood tables outside the latrine.

Immediately after breakfast the elders in charge, who displayed their cast-in-cement smiles, gathered us in a circle in a meadow. I was then tortured with several hours of indoctrination, calisthenics, and camp songs. During one lecture there was a heavyset guy at a blackboard who looked like my dour algebra teacher at Lowell High School. Drawing incomprehensible diagrams all the while, the rotund fellow tried to explain to us everything we needed to know: the function of good and bad in the universe; the ultimate evil of communism; how man and woman could be happy and complete only through the union of heterosexual marriage.

"You see," he said with a flourish of his stub of white chalk, "it is clear from this irrefutable interpretation of the Book of Revelations in the Bible that the second coming of Jesus Christ can only occur in South Korea!"

I grew more skeptical.

My personality was being broken down by this experience. I felt myself starting to waver. My intellectual self was being eroded by the tidal onslaught of group psychology. I was supposed to be helping

Harvey Milk fight homophobes. How did a gay boy like me get in a place like this?

I stroked the copy of "Howl" in my back pocket, hoping that it might keep me grounded. In my time of trial, "Howl" did the trick. I finally broke the logjam inside me during one of our many exercise breaks. We were coerced out onto the playing field for a set of volleyball. This was fine: Volleyball was one of the few sports I did not imagine had been conceived in the Spanish Inquisition. However, the leaders of Camp Revelations wanted us to chant "Win with love!" as we played. I tried.

"Win with love," I repeated weakly as I returned a serve.

"Win with love," I said a little louder when my fingertips set the ball in play.

"Win with love!" I hollered louder than everyone as I spiked and scored.

I had definitely had enough. I broke away from the game and approached the smiling scorekeeper. "Look, time out," I said, sputtering my words. "I don't think I'm cut out to be a member of a cult. I have an appointment with someone in the Haight in just two hours, so could you please get me my backpack and sleeping bag and then drive me back to San Francisco?"

There was complete silence on the volleyball court. I had really tossed a dirt clod in their collective yogurt and granola. My fellow team members tried to quiet me down; the other team started to whisper to one another. One balding and skinny member of the staff ran off toward the main building. A siren began to wail in the distance. I looked around to see if a likely escape route presented itself. Jennie, who seemed to be assigned to me, ran breathlessly toward me.

"Tim, what's wrong?" she asked as though I had just strangled her kittens. "I want you to know how loved you are." Jennie was stroking me like I was a child upset at losing a penny-arcade beanbag toss. She also didn't want to lose her commission.

"Jennie, thanks for the bracelet," I said as I removed her hand from my arm. "But I really need to get out of here. This may be your path, but it's not mine, okay? I need to be around people like me."

Jennie's superior, one of the creepiest of these characters, pushed her aside like a prison warden and walked me away from the others.

"Don't go," the *Kommandant* cajoled. "Don't go. I know your heart is troubled. I know you live too much in your head. Stay with us. It's getting late in the day. Stay with us."

I pulled away as the Boonville camp staff surrounded me, backing me against a California oak. For one crazed moment I imagined they were all hiding something behind their backs. A greenish light emanated from them as they pleaded with me to stay. As my breath raced I saw that the staffers all carried...heads of broccoli. These were not merely ordinary heads of broccoli. These were not merely ordinary heads of wilted broccoli. No, the broccoli they now held over my head had minds and souls and faces. I was locked in a battle with the broccoli brain suckers!

Grabbing me under my armpits, the burliest of the bunch tried to pull me with them back to headquarters. I pulled "Howl" from out of my back pocket and thrust it in their faces. The book worked like a cross to Count Dracula, and they hissed and pulled away. I found a hidden gay power inside me, and I shoved them to the ground. A small earthquake shook the vicinity.

"Back!" I brandished my little black-and-white City Lights book and shouted so loud, they could hear it at the tourist shop by the rest rooms at the Golden Gate. "I am the Antichrist. I am a Communist. I am a fag!" (What else can I say to scare them away?) "I am a Jew!" (Now, I'm not really Jewish, but I was destined to have so many Jewish boyfriends.) "Get me my backpack and sleeping bag now, or I'll call the police!"

Well, with that desperate threat, the camp guards all started smiling again suddenly. I was making too much trouble in the ranks, it seemed. Instantly more accommodating, they pushed Jennie back toward me to handle the situation. I was glad to see her.

"Get me out of here, okay?" I screamed to her. I had shot my wad and was now simply scared. I thought of David back in Southern California; we could be lounging and fighting by his apartment complex's Jacuzzi right now. If I were there, he would bring me back upstairs and patiently try to fuck me. I swore that if I got out of here in one piece, my asshole was his.

"Everything is fine," Jennie said calmly as she walked me toward the gate. "They're getting your things. You'll have to find your own way back to San Francisco. Remember me when you wear that bracelet. Please don't think badly of me." She slipped a napkin-wrapped broccoli muffin into my hand for the journey.

About one second later the camp bouncers dumped me and my backpack out on the dirt road. I had no idea where I was. Boonville, somewhere north of San Francisco, I supposed. I was breathing fast. I looked around. The world was still there, alive, growing — verdant. Everything seemed to be okay; the earthquake I had felt earlier must have just been in my head. I had managed to escape from the bizarre clutches of the broccoli brain snatchers.

Planting my feet on the earth, I slowly reached my right arm out toward the horizon, where the sun was setting. Once again my thumb was out. I worried I would probably get picked up by one of those Northern California ax murderers my mom always warned me about. I would be left in tiny pieces on the off-ramps of Modesto, Fresno, Delano, San Fernando, and Burbank too. But on that day in my life, I didn't care because I knew I had come through something big, some weird kind of trial by vegetable. Now I was back in the world, where I would have to figure out love and God and sex by myself.

And so began about two and a half hours of perfect hitchhiking, where each ride begat the next one and every driver offered a bit of wisdom. The local spirits that protect California hitchhikers chose to teach me a thing or two as they led me back to where I belonged.

First, an Armenian schoolteacher picked me up right outside the camp. He screeched his pickup truck to a halt and shouted, "Get in before they change their minds!" As we drove down toward Highway 101, he told me, "Kid, forget everything those creeps tried to cram down your throat. Wherever it takes you, you gotta follow your own star!"

Within two minutes of being dropped off by the schoolteacher, four hash-brownie–peddling hippies in an old Saab stopped for me. They told me about an excellent book by Hermann Hesse called *Siddhartha* and graciously got me stoned along the way. The hippies left me near Santa Rosa, with the Buddha's Four Noble Truths written down on a truck-stop napkin. I wondered if they knew Meadow?

My thumb went out again. An Episcopalian priest pulled over and invited me into his Dodge Dart. Father S. drove me to Mill Valley as we talked about God and Plato, his hand stroking the inside of my thigh.

Finally, I was picked up by a twinkie gay boy in a rugby shirt from Marin County who was going to the Haight to dance at the I-Beam disco. He shared with me his vision of a gay sexual revolution that will finally seize the keys of the kingdom as he drove me the rest of the way to San Francisco.

At last we rounded those headlands, and I saw the boldly lit Golden Gate Bridge. I wanted to grab all those bridge towers and give them a big kiss, thanking them for letting me escape back to my life. If I could have, I would have tap-danced down the bridge cables as we drove into the Presidio. Scared, shaking, but breathing, I braced myself for my second day in San Francisco.

Twinkie Boy left me at the front door of my friend Neal's house. He was not home. His housemates explained to me that Neal had been arrested for drug dealing and back-alley blow jobs off Polk Street. They were not amused by my knock on their door at midnight. They also didn't buy my tale of epiphany.

"Then they tried to stop me from leaving, but I got out of there in one piece," I explained excitedly.

"Where did you say this was? Boonville?" one particularly dark-hearted housemate asked, grilling me for flaws in my story. "Hon, you just got swept up by the Moonies. Only an idiot would fall for the oldest scam on Market Street."

The Moonies! How could that be? I was embarrassed. The Moonies seduced green suburban kids, not hip sharpies like me. Before my heroic encounter was completely crushed by their derisive laughter, I excused myself to go to bed.

I woke up the next morning on the hardwood floor of the living room in Neal's flat in the remote Outer Sunset District. I was humiliated that my journey into the heart of darkness had been a mere brush with the Moonies. Before my mean-spirited hosts could wake up and torment me, I quickly dressed and got out of Neal's house.

I wandered around North Beach, the souvenir-postcard fog wisping around my ankles. I felt depressed. Disillusioned. What had I expected? What did I want? I think what I really wanted was to have Allen Ginsberg come bursting out of City Lights bookstore, give me a big hug, and say, "Tim! You made it! How 'bout a cappuccino?"

Being a Southern California kid, I thought going to the beach might restore me. I broke the code on the Muni bus map and figured out how to find my way to Land's End. The Geary bus tossed me from side to side on the long trek west. Land's End was the last stop, the edge of a mysterious continent, the edge of buzzing Western civilization. This is where I belonged, Land's End.

It was unbearably beautiful there, the damp rocks decorated with seals bathing in the Pacific. My dark glasses, stylish though unnecessary on account of the fog, were covered over with mist as the waves crashed boisterously against the sharp rocks.

The sky began to clear above as I sang with the seals barking below on their prime real estate rookery. I barked a long, mournful wail to them. They paused in confusion — was I a new kind of seal? — and then they howled back to me. I threw my head back, opened my throat, and again let out a bark. All the crushing failure of the past two days went into that yawning howl. I had cast my vegetarian–no-eggs–no-animal-fat–100%-whole-wheat bread onto the water as I set out to find a world that worked, a world that would not betray me. Those hopes had been crisped into croutons by the Moonies' cynical exploitation. The flurry of seals sang back to me, a lament to match my own. Then some German tourists threw a handful of sardines in their direction, and the understandably fickle seals lost interest in me.

I walked slowly along the bluffs, casting small pebbles down to the frothy sea. Against all apparent odds, the day slowly turned sunny. Leaning over a sign on the barrier that read, DANGEROUS SURF: PEOPLE HAVE BEEN SWEPT FROM THE ROCKS AND DROWNED, I looked down and saw a beach at the bottom of the cliff. Though this area of sand was approximately the size of a compact parking space, about two dozen people had tucked themselves onto it.

I climbed down to this Honda Civic–sized beach. Hopping from the final perilous boulder, I discovered that it was nude beach–arama here at Land's End, a diverse menagerie of dangling breasts and penises.

My exhibitionist streak had already begun to rear its head. I took off my flimsy shorts, hid my remaining eight dollars in my shoe, and started performing a modern dance: the spirit-of-the-seal-rising-from-the-Pacific dance. I had been in enough improvisational movement classes in which we pretended to be animals that I knew very well how to make a spectacle of myself in nature. I climbed on all fours over rocks and threw myself into a handstand on a boulder as I tried to turn my experiences of the last few days into movement.

Climbing over one razor-sharp barnacled rock, I suddenly saw a vision: A pale, sinewy naked man with curly long brown hair was dipping his foot into the ice-cube–cold sea. It was Caravaggio on parade! As this boy-man circled a necklace of seaweed around his neck, he looked directly at me and smiled. I almost fainted — well, almost. I did a grand plié as if I were a stately heron, jumped in the water, and strode toward him through the icy surf. I immediately lost all sensation below my neck.

"Hey! Isn't the water cold?" he shouted to me.

Though I was on the cusp of hypothermia, my mind went into overdrive as my thoughts spoke to me: *What does he mean, cold? Does he mean cold in an emotional sense? Is this a critique of my lack of Freudian oceanic feeling?*

"I…um…oh!" I called out to him, groping for support as I fell backward into the water. I sounded like an idiot. I looked at this guy through my dangling, water-soaked curls. He was so confident, so sure of himself. He had his feet planted on the earth, his nakedness a natural fact. He knew who he was — more than I obviously did. How did he ever get like that? He, like David, was an older fellow. This man with the seaweed adorning him had the hard-won maturity of a person of advanced years. He could have been as old as twenty-five.

"Let me help you," he said, laughing as he pulled me out of the surf. "I'm Michael."

"I'm-m-m-m-m Tim," my teeth chattered as I staggered back to dry land.

"You should be careful here," Michael warned as we collapsed on the warmer sand. "People have been swept from the rocks and drowned!" I thought he was mocking me. Then I got the joke about the sign up above. Turning into a Popsicle had dulled my sense of humor.

I looked out of the corner of my eye, and I saw that Michael had a dog-eared copy of James Joyce's *A Portrait of the Artist as a Young Man* open on his towel. He saw me looking slack-jawed at the open book.

"Oh, I'm a student at San Francisco State," he explained. "I'm taking a class on Joyce. We're starting with the easy one. Have you read *Portrait?*"

For a moment I was tempted to say that I had lived it. "I've read it four times," I said instead in my usual humble fashion.

"Wow!" Michael nodded, impressed, then decided to fish for some information. "As a gay man, I'm not sure I can relate to it that much. Everyone's so hetero in the book."

"I don't know," I replied, knowing full well I had to complete the coming-out call-and-response, as precise as any liturgy. "I'm gay too, but I feel what Stephen Dedalus goes through really speaks to me. The last lines are the most beautiful words ever written about individuality and setting yourself free from your family."

Michael flipped to the end of the book. I trapped my emerging boner between my legs. Sitting at the edge of a continent with a cute boy reading me James Joyce was the height of sexiness to me.

He leaned toward me, cleared his throat, and whispered into my ear the last few lines of the book. Michael then sat back to survey what effect the words had had on me and asked, "You mean that part?"

"Mm." I could barely speak. The feelings of unworthiness had swooped down on me like a rogue wave.

Michael looked at me for a long time, then glanced out to sea, where an ocean tanker was heading out to some distant port.

"Would you like to come to my house tonight?" Michael asked as he looked back in my vicinity. "I live in a small socialist gay men's commune in the Mission, right near Modern Times Books. We compost and everything. Well, we're having a meal tonight. A few of us are thinking about going to Cuba as part of the Venceremos Brigade to help bring in the sugarcane harvest and defeat the imperialist U.S. embargo. Would you like to join us?"

"I'd love to," I replied, shifting on the sand to avoid a sharp rock that was poking me in the butt. "I'm practically Cuban. My sister married a man from Havana. Of course, they were middle-class betrayers of the revolution," I quickly added, toeing the requisite party line. I wanted to ask Michael why his friends were so concerned about Cuba and not about fighting antigay Proposition 6, but I didn't want to lose the invitation. "Great," Michael replied, clearly relieved, then checked his watch. "I'd better go to class. Why don't you come by around 6? You can help me slice vegetables."

Since we didn't have any paper except for the James Joyce, Michael neatly printed his phone number on the inside of my arm with the same fluorescent green highlighter he'd been using to mark up his copy of *Portrait*. "There," he said as he capped the pen. "Now you won't lose me."

Michael put on his clothes and climbed up the path. "See you later," he called, waving from the top of the cliff, then walked bouncily toward civilization.

I fell back naked onto the sand in the dimming light of day, looking up at Michael's clear writing on my skin. Naturally, I immediately proceeded to fall in love. Michael's political commitment and post-hippie communal living was in stark contrast to David's lifestyle.

Talking with Michael, I didn't feel like I was saying something wrong, like I was being judged, as I often experienced when I talked with David. The thought of going to Cuba with my new friend began to appeal to me.

Weaving my future with Michael, I drifted into a sunbaked sleep. I imagined our dinner that night. *There will be a brood of dynamic leftist gay men in attendance. We will eat a delicious ovovegetarian meal that Michael and I will prepare. I'll commit to going to Cuba with them. "Venceremos! We shall be victorious!" we will all shout. At the right moment Michael will invite me into his bedroom to listen to his album of whale songs. Michael will kiss me all over and then fuck me gently underneath the poster of Che with the slogan HASTA LA VICTORIA SIEMPRE!*

The tide came in and woke me up.

Two hours later I was walking in downtown San Francisco, killing time before my date. Carefully checking the bright green numbers marked on my arm, I called Michael to get directions to his house in the Mission District.

"Hi, Michael. It's me, Tim, the guy you met at Land's End." As I spoke, I tucked in my backpack the used copy of an abridged *Finnegans Wake* I had just bought so I could bone up before dinner and impress Michael with my knowledge of Joyce.

"What shall I make for us to eat?" Michael asked. "Do you like broccoli?"

"Sure," I said. "I love it." I hung up, resigned to yet another dinner of broccoli.

Checking my map, I made a detour on Fulton Street so I could see City Hall before I went to Michael's flat. I wanted to check out the building where Harvey Milk was changing the world. Well, at least my world.

When I finally arrived at City Hall, I looked at the vaulting dome high above me. I thought to myself, *Why is this building so huge? Is it because there is a big idea inside? It looks like it could be the capitol of an empire of something, not just a City Hall.*

Looking at the huge building, I felt a huge joy. There I was, a foolish young man, with James Joyce in my backpack and a date for dinner. I felt the wheels of the state apparatus grinding begrudgingly in concert with me. A guy named Harvey Milk, a fag like me, was inside City Hall, tickling the powers that be! I felt so strong. It was as if I were in the Paris Commune with the other radical students in 1871. Or chopping wood with Thoreau at Walden Pond. Or storming the Winter Palace in St. Petersburg. I felt for once that the world was not an enemy, that society *was* perfectible.

My body was in front of City Hall, my head and heart and cock part of this moment in history. I could feel my skin, my feelings, my hopes for the future as tangible as the sidewalk under my feet. For once the big dick of the law and government would not pull the rug out from under me. I had all these powerful feelings and a date for dinner with Michael too.

As I walked away from City Hall, I thought to myself, *Well, I guess I'll have to go back to Whittier pretty soon. I only have three dollars left. Maybe I won't go to New York. I want to come back to San Francisco and make a life in this city someday.*

But for now I went off to my broccoli.

It turned out that Michael was more interested in world socialism than my dick. His boyfriend, Luis, was the leader of the brigade and made it clear that Michael was off-limits. I was shown the door with all

the other comrades at the end of the evening. After
another awkward night crashing at Neal's flat, I hitchhiked back to L.A. the next morning.

A few months later I was working another soul-
killing job at a gas station, trying to make ends meet.
Michael had gone to Cuba. I had received one postcard
saying that Cuba was not the paradise for gay workers that he had hoped it would be. David and I were
not speaking. I was saving money to support my move
to New York City. As I pumped gas into an old man's
Buick, I overheard two other people in a pickup truck
having this conversation.

"Hey, 'dya hear the news?" this obvious jerk in the
truck slurred through his open door. "They got those
two guys up in Frisco. Yeah, some ex-cop killed that
queer Milk and that Dago mayor of theirs, whashiz-
name, Macaroni?"

I dropped the gas nozzle to my side.

I knew it was time to leave California.

I was covered in gasoline.

GOOD WITH WOOD

I ARRIVED IN NEW YORK CITY on a nonstop red-eye flight from LAX to JFK. Having cleverly sold my resurrected Volkswagen Bug for a little more than it was worth, I used the money to buy a one-way plane ticket to New York. I had $462 left over to start my new life in Manhattan.

Not once in my life had I left the West Coast, so I gripped my airplane seat armrests tight as the American Airlines jet flew over the Grand Canyon, and for the first time I began the journey "back East." These words, "back East," were spoken with a mixture of terror and pity by my parents and grandparents to describe the old world of our ancestors. They made it sound like the Forbidden Zone from *Planet of the Apes*, a scary world of shadowy figures, apocalyptic sensuality, and unpredictable events. Of course, this had made me even more desperate to go there.

My mom had broken into tears as I packed my bags the night before I left. Sulking, she silently watched *The French Connection* on TV. After Gene Hackman chased the drug dealers through the gray, gritty streets of New York for the umpteenth time, my mom finally snapped. "You can't go to that terrible place. I won't let you go back East!" She began to quietly sob, her quick fingers never missing a stitch as she knitted yet another polyester blue afghan for me.

"Mom, I have to go. It'll be okay." Trying to distract her with a treat, I sat down on the ottoman and asked,

"Do you want a foot massage?" She nodded, sniffling. I rubbed the hard calluses on my mom's toes, twisted from a lifetime of standing all day in high heels behind the jewelry counter at the May Company department store. We watched the amoral hopeless conclusion of *The French Connection,* my mom breaking into sobs from time to time as my dad snored in his La-Z-Boy on the other side of the room.

The moment my parents went to bed, I sneaked my dad's car keys off the kitchen counter and drove the few miles to Fullerton for a final encounter with David.

"So you're really going," David said sadly, not wanting to believe it as we sat in the hot tub of a house he was looking after. This palatial home was in the district of State Senator John Briggs, architect of the dreaded Proposition 6, which had obsessed me at the time. "I wish I could go with you."

"I need to go alone, I think," I replied, sinking my head under the foaming water of the Jacuzzi as a way of avoiding the subject. "For now, at least."

We dried off in the warm night, daring the neighbors to look at our naked skin. David invited me into the house, and we made love in the plush master bedroom. We fell onto a water bed, so soft that it made me feel weightless, as if I were floating in a solar system of our own making. David bent my legs against my chest, poking his erection against me as he tried to divine whether I would let him in tonight.

For some reason my body opened to him this time. It was almost as if a switch in my mind had flipped from off to on. The curtain rose all at once on that part of my flesh. I was leaving, and now it was okay for him to fuck me on that sloshing bed. As David's body moved in and out of mine, the entire bed flowed from one side to the other. The tidal pull of the moon moved David and me against each other during that long night. This was how we said good-bye.

Twenty-four hours later the plane circled low over Long Island, past the murky swamplands of Jamaica Bay. I pressed my face to the window as I slurped up this new wet and cloudy world. It looked so old, so wet, a place where things hide under rocks.

As I peered out of the buzzing Boeing 727, New York scared me with its lush untidiness. It was as unfamiliar to me as my "back East" grandfather when he visited once a year from Michigan. Grandpa Miller smelled funny, talked loud, was barely literate, and had huge tufts of gray hair coming out of his ears. New York was full of sights that reminded me of the scary hair that spilled out of my grandfather's ears.

Pushing my way out of baggage claim at Kennedy Airport, I set foot into the tropical July air of NYC. You could see the humidity almost hovering in front of your face, daring you to breathe its dampness into your lungs. I felt my skin pour sweat under my arms and in my crotch. New York was a place I might get a rash.

Knowing enough to brush aside the scam artists trying to waylay me into their unlicensed cabs, I dragged my ass (and my avocado-green polished plastic suitcase stuffed with rantings and poems) into Manhattan on the boring yet reputable Carey Bus. I didn't know a soul in New York. I would need to scrounge up a chaotic series of dives for the next few weeks as I tried to get my life together.

My life in New York City would eventually be measured by a nomadic journey through apartments, friends' couches, and the many beds that I would lay down upon with the men in my life. The map of the dozens of places

I lived in in NYC resembled a Rorschach test. The globs and amorphous shapes that detail one faggot's progress had the look of a medieval map, complete with the warning "beyond here there be dragons."

The search for an apartment in New York with room to lay your head (or get head, for that matter) is rated just below the quest for the Holy Grail in difficulty. The challenge to find a home began the minute I set a tender foot on the greasy pavement of the island of Manhattan for the first time, in 1978.

At the Port Authority bus terminal, balancing a pay phone that was as slick as a fish from the previous user's perspiration, I called the number of a friend of a friend of my friend Rachel in Seattle. She had decided to look after her goyisheh "Tim from California" and had assigned a string of her Long Island Jewish pals to keep an eye on me these first days. Their job, should they decide to accept it, was to make sure I didn't end up floating in pieces down the Hudson.

I spent my first night in NYC with this friend of Rachel's, a nice fellow named Kenny. He let me stay with him where he was house-sitting, an apartment at the International Ladies' Garment Workers' Union Building at Twenty-Third Street and Eighth Avenue. Kenny was a metalworker, and he was out of the apartment a great deal. A little afraid to go outside that first night, I repeatedly listened to Joan Baez's song "Farewell, Angelina" and stared through the Chelsea gloom at the glowing Empire State Building, which poked out of the July thunderclouds. Tossing and turning the whole night, I lay in the chaste bed that Kenny shared with me.

After three days with Kenny, I had to find somewhere else. I quickly met a feral Irish-American guy as he cruised me in front of the Manhattan Savings Bank on Broadway and Eighth Street, where I had just opened an account. He said I could stay with him for a couple of days. What a clever nineteen-year-old was I! I moved to his place at Second Avenue and Tenth Street. The windows of the apartment looked directly into the Second Avenue Deli. The smell of a thousand years of Ukrainian borscht from the deli permeated the walls. I spent the next five nights bouncing up and down on the dick of this Irish-American man from New Jersey. To this day, and with my usual self-importance, I can't go by this building without mentally installing a plaque outside that reads, IN 1978 TIM MILLER GOT FUCKED IN THE BUTT HERE FOR THE FIRST TIME IN NEW YORK. I remember that each rise and fall of my body as I plunged down onto his cock brought the sight of the deli man across the street carving the lox so thin you could read *The New York Times* through it. Things got too tight here. So off I went.

I went to the Gay Roommate Service. They gave me, for a reasonable twenty-five dollars, an extensive list of psychotic men with broom closets to rent. Most of these men offering rooms to rent were interested in home-delivery sex service. After the sixth time I was groped within minutes of entering a strange man's horrible apartment on MacDougal Street, I finally found a room that was available from the Gay Roommate Service bulletin board, and I moved to 13 St. Marks Place. It was an apartment building right across the street from the New St. Marks Baths, the gay bathhouse of choice at the time. Speaking of historical plaques, there was a doozy on the baths' exterior that announced that James Fenimore Cooper had written *The Last of the Mohicans* here.

Thrilled with the literary surroundings, I moved into 13 St. Marks Place with Charles, an insane novelist-cabdriver just out of Harvard who lived for his pursuit of Puerto Rican boys. He drove around New York in his cab with the meter off, shuttling Latin beauties from Jerome Avenue to Atlantic Avenue on their mysterious pursuits delivering small brown bags. Charles was always being cited by the taxi and limousine commission for giving these boys blow jobs on his breaks in the back of his cab.

As I schlepped my bags up the looks-like-we're-in-Italy spiral staircase, Charles tossed me a copy of the galleys of a new gay novel I had read about in *The Advocate* called *Dancer From the Dance.* "I got this advance copy from a friend in the publishing biz. This book takes place next door." Charles sighed, a 22-year-old playing the bored grande dame as he sipped his cocktail, a too-strong Cape Cod. "Read it and weep. The book recounts the highlights and hardships of gay life in New York. I'll quiz you in the morning."

I sat out on the fire escape all afternoon, chewing up the novel as a guidebook for gay life. It was exciting to read a new book in galleys, as if I were getting a sneak preview. I had never read a book that was set on the street where I lived. The author's words ricocheted inside me as I surveyed the circus atmosphere of St. Marks Place. Unfortunately, the day after I moved in, Con Ed turned off the electricity. (Charles hadn't paid the bill in five months.) For fiscal security I knew I had to leave St. Marks Place, and I immediately decided to move downtown. I took the book with me as plunder.

I tore a tiny slip of paper scrawled with a phone number off a sign in the Broome Street Bar. It had promised a raw loft space to share with other artists. I called the number, and the man who answered, a painter, said I could move in. Lugging my paltry belongings to 393 Broadway at White Street, two blocks below Canal Street, I found myself catty-corner to what was soon to be the hip nightspot the Mudd Club. I arrived at a 2,000-square-foot empty loft space that was jammed with hovering nineteenth-century sweatshop ghosts. Five hundred dollars a month divided four ways with three painter loft mates kept the rent a reasonable $125.

While I was living here in this raw space, the Talking Heads never left the turntable. Gulping gallons of coffee down our throats, my loft mates and I began cobbling together individual rooms and installing a makeshift shower with a garden hose hanging from the ceiling.

For my room I began to construct a kind of fanciful tree house in the middle of the loft out of scavenged packing crates from Chinatown and a bunch of fabric I had found in a Dumpster on Lispenard Street. I built a winding ladder that brought me to a second-floor platform, where I put my sleeping bag. A giant wooden cable spool served as my desk, and cinder blocks snitched from a construction site held up my one bookshelf. I cut a porthole with a borrowed jigsaw and mounted a scavenged telescope there so if I wanted to, I could spy on Meryl Streep, who lived on the other side of Broadway. My slightly rusty carpentry skills from childhood came in quite handy as I realized my fantasy home on lower Broadway.

As I grew up I had discovered that out of the meager list of approved-for-boys activities (Little League, Boy Scouts, vivisection), the only one I had been good at, other than beating off fourteen times a day, was carpentry. It was the one place my dad and I had a slim chance of connecting, where his expectations and my homo predilections could look each other in the eye and exchange a manly handshake.

Under my dad's watchful eye, I built bookshelves, napkin holders, birdhouses that no bird thought were safe to go into, and glamour-filled split-level tree houses decorated with throw rugs! I'd invite my little friends into my treetop lair, pull up the rope ladder, and try to convince them that we should cover ourselves in corn oil and play naked Twister. This tree house was the prototype for the loft room I would build at 393 Broadway.

I loved going to the lumberyard with my dad. It was like church. Better. More authentically spiritual. Sackett & Peters Hardware and Lumber was a gothic cathedral of two-by-fours, a delicate abbey piled high with a maze of construction-grade plywood. The sunlight slipping in between the spindly fir strips dappled our bodies as my dad and I searched for just the right piece of maple wood.

Most important, lumberyards were staffed by sexy men in sleeveless orange fluorescent vests showing their great arms. Their job was to meet your every woody need. The lumber workers sauntered godlike as they led you into dark hallways to offer you their mahogany. They'd turn the plank over in their hands, show you the wood's true line, stroke the smooth sides, measure out in inches exactly how much you needed.

Then they would take the wood to an enormous table saw, a fierce machine that could rip and tear the wood. In an explosion of grating sound, the sawdust covered your skin. The tickling of the sawdust and its

earthy smell made me shiver with pleasure. I breathed
it deep into my body.

In my life journeys through teenage blow jobs,
synth-pop music, the Reagan-Bush years, and the rise
(and fall) of the Queer Nation goatee, I have always
tried to stay close to my carpenter roots.

Once I had solved the dilemma of where to live in
New York, I was confronted with an even more daunt-
ing chore: finding work. The moment I had swept up
the last pile of sawdust from my room construction, I
began sifting through the crummy dead-end jobs that
presented themselves to me:

I was a bellboy at a residential hotel on Central
Park South. Every Tuesday the retired dentist on the
fourteenth floor (it was really the thirteenth; could
that fool anyone?) would push his bourbon-drenched
face into mine and try to kiss me. "You can't kiss me
in the elevator, Mr. Rothbart!" I would say, trying to
tame his octopus arms. "Think of your wife! Your
grandchildren!"

I spent two weeks as a falafel maker on MacDougal
Street. The owner of the place, a Hungarian with a
heavy accent, criticized everything I did: "You stupid
boy, you must put hummus evenly on inside of pita
bread. You would have been worthless when Russian
tanks rolled into Budapest!"

I worked with my new friend Mark, who shared my
interest in performance art, as juice boys at a busy midtown healthy eatery called the Curds and Whey Café.
The unctuous manager explained my precise time
schedule to me: "From 9:05 to 9:08 you collate juice filters. From 9:08 to 9:11 you take the carrot inventory."

I analyzed my employment situation as I was
putting the finishing touches on a New Orleans–style

veranda for my room at the loft. The sunporch was cantilevered out toward the wide windows so that I could peer up and down Broadway. As I hammered in the final galvanized-finish nail, it all became instantly clear: What I was doing for myself I could do for others! My whirlwind job and house hunting had taught me something very important about New York City: It was hard to make money, hard to find a place to live, and harder yet to have enough room in your apartment to even put a bed. I decided to turn these realities to my advantage.

Certain that my parents had not raised me to become alienated labor back East in lousy jobs, I gathered my tools, chisels, saws, hammers, and sexy carpenter belt and resolved to start my own carpentry business. I decided to become a builder of loft beds. With a newfound entrepreneurial zeal, I designed an advertisement, which I photocopied and that had the look of a ransom note: CARPENTER-PERFORMER-HOMO-SEXUAL AVAILABLE TO BUILD LOFT BEDS THAT WILL CREATE A NEW YOU! The phone started to ring almost at once.

I quickly became fluent in the lumberyards of lower Manhattan and discovered their specific pleasures. Prince Street Lumber had the cutest staff, but they charged the loft yuppies too much for their hardware. Dyke's Lumber in Midtown had the funniest name but an inconvenient location. Bowery Lumber was my favorite because they offered free delivery on any order over twenty-five dollars.

I had noticed in my search for a place to live that few people in New York really had enough space in their tiny apartments to sleep properly. Some unfortunate people resorted to dangerous folding futons that seemed to have been designed by Torquemada as instruments of torture. These futons accounted for dozens of severed fingers each year. Most folks with tiny apartments more sensibly decided to have special raised sleeping shelves in their apartments that were called "loft beds" whether they were in a loft or not. Somebody had made up the term in an effort to make it sound glamorous, as if we were in Paris: "Darling, let's retire to the loft bed, have a cappuccino, and bump our heads." Clearly there would be a market for my loft-bed construction business.

No solution to the space problem was too bizarre for me: I'd build loft beds anywhere. I'd build beds in hallways or in closets. A bed built out over the stove in a studio apartment's kitchen was very practical in a Lower East Side tenement without heat. You could make some potato latkes and keep yourself warm in bed at the same time. One loft bed I craftily hung from the ceiling by chains attached to meat hooks in a bedroom painted slate gray. This bold design became very popular on certain streets in the West Village and Chelsea. The reassuring stability of the chains provided numerous secure places for bondage toys, which solved the age-old problem that has confronted mankind: "Where do I attach my handcuffs or wrist restraints so I don't have to pretend I can't escape?"

I would build hundreds of beds for the people of New York City. Beds for people to sleep on. Beds for people to fuck on. Beds for people to get pregnant on. Beds for people to get sexually transmitted diseases on. I had found my vocation.

I was walking through SoHo on my way to Prince Street Lumber one day when I happened to notice a photocopied flyer advertising something called Open Movement. From the vague description, it seemed to be a kind of improvisational dance and performance-art jam. I instantly became so excited that I dropped my newly purchased screw gun.

I went the following Tuesday up the steep stairs at 99 Prince to Open Movement. My hands paused for a moment on the rough surface of the door to the loft. Pulsing Steve Reich music vibrated under my fingers as I heard the distinctive murmur of bare feet on hard oak floors inside. I thought of David waiting for me behind another dance-studio door two years before on my eighteenth birthday.

I pushed my way in. The loft was a swirl of amazing motion. People perched on each other's shoulders before they were flung through space and landed, silent as a cat. The improvisational movement of dozens of fingers became a tangle of imagined flames that spread from body to body. As the participants moved, their faces shifted and contorted into revealing glimpses of each person's monster self, and then their bodies transformed as they fell almost weightless through space. I looked around the room and instantly recognized some of the people amid the explosion of bodies. That guy, he dances with Merce Cunningham! Over there, she was in *Einstein on the Beach*! I saw those two skinheads at my favorite punk dive, CBGB, last night! It was as if I had stumbled at last into the club I wanted to belong to.

I quickly got into my sweatpants. I had stopped wearing my Patti Smith T-shirt — she seemed too commercial at this point — and slipped on a torn-up Harvey Milk campaign shirt instead. This would telegraph to people that I was a gay boy, politically motivated, probably Californian.

I walked into the maelstrom of bodies and felt the breath of the movement surround me. Using my deepening interest in Zen meditation to calm my over-the-speed-limit heartbeat, I put all my awareness into sensing the floorboards under my feet: the cool texture of the grain in the wood, the seam where the tongue and groove connected the boards, the energy that journeyed through the oak into the souls of my feet. I dipped one toe out to the side. The water felt fine. I dived in.

This gang of performers would become my rocket ship and cradle, my community and witness. Improvising with Peter, Charles, Ishmael, Joanne, Mark from the Curds-n-Whey Café, Stephanie, Irene, and others gave me a safe place to take big chances. A place to meet men, make art, and grow up. The three-car pileup of movement, sex, and performance carried me through these first years in New York. This was the fuel core that kept my motor running and showed me I could eat art for breakfast.

In 1979 my fellow art conspirators and I would liberate PS 122, an old abandoned school building in the East Village, and create a performance space just for these kinds of adventures. Surf's up!

I began to make a new full-evening performance each week. In these pieces I got to do things that I had always wanted to do. I did a crazed punkish barking-seal dance with Peter after we had placed clothespins on each other's nipples as I told the story of meeting Michael at Land's End. Inspired by Polish theater director Jerzy Grotowski, I was part of numerous collaborative projects in which my friends and I would go to the countryside for a week at a time, not speaking, communicating only with our bodies. During one of these paratheatrical trauma sessions, I saw Mark, who would later run PS 122 for the rest of the twentieth century, running bare-assed down the endless sea as if chased by demons.

We would try anything, no matter how risky, if it might pull us to a more authentic way of being. In my desire to channel Russian futurist Vladimir Mayakovski, I chained myself inside a foot locker and set Russian newspapers on fire all around me. Only a quick-thinking audience member with a bucket of water saved me from the burn unit.

No part of life was off-limits in these pieces. It was all ground meat ready to be made into hamburgers. (In fact, cooking hamburgers became a regular feature of my performances in that period.) My emerging identity as a gay man became the fodder of choice for my pieces. I even created a command performance when my parents came to New York to visit me. It was a piece especially for their "enjoyment" called *Pretty Boy/Big Building/Grand Mal.* My parents' jaws lingered around their Hush Puppies, sensible for New York walking, as I performed naked, put my mom's lipstick on, and smoked a cigar of my father's while telling stories from my sex journal mixed with family reminiscences.

My mom tried to find something nice to say after the show: "Well, honey, I liked the part where you talked about Whittier. Did you have to take your clothes off, though?"

"Son," my dad asked incredulously after the performance, "can you make any money doing this kind of thing?"

Naturally, I wasn't making any money doing this. I still relied on my small construction business. I invited some of my artist friends from Open Movement to work with me to augment their income from waiting tables. As we labored doing loft renovation, we would try to see the act of carrying sheets of plywood up six flights of stairs as a kind of "endurance" performance piece, in the tradition of durational body art. That worked. Once.

Running your very own carpentry business when you're a young queer performance artist takes much too much work. The burden was too great, Manhattan too vast, the money too meager.

In the summer of 1980, I debuted one of my new performance pieces at Club 57 on a bill with my friend Keith, fresh from rural Pennsylvania and now a student at the School of Visual Arts. In my piece I pulled a gun out of a box of bran flakes and threatened the audience; Keith did another piece from his *Lick Fat Boys* performance series. When I received my five dollars after the show, I realized I needed to get an actual job. My carpentry business was simply not cutting the maple wood.

Somberly I closed shop and gathered my saws, hammers, chisels, and carpenter belts (I had two carpenter belts now, one for day wear, the other for evening) for the last time. I went to work for a contractor named Frank di Martini, who often came to Open Movement to meet girls. Frank needed an extra hand, and my life as a Brooklyn construction worker began.

I now became a part of the subculture of a small construction company in Brooklyn. It was such an intense testosterone scene on the construction jobs, a mix of carpenter-jocks, ex-hippies, intensely butch dyke union wanna-bes, and one fag. All of us shared one thing: We were good with wood.

Frank di Martini was a cheerful, compact, ponytailed, rippling-muscled, sensitive New Age guy. He insisted on having at least one sweet and emotionally tuned-in gay man on every construction crew. I suppose that was me. This was Frank's version of queer affirmative action. I think he mostly wanted to have someone to talk to at lunch about things of mutual interest: metaphysics, love trouble, the latest Sondheim opening on Broadway. Frank would share with me the feelings that crosscut his life. Drilled into hidden places. Chiseled into his sense of self.

There was a darker side to this, though. I think Frank also wanted to have access to my Homo Sensitivity Gold Card. We were all given those plastic cards at birth, whether we know it or not. Frank thought he could borrow it from me if things got bad. It might help him meet his emotional payroll. We would use it to divide our feelings into lines on our lunch break over foot-long submarine sandwiches.

Okay, I know there are some people who would criticize me for idealizing this male universe I had landed in. They would say to me, "I think you are giving too much energy to a basically oppressive heterosexist job situation!" They might have a point, and I may be destined to end up on Oprah Winfrey's "Queer Carpenters Who Give Too Much on the Job" show.

Sure, I was giving, but I was also getting. I was getting the vibe of a world of working men in Brooklyn. Part of me had always wanted to be accepted by these guys who reminded me of my brothers and cousins. It was sexy too, being surrounded by all these straight men and their tools all day long. Mostly, I was out on the construction sites, except, of course, when hardened union guys from Queens were around. I was honored that in some way my queer gifts were being acknowledged and honored amid the whir of the saw and the bam-bam-bam of the nail gun.

The first day on the job with Frank, we did eight hours of demolition in an ancient basement on Adelphi Street. Yuck! The Pleistocene dirt of Brooklyn covered me from head to toe. This grime was made up of the grit of the writings of Walt Whitman and Hart Crane. At the end of the day, covered in their poems and black soot, I sat on the D train heading over the Brooklyn Bridge back to home on the Lower East Side. I caught a glimpse of my face in the shutting subway door. I didn't recognize myself. I was filthy, and there was a raccoony splotch of white where my face mask and goggles had been. I looked like those Welsh coal miners in the classic 1941 film *How Green Was My Valley.*

At the first stop in Manhattan, some artist friends got on the train and sat across from me. As they chatted amiably, they had no idea who I was. They didn't recognize me. I had become the invisible worker, someone who earns his keep with the sweat of his brow.

This realization of born-again working-class identity went straight to my head. Before too long, in that crucial summer of 1980, I became the head co-foreperson carpenter at the People's Convention in the South Bronx, a protest shanty town designed to expose the hypocrisy of the middle-of-the-road Democratic Party, which was soon to be holding its own convention in New York. My partner foreperson carpenter was a fabulous dyke named Marty. She was a performance artist too. Marty and I were Dyke and Fag Carpenter People's Heroes, ready to build a new social experiment in the bombed-out South Bronx.

That summer Marty and I marched with thousands of others in defiance of the corrupt Democratic Party Convention at Madison Square Garden. I took off my red plaid sleeveless shirt, the one I always wore on construction sites, and waved it over my head to show my politics and attract the cute man with the trust fund representing the Socialist Worker's Party. We poured past the Garden as we manifested our demands for social justice. Economic empowerment for all workers! We will seize the means of production!

(I do miss communism every now and then.)

But my friends on the subway couldn't see any of this. They probably thought I was just some working grunt on my way back to the wife and kids in Washington Heights. Had they only looked closer, though, they would have noticed the manifesto-red nail polish I was wearing that particular day. I had crossed over from my art life, and I now dwelled in a different world. I was now part of the realm of dirt and dust and beer and...blood!

Earlier that afternoon, while the jackhammers had pounded, Mike from deepest Brooklyn was starting to space out after his five-foot-long submarine sandwich lunch and four Budweiser and two Amstel Light (because he was dieting) beverage break. His blood sugar was not doing well at all. At about 2 p.m. he slipped on a rock, and his Sawzall, which was on at the time, tore a hunk of meat from his leg. Screaming in pain, he was hustled off to the emergency room. Those of us remaining exchanged nervous glances as Frank picked up a bucketful of sawdust and threw it over the spreading red pool of blood and said, "Back to work."

Now, every carpenter knows this is the tightrope we walk. The tools that can cut through brick and wood can also cut through our meat and bones. It is a blood contract, and nobody really knows the terms of it.

While I was going to Brooklyn throughout 1980 to rebuild brownstones, I was also seeing this guy named

John. I met John because I saw a postcard up in the Laundromat on Second Avenue for a performance-art piece he was doing. It caught my eye during the spin cycle. John was so beautiful with his mess of androgynous curls glowing in the photo. He extended one dancer's arm out to the side, fingers reaching all the way to New Jersey. I had to meet him. I got his phone number.

"Yes, in Manhattan," I said to the telephone operator. "I'd like the number for the attractive man on this postcard doing minimalist dance." (Directory assistance is amazing!)

I called John up. "You don't know me," I said, "but I think we should get together and talk about the new directions for gay men's performance in the '80s. I'm putting a festival together at PS 122." Okay, so it's been a recurrent pickup line in my life.

"It sounds interesting," John said cautiously. "Why don't you come over, and we can talk about it."

On my way to John's apartment in the East Village, I walked down East Sixth between First and Second. This is the block with all the Indian restaurants. Shagorika. Kismoth. Taste of India. Passage to India. The Gastronome Gandhi. Gandhi to Go. They're all there! I used to imagine that all these restaurants shared the same kitchen. I was sure there were block-long conveyor belts delivering huge piles of *poori* and *papadam* like stacks of laundry to each small restaurant. In the soon-to-arrive delusional paranoid days that began with the election of Ronald Reagan, I was convinced that one of his operatives (Ollie North, perhaps) was going to sneak back there with a clutch purse full of plutonium and dump it into the common vat of *mulligatawny* soup. In one fell swoop he would wipe out all the queer performers in the East Village because these cheap restaurants were where we ate.

I got to John's house, 306 East Sixth Street. He buzzed me in.

"How many flights is it?" I shouted as I climbed the many stairs leading to his apartment.

"Just keep on coming," John called down. "You've almost made it."

"Whew," I gasped, "that's quite a hike."

John extended his hand.

We had tea. We ate cashew chicken from the one Chinese takeout restaurant on the block. I was very drawn to John, so I cast my net wide and tried to pull him to my shore. John resisted me. I think he knew I was going to be big emotional trouble, so he struggled to avoid the coastline of my side, to miss the shoals of my chest, not to get pulled down by the undertow to my dick and butt.

John tried, but it didn't work. Sorry.

Who's the fish and who's the lure really in all of this? I don't know. I know we sat on wood boxes. John and I shifted near each other, and the inevitable thing happened, the only thing that could have happened between John and me: We began to fall toward each other, obeying the law of gravity and the even greater law that governs falling bodies. It was like when NASA's Skylab was going to fall from outer space and crash to earth. They could try with all their might to keep it from falling, but down it came anyway. Nobody really knew whom the debris would hit when it plunged into Western Australia. What if a big piece had hit a future boyfriend of mine, who was then a little boy in Perth dressed in a Catholic boys school uniform? I didn't care as long as it didn't hit me or anyone I loved in the head.

That kiss with John happened as we hit the earth's atmosphere. Then came the opening of clothes and the rush of feeling as we entered each other's undiscovered countries.

"Can we go into your bedroom?" I asked, a little uncomfortable on the wood boxes.

"You want to?" John asked, rubbing my close-cropped hair.

"I think so."

There was a voice inside that was telling me to wait. I wasn't sure if I had a passport for this journey. My papers probably aren't in order. I'd better turn back. I'll just leave now. Well, on second thought, maybe John and I can just sneak over the frontier at night. Hope for the best. So we kissed. And ate each other's butt holes, of course. And fucked each other.

That night as I slept next to John, I dreamed so vividly, the dream came with specially composed dream-sequence music. I dreamed I was in a graceful world, rolling fields of grass extending as far as the eye can see. Feeling John in bed next to me, I began to believe that this was a world we might get to live in together. On these fields of grass was humanly designed architecture, like the perfect college campus — the University of Iowa, maybe. It was all the colleges I never got to go to. I walked through this grassy dream looking for John while strange and beautiful music played from hidden speakers in my head.

We woke up the next morning, and I had a bright idea. "Instead of us making two separate pieces for my gay men's performance festival," I suggested, "why don't we start making a performance together that chronicles our relationship?"

"I don't know if that's a very good idea," John said, looking skeptical. "We just met. Maybe we should get to know each other first."

"Oh, c'mon. Don't be so conservative. We have a responsibility as young gay men to create representations for our generation. We can show how we reference more through the Talking Heads than Donna Summer. This could be an awesome 'personal is political' gesture!"

(I had been doing some actions lately with Fags Against Facial Hair. Upset that West Village mainstream homosexuals were invading our bohemia, we had gone around the East Village spray-painting DISCO SUCKS and CLONES GO HOME on the sidewalks. Horizontal hostility can be a thrilling energy source at twenty-two. I was getting more excited by the minute.)

John stretched long against the sheets. "Let me think about it. Want some coffee?"

"I don't drink coffee," I replied with certainty. Though I was still in my anarchist–vegan–herbal-tea period, I pondered the offer for a moment. Suddenly coffee sounded quite grown-up and postcoital. Backpedaling, I said, "I mean I don't usually drink coffee. I would love a strong cup right now, though."

In spite of the coffee, three weeks later we premiered *We Had Tea, We Ate Cashew Chicken*, chapter one of our *Live Boys* series of relationship performances. This initial performance detailed our first date and sex through the metaphor of everything we ate and drank that night, including each other's come. During the coming year John and I would make a number of pieces that chronicled our relationship in its many phases. The most successful of these ran for many performances and was called *Live Boys: I Walked Down Second Avenue. I Fucked Him in the Ass. I Love New York.*

John didn't want to love me. He had been burned by men many times and was cautious about opening himself to me. But I forced him to. For a while it gave him a lot of pleasure. Later it would give him a lot of pain. But for now, for a few powerful months together, how we loved to fuck each other!

While I was seeing John, Frank di Martini & Company was doing a job in the Fort Greene section of Brooklyn. We had done a massive renovation, and now I was working all alone on this site, doing the finish work on some doors and the parquet floor. Most people don't know that I am an expert door hanger. (I know, it's a fascinating subject.) Now, door hanging is a very useful skill because everybody needs doors. We need doors to go from one room to the other, sure. But we also need doors to go from one time of life to another. So if you know how to make a doorway, you'll always have work.

I had framed out a door at this brownstone and had left a space above for a transom. I was waiting for the stained-glass artisan, who was late (as artisans will be). Finally Gene, Mr. Stained Glass, arrived with his wide grin and wider shoulders. His long hair and two-day stubble made him look like one of the cuter of Jesus' disciples just fresh from a workout lifting rocks in the desert. He stripped to the waist as he installed his piece...of glass.

I pretended great interest in how he was deftly placing his work of art. It gave me a reason to be close enough to him to sniff the aroma coming up from his shucked-down overalls. The stained-glass commission he had fulfilled was a sort of reedy-lake-mallardy-duck-on-the-wing thing. We admired it. Then, out of the corner of my eye, I saw he was admiring me quite obviously. Then Gene the Stained Glass Hunk spoke.

"So...uh...do you like being a carpenter?"

"It's okay," I replied, flinging a slug an electrician had left on the floor.

"You really seem to have a knack for it," he said, examining my rather skillful work on the doorjamb.

"I'm good with wood," I replied, looking him in the eye.

Well, with that line, he had to make eye contact, right? So he glanced up and moved slowly toward me, brushing a fleck of wood off my cheek. His hand reached around my shoulder, and he pressed his body to mine as we leaned against the door frame. The heat of his body made my face turn red, like a bursting cartoon thermometer.

"You really know how to hang a door," Gene said. "Let's see if it swings."

Suddenly we were kissing and grabbing and poking. Soon our cocks were in each other's mouths as we stirred up the sawdust below our feet. The smell of the wood was in my nose and on my skin. It took my breath away. We offered each other our mahogany. We turned each other over in our hands. We showed each other our true line. We stroked our smooth sides. We measured out in inches exactly how much we needed.

It was clear to me that Stained Glass Man was about to come on my pricey birch-veneer clamshell molding. I breathlessly said, "Not there! Shoot on the inexpensive knotty-pine door saddle!"

We both came by the door hinge. Lazy dollops of come, like a dentist's office abstract expressionist painting, meandered slowly down the length of the wood. At that moment life seemed like a graceful and interesting place, where I could work hard and then mark what I had created with sex. The ab-ex look was quickly turning very Francis Bacon as the come lost its shape and melted to the floor. We looked at each other and laughed, brushing ourselves off and pulling up our pants.

"Do you want a cigarette?" Gene asked me, lighting one for himself.

I thought for a moment that this could be an opportunity to re-create myself, much like I had recently done with coffee. I could become a man who smokes cigarettes after sucking off hot artisans on construction sites. It was yet another possibility that presented itself to me. But I decided to take a rain check for the moment.

"No, thanks," I said, wiping my mouth. "I'm careful with my voice. It's my instrument for my artwork."

Stained Glass Man chuckled, hoisted his tool bag, pecked me on the lips, and went off to his next delivery.

I grabbed some sawdust and threw it on the dripping splooge. I got down on the floor and rubbed the queer come into the arrogant pride of these rich people's brownstone. Put that on your croissant, Class Enemy!

For the last part of my job that day, I needed to shave one thirty-second of an inch from the back of some of the pieces of parquet floor to make them fit flush around the door. For this job, I was going to use my hand electric planer. A hand electric planer has eight to twelve razor-sharp blades whirring five million times a second. It's basically a death machine. Now, this was not exactly a case of using the right tool for the job. In fact, it was completely the wrong tool. But since I'd enjoyed an unplanned sex break, I was in a hurry and needed to finish up.

I carefully held the first piece of parquet floor between my fingers. Errrh! One thirty-second of an inch shaved off. Good. Glued and installed. Good.

I gripped the second piece and carefully brought it close to the whirring blade held in my lap. Careful. Careful. Careful...

Now, if we were looking at this scene from outer space, what would we see? We would see a young queer carpenter in a hurry about to make a grave error. From space we would see the swirl of sawdust from where two bodies had recently been, the lingering heat of two men's mingled breath as visible as any nebula's gases on the opening credits of *Star Trek: The Next Generation*. From outer space we would see that in 1897, the Italian workman in the Bronx who had fashioned this piece of parquet floor had noticed a hard little oak knot on the underside. Uh-oh. I want you to all watch that oak knot very carefully now as it moves toward that leering blade. Closer. Closer. Closer...

The knot hits those blades, the machine jams, and my hand is pulled into the planer's teeth. Blood spurts everywhere: a tidal wave of gore.

I have cut off my entire arm, I think. *No, my arm is still there. My hand. No, my hand is still there. My fingers. No my fingers are still there. Wait, the end is gone. I've cut off the end of my finger.*

What could I do?

On automatic pilot I decided to go St. Something-or-Other, the Catholic hospital by the De Kalb entrance to the subway. Now, I believe whenever you cut off a part of your body, you should first find it, then put it in a teacup of ice, and then remember to bring it with you to the hospital. They can do amazing things with these cut-off parts. (I've seen the John

Wayne Bobbitt penis-restoration video.) I picked up the bloody tool and poked through the blades. I found the cutoff piece of finger, but it seemed like it wasn't going to be much help. It didn't look so good: sort of like a little spoonful of steak tartare. I left it in the electric planer.

I tore off my red work shirt and wrapped it around my squirting finger. Bursting out the door, I ran down the street leaving a trail of blood behind me. If anyone was looking for me, they'd know where to find me that way. Each drop of blood on the pavement was for someone in my life. This one, for John. This one, for David back in Los Angeles. This one, even for Vinnie, smug in his bungalow in Hollywood. This one, for Frank di Martini. This one, for me. All these, for everyone at Open Movement.

As I ran down the street, I remembered all the jobs I'd done in this neighborhood. I put two doors in that brownstone for a Wall Street stock analyst. I made the cabinets in a bathroom in there for this fuck buddy of mine who did public relations for the Brooklyn Academy of Music. I was proud of the window sashes for the yuppie family across the street.

I finally arrived at the Catholic hospital and rushed breathlessly toward the emergency room, my hand clutched to me like a relic of the one true cross. I burst through the doors and screamed, "I've cut off my finger! I'm bleeding to death!"

Everyone in the emergency room was screaming too. The nurse and orderlies were weeping and throwing themselves on each other. This seemed an extreme response to my admittedly bad problem. But they weren't paying any attention to me. They crossed themselves and said "El papa" this, "El papa" that.

Finally a formidable nurse with a faint mustache
and the name RAMIREZ on her breast screamed over the
loudspeaker, "The pope has been shot in Rome! Let us
all pray."
They all fell to their knees.
My mind took this in and quickly made a checklist
of the situation: I have cut off the end of my finger. I
have run bleeding through the streets of Brooklyn. I
have come to a Catholic hospital emergency room six
minutes after Pope John Paul II has been shot at the
Vatican! Is this fair, God, really? We have to talk.
An old woman with cataracts was weeping uncon-
trollably next to me as she grabbed at me, thrusting
her rosary into my bleeding hand. I had never felt
more like a WASP in my entire life. At long last the
commanding Nurse Ramirez glided toward me. She
gathered me unto her and put me in an examining
room. Capably, she placed my whole hand, red shirt
and all, into a metal bowl and poured a bottle of anti-
septic on it. She began to peel the cloth away, unwrap-
ping my finger like the Mummy revealing himself. My
finger was chewed up pretty seriously. It looked like I
had stuck it into a garbage disposal and then dipped
it in a bowl of salsa ranchera.
Nurse Ramirez remained calm. "Young man," she
told me, "we're going to cut off some skin from your
arm and sew it onto the end of your finger."
My eyes replied, *Yes! You're beautiful, Nurse
Ramirez.*
She grabbed a scalpel and neatly cut a nickel-size
piece of skin from my upper arm. Peeling it off like a
Band-Aid, she then flopped it onto the end of my finger
and sewed it on with deft strokes. The exposed flesh on
my biceps looked like a science project, like a cow I

once saw at the county fair with its stomach exposed so you could put your hand in it. The flesh winked shut as Nurse Ramirez stitched the wound closed.

"Sit!" she ordered me. "Keep your finger extended over your head. "Wait here for twenty minutes, then call someone to bring you home."

The woman with the rosaries sat next to me. She was calmer now. Patting my shoulder, she said, "I will pray for you even as I pray for the pope." The TV news reported to all assembled that the pope would live, and so would I.

I waited exactly nineteen minutes and then walked slowly to the pay phone on the wall. I called John and hoped he was home.

"Hello?" he said sweetly after the fifth ring.

"I'm in a Brooklyn emergency room," I panted. "I cut off the end of my finger. I'm lucky I didn't die. Please help me." I felt the tears start to come.

"I'll be right there, okay?" John knew the right thing to say. "I'll get there as soon as I can, and I'll bring you home." I don't think any words had ever soothed me so much in my life up to that point: John will bring me home to the East Village.

"Okay." I stifled a sob, wanting to be a big boy. "Hurry."

A half hour later John walked into the emergency room. I can still see him now, this most confusing man in my life. How much I loved and resented him for his gentleness! I can see him as if he were in front of me. John's beautiful face, so generous with his smile. His brown curls tumbled down his forehead and made a place that I would have liked to hide in. John had on his old winter coat even though it was May. It was cinched up with a wide belt.

"I guess my finger slipped," I said, holding up my enormous bandaged hand. "Do you think we can use this in a performance?"

"Don't think about that right now," John cooed. "Let's get you home."

He helped me up from the plastic seat, which was damp from my nervous sweat. We went outside to Flatbush Avenue, the afternoon light making Brooklyn look good, and John hailed a cab. This was a luxury not usually indulged. Feeling special, I nestled down into the seat like it was a stretch limo and leaned my face against the window as we crossed the Manhattan Bridge. The suspension cables framed my view of New York, chopping the skyline into little shapes, like the slices of pizza John and I loved at Stromboli's. The bits of Manhattan visible through the thick bridge cables were manageable bite-size pieces, just like the end of my finger back in the electric planer.

The cab left us at St. Marks and Second by the Gem Spa newsstand, where I often browsed the porn magazines. John quickly bought a half dozen bialys for us to snack on from the woman at the Second Avenue bakery who loved us and pretended we were yeshiva boys.

Walking quietly down the street, I felt so old. I leaned on John. I felt scarred and scared by this day. I looked up at the buildings of the Lower East Side. I had built beds in so many of them. And I'd had sex in all the rest. I knew their insides. I knew where the studs hid under plaster walls, waiting for the nail. I knew which brick would take which exact spike. I knew what dwelled in the mystery under the floorboards, the dark places between the joists that we walked on every day of our lives.

I had sawed and screwed. I had nailed and pounded. I had opened my body, and the blood had started to pour. I would try, but I would never be a carpenter again. I might even build another bed or two, but I would never really be a carpenter again. But I would always know, inside me, that there had been a brief time in my life when I was good with wood.

We walked on to East Sixth Street. I felt the sticky blood still on my arm. On my pants. On my shoes. I felt this blood on Sixth Street. It was slippery under my feet. It was hanging over my head. I saw my boyfriend John that day in May of 1981 on East Sixth Street. I looked to the East River. For an instant I saw the blood that was about to rise up from that river. I saw a wall of angry blood that would sweep away so many. I saw this for a second, a deluge about to come.

John nudged me and asked, "Are you okay?"

"Oh, yeah, I'm fine," I replied. "Can we stay at your house tonight?"

"Sure."

We walked into his building and climbed up the stairs very slowly. We went into his apartment. John carefully took the clothes off me and helped me into the bathtub in his kitchen. He took his clothes off too and then got in behind me. The water surrounding us both, John washed the blood from my body.

THE MAW OF DEATH

MY MANGLED FINGER HEALED SLOWLY. As Nurse Ramirez
had instructed me, once a day I poured hydrogen peroxide over it and watched it fizz away the infection. I
had spent the past few years in the area of pure art, so
the ritual finger soaking was the closest I had felt to
my childhood chemistry set in a very long time. I
became familiar with a world of science in which my
body was subject to the predictable effects of certain
outside agents. I took it on as a project, carefully dripping the peroxide onto my wounds so they foamed up
like a draft beer.

Slowly I began to regain the use of my right hand
for simple maneuvers. It would be months before I
could use my finger again confidently in sex. To this
day, when that scar tissue on my right index finger
strokes the litchi nut–like surface of a prostate gland,
I often have flashbacks of that terrible day in
Brooklyn. Add dropping barometric pressure to the
mix, and the throbbing in my finger might make me
pass out from the echoes of that traumatic experience
with the planer.

John and I continued charting the ebb and flow of
our relationship in performance, though the intimacy
of the finger story ended up on the editing-room floor.
As if we were cave explorers in a Kentucky cavern,
John and I used these pieces to spelunk deep into the
myths of our meeting, our neighborhood, the torch

passing to a new era of queer boys, and our ever-volatile love life together.

Turning the sweat and feeling of real life into something called art is a tricky alchemy — trickier by far than slathering hydrogen peroxide on your stitched-up index finger. Juggling art and life is a little like playing Russian roulette with a bazooka: thrilling, but you'd better not press your luck. For John and me, this activity accelerated the usual tensions that exist between two ambitious and wounded young men. Our boundaries, egos, and unresolved intimacy issues were challenged by each other in the full glare of a ticket-buying audience. We were little boys sitting on top of several stacked Manhattan phone books as we tried to drive our sixteen-wheel emotional trucks through each other's lives.

In the summer of 1981, John and I finished the final chapter of the *Live Boys* performance series. This one was titled *Live Boys: I Hate Your Guts*. The *SoHo Weekly News* ran a huge photo of John and me next to the review with a headline that blared LIVE BOYS GO BUST. The intrepid photo editor had torn the photo in two and left the jagged edges bracket the review. This was not a happy time.

In the final piece we engaged in a too-real fistfight that left me with a split lip and John with a broken heart. This performance at an upstate New York arts festival ended with our removing the pajamas we always wore in the pieces. We told the audience we would burn and bury them the following day in a private ritual to show that we had ended our relationship. The people watching this spectacle were left silent and stunned as John and I left the stage.

The next morning our shovels cut deep into the loamy soil of a meadow in the Catskills. John and I dug a good-size hole and placed our threadbare blue pajamas, worn out from dozens of performances, into the pit. Then we set our *Live Boys* costumes on fire. The cloth sputtered and glowed as we were surrounded by its polyester smoke.

"I'm glad we're being grown-up about this," I said, stirring the glowing ashes.

"Um." Tight-lipped, John turned and walked back alone the way we had come.

John and I entered a strained, protracted breakup period. Like two guys on a bomb squad, we carefully tried to defuse the tangled-up parts of our lives. Our communication ground to a halt except for every ten days or so when we would indulge in that dangerous yet seductive pastime: sex with your ex. That would usually make the bomb explode.

A few weeks into the breakup, John was getting his teeth cleaned at his dentist in Midtown. Under the hygienist's vigorous scraping, his gums started to bleed and wouldn't stop. She applied gauze, but nothing seemed to staunch the flow. The dentist became quite perplexed and admitted John to Bellevue for tests.

"It seems my blood has lost the ability to clot," John told me over the phone from the hospital. "They want to check me for all kinds of things. They're testing my blood for platelets, whatever they are."

"Well, I'm sure it's no big deal," I lied, vaguely aware of some disturbing rumors that had been afoot about some gay men who were sick. "I'll come by later today and visit."

I try to remember how it felt as this particular ship sailed Titanic-like into my life. Was it dramatically sudden? Or did it slip in slowly like the acupuncturist's needle we would all be poked by soon to boost our immune systems? Had I experienced any prescient dreams? Did I have the slightest clue about what was slouching toward us?

I was twenty-two years old.

Mostly, I simply could not believe that *anything* could stop me from making my performances about Russian futurism and New York homosexuality. Surely this "gay cancer" would affect only West Village mustached disco queens who went to the baths every day, not youthful, smooth-faced East Village anarchist performance artists in skinny neckties.

I went to Bellevue to visit John. I had never realized how close the hospital was to the East Village. Bellevue had been biding its time, waiting to pounce on us a few blocks downtown. John was sitting in a shared room high over the East River, reading *The Village Voice*. He looked uncomfortable in his shapeless hospital smock.

"Hi, babe," he said, brightening when he saw me. "You didn't need to come by. I'm getting out later today."

"Oh, that's okay. I wanted to." I had actually been incredibly nervous on my way there. Hospitals completely freaked me out. "I brought you some bialys with extra onions on them."

"Thanks," he said, a little confused by my gift. He looked at the bag as if he had never seen such a device before. We sat in silence and shared a savory bialy. I looked around the room to find something to talk about.

"Wow, look at that barge full of garbage coming down the river." I pressed my nose up to the window and stared toward Brooklyn. John wasn't buying it, so I turned back. "John, I feel so awful that we broke up in such a bad way. I'm sorry you're not feeling well now."

"I'll be okay," he said, looking away as he smoothed the sheet over his long body. "I'm sorry we broke up too. I guess it's how it was meant to be."

A nurse came in with some paperwork for John's discharge from the hospital. I grabbed at this moment as an escape hatch. "Well, I should go. I'll talk to you tomorrow."

Distracted by the nurse, John waved good-bye over her vast white back.

As I walked down First Avenue, I felt numb from the weight of this visit to Bellevue. It seemed like my feet were stuck in tar, it was so hard to move. I felt as though my life had suddenly shifted to a different planet with a heavier gravity than Earth's. It took me a long time to get back to the neighborhood.

John got out of the hospital, the situation with his blood taken care of by some medication, and he began work on a performance called *Surviving Love and Death*. Things seemed back to normal for the moment.

There were pressing problems of the immediate variety, though. Once again I had nowhere to live. For more than a year, I had been living at 309 East Fifth Street. This apartment had been the perfect digs for me. Conveniently located at the corner of Second Avenue, the flat had three rooms with five windows on the street. It was on the same block as the police station. I loved the feeling of security the cops provided! My destroy-the-state sentiments went out the window when it came to personal safety. The rent for the Fifth Street apartment was only $140 a month! I was so happy there. I was in heaven, but I couldn't stay: It was a sublet, and the gig was up.

Once again I called the Gay Roommate Service to try to find a new place but ended up once again being pawed, this time by bizarre men in Hell's Kitchen. I couldn't find anything.

I complained to my photographer friend Dona as we hung out in her darkroom while she processed film of photographs she had taken of some recent performances. Dona looked like a mixture of Pebbles Flintstone and a particularly gorgeous Irish Republican Army terrorist. She suggested I check out a landlord on Avenue B who had just bought two big beat-up buildings.

"He's a profiteering slimebag who should be garroted and dumped in the East River," Dona said with characteristic nonchalance, "but you're desperate, and the apartments have large rooms. Keep moving those prints around." I followed Dona's orders as the photograph slowly revealed its image of John sitting on a child's wooden chair in a recent performance.

Dona saw me looking at the image.

"Love sucks," the twice-married and soon-to-be-a-major-lesbian Dona said. "Trust me. Go check out this guy with the apartments."

Dona was right. I *was* desperate, so I pushed my way past the junkies of Avenue B. I went and threw myself on the mercy of the landlord.

"So you want an apartment?" he said, torturing me just for the fun of it. This landlord was direct from central casting, right down to the giant belly and chomped-on unlit cigar. He stroked the flap of hair that swept up and over from his ear to cover an almost totally bald pate. My eyes couldn't resist creeping up to this engineering miracle. How did he keep it there? "Why should I help you?"

"I'm clean and loyal and reverent," I said earnestly, "and I'll give you a $200 finder's fee."

He threw me a set of keys. For once, thank God, I managed to catch something tossed to me. "Check this one out around the corner. If you're not back in ten minutes with the money, I'll call the police."

So I moved to 234 East Fourth Street, at the corner of Avenue B, which from now on I will refer to only as the Maw of Death!

The huge metal doors of the Maw of Death clanged behind me as I tiptoed down the dark, boric acid–filled hallway with my polished avocado-green suitcase. The walls were filthy and smelled of paleolithic piss from a Times Square toilet. Abandon soap, all ye who enter here!

The building was equipped with a rich array of drug dealers, armed people lurking in the hallways, and a particularly active Santeria chapter, which at the time seemed to me to be the Lower East Side version of voodoo meets the Virgin Mary. This Santeria chapter was very big on blood ritual. Often I would come home and find the headless bodies or severed heads of chickens, goats, and the occasional unfortunate piglet.

Rebounding from a recent divorce, Dona had planned also to move to 234 East Fourth, but then someone carved a death's head on her door and hung a piece of piglet entrails from her doorknob. Dona was smart. She didn't move in. I am embarrassed to say, I signed a lease for the Maw of Death!

As I snooped around the fragrant building, I noticed there was a family of twelve next door and a punk-rock band above. A boy named Martin lived to my left. In a quick glimpse I had of him as I staggered up the stairs with an armful of synth-pop records, he had registered as a serious cutie pie. He was blond. With a vengeance. Martin would prove to be the one good thing I would find in the Maw of Death.

The day I moved in, someone cooking his heroin over a candle in the derelict building next door started a fire. The abandoned tenement was being used by an army of junkies as a shooting gallery. Soon disaster-movie flames were shooting close to the *Peter Pan* cartoon curtains I had just hung in my living room. As the fire got worse, the junkies started throwing themselves out the windows, scampering down the red-hot fire escapes. They looked like roaches jumping out of a toaster when you turn it on or shake it. I continued to hang my pastel drawing of Allen Ginsberg on the wall and glanced out my window as the firemen doused the flames, thinking, *Gee, at last, a home of my own.*

There was a knock at the door. I jumped off the overturned garbage can and walked down the long hallway.

"Who is it?" I called through the door, not wanting to be murdered my first day in a new place.

"It's me — Martin," a voice answered, "your neighbor from next door. I just want to say hi." I peeked through the eyehole and saw his handsome mug fishbowled all out of proportion. I undid the three locks.

"Hi, I'm Tim."

"Welcome to the building," Martin said, laughing. I wasn't sure what the joke was. "Would you like to see my apartment?"

"Sure, just give me a second." I went back in my place and changed into a clean sleeveless shirt that I thought I looked cute in.

Swapping small talk, we went next door. Martin was an English boy who grew up in Florida, where he had acquired his beefy muscles and American demeanor. He had about thirty earrings, a great smile, and truly the most ambitious haircut I'd ever seen. The sides of Martin's head were shaved so close that you could see the capillaries faintly pulsing red under his scalp. His long curly hair was greased with enough hair goop to lube a tractor trailer and was pulled straight back, taut as a trampoline, by a hardware-store hose clamp.

"Well," Martin said as he invited me into his spacious apartment, "ta da!"

His flat was decorated in what I think I would call "latish *Nuevo Wavo* junk shop": aqua walls, twinkly lights, a stuffed tattered marlin hanging over the bed next to the bas-relief of the Jetsons. Martin and I looked at his paintings, for he was, of course, an artist. He created images for record companies and had done the covers for a singer friend of his who was starting to get attention in European discos. Her name was Madonna. I'd never heard of her. He showed me the cover art he had done for an extended-play mix.

"She's in town from Paris," Martin said. "I'll call her, and we'll go meet her at her health club tomorrow."

Then we did a large but not unreasonable amount of cocaine. Clearly we could have kissed right then via the usual neck-rub strategy. But we didn't. Martin and I just talked, quietly watching the fire burn down the building next door. Then we listened to our favorite song of 1981, the Human League singing "These Are the Things That Dreams Are Made Of."

And that's how we met. And that's how we became friends. I would live next door to Martin at the Maw of Death for a year and a half. During that time many terrible things would happen there:

Three people would kill themselves by jumping into the central air shaft of our building.

Once a week Hector, our super, would run through the hallways pounding on our metal doors with his machete, cursing us in Spanish.

Martin had to fight off a bunch of junkies in the stairwell by kicking them in the face with his newly fashionable pirate boots.

Finally, most horrible of all, I went out on the landing outside my door one morning and saw finger trails of blood going all the way from the fourth floor to the first. This blood ended up rhythmically dripping into a sticky red pool by the torn-out mailboxes.

There was something wrong with this building, something terribly wrong. The Maw of Death reminded me of the building in the movie *Rosemary's Baby* but without parquet floors, Mia Farrow, or million-dollar Central Park West views.

The problems were not just with the Maw of Death, though. My personal and creative life was going nuts too. Since John and I had broken up, I was trampling with big muddy shoes through a number of men's lives. I was a mess of hungry desires, clumsy gestures, and unowned feelings. Things did not improve when I began a performance project called *Cost of Living*, which explored suicide and required me and several other artists to throw ourselves out of an airplane 3,000 feet above New Jersey. Every confusing moment of my life could be explained away by shouting, "I'll put it in a performance!"

John had begun hitting me hard with his fist every now and then when we were in public together. Not accepting that we had really broken up, he came to my apartment in the Maw of Death at 4 A.M. one night and slipped a note under my door. It was a proposal of marriage. My life a shambles around me, I felt my structural supports were starting methodically to unhinge, as if an unseen magnetic force were pulling the screws loose.

Finally, I couldn't take it anymore. My personal situation a mess and my apartment under siege by the forces of darkness, I decided to abandon the Maw of Death. I knocked nervously on Martin's door to tell him that I was jumping ship.

"Martin," I said, "don't be mad, but I'm moving out."

He seemed unfazed. "Oh, I'll miss you. But my friend Madonna, the singer, she really needs a place to stay until her first American album comes out. She was hoping an apartment in my building would become available."

Whatever. I put my stuff in storage and left the country for my first big solo performance tour for several weeks in the United Kingdom. I just counted myself lucky that I had broken my lease with the Maw of Death.

When I came back to New York in time for Thanksgiving 1982, I found a new apartment. It was only eight feet wide, but it was on a good block, Mulberry between Prince and Spring in Little Italy. There was no light or cross-ventilation, but it was only $255 a month. Also, at the same time, I broke down and got a new boyfriend.

I met him at my friend David's Christmas party on the Upper West Side. Since the first of my final breakups with John when we burned our pajamas the previous year, I had decided I was unsuited for married life. I had confined myself to short-term romances with mysterious men on Lower East Side rooftops as a

kind of damage control. This was a stopgap method of
bailing the decks as the ship was listing to starboard.

I went to the Christmas party under duress — my
host's threat of ritual suicide if I didn't show up — and
took the train uptown, planning to stay only long
enough to drop off a present. My friend Beth came
along with me for immoral support.

"Will it be *all* gay men at this party?" Beth
inquired, knowing the answer already.

"What do you mean by *all*?" I asked in a lawyerly
fashion. "Don't worry, I'll look out for your interests." I
was true to my word, because a few weeks later I helped
match Beth up with her future husband, Greg, a video
artist helping me with my suicide/skydiving project.

The trip so far uptown to 109th Street had the feeling of a search for the source of the Nile. I pored over
the subway map to try to figure out which way to turn
when we got out on the street. I opted for the express
stop at 96th and then a walk uptown. The eternal New
York December smell of salty roasting chestnuts on
rickety carts mingled with the warm breath rising from
the subway grating. I felt completely like a New Yorker,
even though I was counting the seconds to go home to
Los Angeles for the holidays and work on my tan.

I buzzed David's apartment, and Beth and I hauled
ourselves up the many flights of stairs. We were greeted warmly at the door and invited into an apartment
full of grown-up furniture. David was from
Springfield, Illinois, and had re-created on 109th
Street Abraham Lincoln's house. The party was in full
swing as the eggnog and egos flowed. Lots of fellow
performers and choreographers were there, a few of
whom I had complicated relationships with.

Slept with him. Haven't spoken since.

Didn't sleep with him. Haven't spoken since.
John was there too. It was the first time we had been
at a social engagement since I refused his proposal of
marriage. We nodded to each other diplomatically. He
looked quite beautiful, and I felt like I was sinking in
a pit of "Oh, God, what have I done!" This was a sentiment that was echoed in our favorite Talking Heads
song, "Once in a Lifetime," which John and I had
always ended our shows with.

There was another buzz at the door, and two new
people came in, an enormous man with a blast of
black hair accompanied by a more reasonably dimen-
sioned handsome guy whom our host greeted as
"Doug." I had been hearing about this Doug character for the past few months as he had begun to sniff
around the corners of the downtown performance
scene. Doug was a graduate student at New York
University but carried the cachet of being a native
New Yorker. His arrival at the party had been greeted
by all of the faggot performers looking up from our
figgy pudding with thought balloons appearing over
our heads saying, FRESH MEAT.

How do you describe your first look at a man that
you are going to see when you open your eyes the next
few thousand mornings? It's hard to find your way
back clean to a memory, with all the slightly fictional-
ized tellings at dinner parties and in a novel or two.
Maybe the quest for truth is hopeless, like it was for
poor Heinrich Schliemann, the nineteenth-century
German explorer, getting dust in his eyes trying to find
the ruins of the city of Troy.

Well, Heinrich, you gotta fucking well try.

Doug was a Bronx beauty. His wild froth of curls
spilled over his forehead and into his eyes. (Me and

my hair fetish!) He had a great nose that gave his face
an approachable generosity, crying out so that all the
goyim could hear, "New York ethnic!" His compact
body was dressed up in a retro sweater-vest and bow
tie. This gave him a sexy look, sort of like a Jewish
Jimmy Olson, boy reporter. I detached myself from the
mantle and made my way toward him.

"Hi. I'm Tim," I said, sipping my eggnog loudly.

"Hello, I'm Doug," he replied. Gesturing to his tall
friend, Doug added, "This is Takis. He's Greek."

Takis easily picked Doug up off of the ground for a
moment and said, "And you, Doug, are my Jewish
roommate with a big nose from the Bronx!"

"Beware of Greeks bearing Jews!" I commented
cryptically as Takis set Doug back down on the polished wood floor.

(I'm pretty sure this is what happened. I know I
actually made that fall of Troy pun, and that is not
just payoff from my Heinrich Schliemann reference a
few paragraphs earlier. I can't be certain that Takis
was actually picking Doug up when I said it, but it
works better that way, don't you think?)

Throughout the '80s and '90s, Doug would always
claim that I never really properly "fell in love with
him." All I know is that I levitated my way through
this Christmas party as Doug and I flirted under the
gaze of everyone.

"How long have you been in New York?" I asked
him.

"Forever," he replied. "I was born here. Where are
you from?"

"Los Angeles. Whittier, actually." And then I quickly added, "Richard Nixon's hometown" to pull
Whittier out from the pit of suburban banality.

"Wow, Whittier! That's exotic. You're probably a WASP. I've never met one before."

"Yes," I said, ready to play along. "I was born during an Apache attack in a covered wagon on the Santa Fe Trail. Seriously, it would be nice if we could hang out sometime. I'm going to California for Chris— I mean, the holidays, tomorrow. Maybe when I get back?"

We exchanged addresses and phone numbers. I thought about changing my flight and trying to call Doug the next day but decided a nice note with the greeting "Happy Challahdaze" would be more appropriate. Before I left the party, Doug and I gave each other a little hug, and as I put on my scarf to go, I saw John looking at me from across the room. I felt like I had just broken the punch bowl. But then John, ever gracious, smiled, mouthed the words "Merry Christmas," and went back to his conversation. Beth and I left.

"I have a vision," Beth said, channeling Yenta the Matchmaker. "I see you under a canopy. With a *man!*" She playacted having a heart attack.

"Do you think he liked me?" I asked Beth, looking back up one flight of stairs.

"He liked you," she said, back to her normal voice. "Trust me."

I ran down the stairs in four-at-a-time leaps, exactly like who I was at that moment, a guy who had just met someone with whom he was going to spend years of his life.

When Doug and I met, in 1982, I was a person who thought of himself as only a few weeks free of the Maw of Death. The early reports in the *New York Native* of gay-related immune deficiency heralded a time when doom was underneath every newspaper headline and turned-down bedsheet. The scary episode with John's blood not clotting had left a fearful question mark about what was happening inside his body. This meant that I had some major questions about my own situation. How did I manage to live in my 24-year-old body, terrified constantly that I might not make it to twenty-five?

Denial worked wonders.

Somehow I can't quite separate the Maw of Death from the events of that time, the new disease, and the new boyfriend. If I want to remember that time, I also have to go back to 234 East Fourth Street. I need to know what unstoppable forces got unleashed in that building, the *Raiders of the Lost Ark* special-effects Four Horsemen tornadoing up to the sky. When I remember the day I met Doug, the memory is inextricably linked with the Maw of Death and my friend Martin, the one good thing I found there.

Martin and I didn't become good friends while we lived at the Maw of Death. Since we were already practically roommates, we kept a kind of neighborly distance. It was only once we had both left the Maw that it felt like we could become better friends — and begin to flirt in earnest, even though I was already seeing Doug.

The affair with Martin began after Doug and I had been seeing each other for six months. Things were not going so well. I had been so excited about our first date. I called Doug as soon as I got back from Los Angeles to invite him over. Buzzing around my new digs on Mulberry Street, I plugged in a large lightbulb sculpture to make some mood lighting, but an electrical short blew all the fuses in my apartment. Doug arrived to my hastily improvised candlelight.

"Hi," he said, offering me a bottle of wine with his right hand so we had to shake with our left.

"Hi," I replied, immediately dropping the bottle. "I blew a fuse. Come in."

During our date Doug began to tell me about his extensive study of French deconstruction as part of his Ph.D. program at NYU. He had been reading French philosopher Guy Hocquenghem's important work *Capitalism, the Family, and the Anus*. Covering up my lack of fluency with this area of inquiry, I countered, "Oh, those frog theorists have to write all these books just to explain why they like getting it up the butt." To cover my nervousness, at this point I started swinging from my chin-up bar in the kitchen doorway. Doug took action and kissed me as I swung gently back and forth. As it so often has been the case in my life, it felt like going to my bed was the next logical step.

The squabble about language theory and anal sex had set a tone for our evening. Despite our valiant efforts, Doug and I came up against a brick wall as we tried to fulfill my preferred sexual agenda of fucking each other. Doug couldn't relax and let me inside him. Ever practical, I proposed he fuck me then, but I didn't know the proper dirty talk that would make Doug want to do this.

This clunky sex dynamic between us, along with my busy schedule and Doug's ongoing relationship with his boyfriend of five years in Boston, kept our relationship on an alternating current during our first nine months. We had a serious discussion about our problems at a café on Mercer Street.

"Our sexual relationship isn't really working," I said, slurping up my iced mocha coffee. "Plus, I may have been exposed to herpes anyway from this guy I had sex with in London. I just want to become a virgin again."

"I think we should be patient with each other," solution-oriented Doug said. "We've only been seeing each other a little while."

"Well, okay," I said, not wanting to let this man go in spite of our troubles. "But let's take it slow because I'm really busy the next two months jumping out of airplanes for my performance, and you still have a boyfriend in Boston."

Doug and I began a long, tentative courtship. Since Doug was continuing to see his boyfriend, Chuck, in Boston, when Martin and I ran into each other as we rode our bikes on Lower Broadway, I felt free to pounce on him. We were so happy to see each other. We hugged and bought each other an icy-cold V-8 juice as we sat down and talked.

"It's great to see you!" I shouted. "Wild hair!"

He had several barrettes lined up along his creamed-back blond locks. He was the first person I ever saw work this look. "Isn't that Dona's bike?"

"Yeah," he replied. "I bought it from her. I love it. Want to go for a ride?" Martin dragged out the last word suggestively.

It was August, and August is a very strange time in New York. It is so hot. It is so humid. In August it feels like life and time have stood still. The hot breath of a subway in August can carry you away from who you think you're supposed to be. Everything is up for grabs in August, and all the rules can be broken. A fellow can spend the entire month of August doing nothing but riding his bike down Park Avenue South, chasing a lunatic blond doof with a great butt through the lower twenties. I was twenty-four then, racing through my lower twenties too. I was glad to be on my bike this August in New York.

One steam-room–hot evening, Martin and I got on our bikes to catch a midnight showing of the movie *The Draughtsman's Contract* on the Upper East Side. We pedaled around Grand Central Station, past the Pan Am building, then through the Helmsley-Spear tunnel. We were impervious to cab and cop alike as we raced though every red light. We got to the movie theater with just enough time to make out a little bit on the stoop of a building at 61st Street and Second Avenue. Now, we didn't sleep together that night. I'm not sure why. I think I was a little scared to have sex with Martin.

The next day I called my friend Dennis, who wrote obsessive, beautifully crafted stories in which teenage boys have their ass flesh carved up with razor blades during reckless sex in our native Los Angeles. I thought he might be able to advise me in my dilemma with Martin.

"Dennis," I said, "I need to ask you a question. What do you think this safe-sex stuff consists of?"

Dennis, who may or may not have been an expert in such matters, gave some long thought to this. We were new at this then, in 1983. "Hmm," he said finally, "safe sex, eh? Well, I think, basically, you can do whatever you want. But whatever you do, don't suck, fuck, rim, or kiss him."

This gloomy information sobered me. It was a very complicated time. But it was complicated for other reasons too. I was more involved than I thought in my on-again, off-again relationship with Doug. We were not completely boyfriends yet, but it was definitely on the verge. But Doug was off in Boston with his "ex-boyfriend" (Doug called this guy "ex," but he didn't seem so ex since Doug still went on all-expense-paid trips to Martinique with him).

So I was alone in New York in August. And I was much taken with my friend Martin and our wild rides uptown. We were Martin and Tim: the two who had escaped the Maw of Death!

The next day the asphalt on Mulberry Street melted my sneakers as I walked to meet Martin at the subway. We had planned a beat-the-heat trip to Brighton Beach. I had recently purchased on Fourteenth Street a handsome blue-and-yellow inflatable raft to ride the waves.

When Martin and I got to Brighton Beach, we blew up that surf rider, got on it together, and floated way out beyond everybody else. We just bobbed there, told stupid jokes, kissed a little bit, showed each other our dicks underwater, and waved to people far away back on the shore. It felt so private. It was like we were on our own little island floating off the coast of America. It seemed like we might never have to go back to Manhattan. I could forget about everything else troubling me in my world. Martin and I could just stay on our surf-rider island for the rest of our lives.

But we did have to go back. It was getting dark. So we paddled toward the shore and lay kissing on the deflating raft as it hissed out its breath all around us. Then we got on the F train and headed back to Manhattan.

When Martin and I got back to Little Italy, it was so hot, the rats had passed out on my front stoop and paramedics were administering oxygen. We headed straight for my apartment, took off our clothes, and got in the shower together with only the cold water on.

Finally, we began making out the way men are supposed to, the water covering our supple naked bodies
as they tried to squish inside each other. This was very
nice. Martin was a big blond guy, what today I would
call a dude. He had more yummy body than I knew
what to do with. We sucked and nibbled and supped
at each other's table. The shower's sharp spray was on
my back as I sucked his dick.

"Yeah," Martin whispered, stroking my hair, "suck it."

I started to weird out. The pointed pricking of the
water spray was cutting into my skin, tattooing my
crime of infidelity on my back. The water began to
feel too wet. I started to think, *Oh, Douglas is coming
back to New York tonight.* I began to feel a little guilty.
I'm like that sometimes — Mr. Guilt. It happens when
I feel Goofus and Gallant battling around inside of me.
I get ripped in two by the apparent contradiction
between what I *want* to do and what I think society,
God, family, and boyfriend tell me I *should* do. More
often than not, this creates a psychic meltdown, and I,
as they say, act out. In my current situation something
felt not right. The fact that I was losing my hard-on
told me so.

"Martin, I think we should stop."

Martin probably knew what was going on in my
head. He just looked at me sweetly and smiled, shrug-
ging his shoulders. "Rub-a-dub-dub," he said.

Three men in a tub, I added in my thoughts.

We got out of the shower and dried each other off.
It was torture having to put clothes on in the heat. If
only we could walk naked hand in hand out onto
Mulberry Street and buy an Italian ice at the corner.
Instead, in our black cutoffs, we went out into the hot
wet night and had one last freezing-cold V-8 juice.

Later that night Doug came over after his train got in from Boston. I could tell that something important had gone on while he was there.

"What happened with your Boston boyfriend?" I tartly queried, covering up the shame I felt for philandering with Martin.

"We finally broke up," Doug replied. "I kept thinking about you. I want us to keep trying, Tim."

"I'd like that." I knew I should say something more poetic, but this was the best I could do. Happily, it was enough. It was clear to me that Doug was a man, a mensch, as he had once named me as a way of explaining why he couldn't dump me. That was a thing to be cherished. That night Doug and I made out like nuts on the floor of 241 Mulberry Street, though he still grimaced when I tried to fuck him.

Later that year I ran into Martin at Rockefeller Center, and we had a very good talk.

The next year Doug and I moved in together.

The next year John began to get sick for the first time.

The next year I caught just a glimpse of Martin. On a new bike. Racing down Broadway with an even more ambitious haircut.

The next year Martin was dead. Of you-know-what.

I had been out of New York a lot, so I didn't hear about it when it happened. Didn't do the hospital time with Martin. Didn't see the *National Enquirer* invade his hospital room to flash his now-famous friend Madonna's photo as she left his side. It was only later that someone broke the news to me, and I sat down on the street and said, "Oh, shit." This was the first person I knew who had died. I *knew* him. I knew his big

blond body. I knew the nice fleshy place on his belly.
My fingers had found their way over his skin, and now
that was gone. His paintings for album covers. Our
bike rides together. The life between us. It was all
nothing now.

"Oh, shit."

See, I had actually thought that *all* of us — Doug,
John, Martin, and me — just might escape the Maw of
Death.

I was wrong.

A BUDDY SYSTEM

DOUG AND I MOVED IN with each other on Gay Pride Day 1984. Rising early that Sunday morning, we crammed our belongings into a friend's van and moved into a sublet loft at Bond and Lafayette as an experiment in living together.

Groaning under the burden of dozens of milk crates bulging with magazines and books (their combined weight could have capsized an aircraft carrier), we piled our boxed worldly possessions in the middle of the loft floor. These cardboard containers looked like a child's set of building blocks as they sat there, full of possibility. One box was full of Doug's Foucault; the other stuffed with my Wagner recordings. Like kids in kindergarten, we could arrange these boxes to make a castle or a skyscraper or, in our current situation, a life together.

"Well," Doug said, wiping the June sweat from his forehead, "here we go."

"Yeah," I sighed as I collapsed onto a packing crate. "I hope we don't kill each other. I've never lived with anyone before. I can be a little controlling every now and then."

"Really?" Doug mugged a face of mock surprise. "Let's just take it one trauma at a time, okay?" He sat down next to me and draped an arm across my legs. We sat quietly side by side on our belongings for a long moment.

"Hey, Dougie, let's catch up with the parade in Midtown," I suggested, never having missed a gay pride march since 1977. "We can unpack later."

Doug and I locked up *our* new house for the first time. I turned the key in the top lock. Doug did the bottom. Creaking down to Bond Street on the ancient elevator, we poured out onto the street the instant we got to the ground floor so we could get uptown pronto.

"Tim," Doug whispered loud enough for a cabdriver to turn his head, "look at that guy. I think it's Robert Mapplethorpe."

"Be cool," I hyperventilated. "Let's keep walking, looking straight ahead. His studio is on Bond Street. He's our neighbor."

Doug and I walked down Lafayette Street. At the last moment I peeked over my shoulder and saw the notorious photographer climb into a taxi going uptown. We, on the other hand, jumped on the Lexington Avenue subway. Conveniently, the Bleecker Street stop was right outside our new digs.

Doug and I caught up with the march just as it was passing 42nd Street and immediately joined in with our friends Barry and Stephen, who happened to be marching by with the gay writers' contingent. There were dozens of placards with giant photo blowups of queer writers. Barry sweetly let me carry Marcel Proust for a while.

"*Mazel tov!*" Stephen said enthusiastically, giving us each several dramatic continental kisses. Italian-American by birth and Jewish by his marriage with Barry, Stephen had a double dose of energetic warmth for us, his adopted younger gay bothers. "Congratulations on your new life together! I shall get you an appropriate housewarming present, maybe a replica of Shakespeare's First Folio. They're on sale at Macy's." Stephen was carrying a huge poster-size engraving of Shakespeare, claimed today as an honorary queer.

Doug and I ran with the others on an impulsive storming of the New York Public Library. In a blizzard of placards and rushing bodies, the gay writers made a mad dash up the stairs that would have fit right in the Eisenstein film *Battleship Potemkin*. A quick montage would follow of photos of Gertrude Stein, James Baldwin, Oscar Wilde, and dozens of others pushed boisterously onto the portico. Draped over one of the huge lions that were supposed to be guarding literature from the homosexual horde, Doug and I waved Marcel Proust together as the march surged along Fifth Avenue.

We were two more-than-cute-enough young men. Doug would often undercut that impression of himself, but I consistently exaggerated it in myself, believing I was handsomer than I actually was. Both of us sported bumper crops of curly hair. Our closely trimmed sides from a five-dollar Astor Place haircut gave our curls up above the look of hats clapped on our heads. Doug was in his frayed denim short shorts, showing off his Betty Grable legs, part of his post-Bronx makeover.

As I tapped my red Converse high-top tennis shoes nervously on the lion's pedestal, my lanky body was all akimbo angles and desires. I leaned against Doug while he took a turn waving our poster of Mr. *Remembrance of Things Past.* I was not aware, as I threw my arm in a proprietary manner over Doug's shoulder, that this might have been an unconscious way of my saying, "I'm taller than you." Doug and I were full of bumps and grooves as we abutted, a walking advertisement for opposites that attract. Natural surfaces where our differences complemented each other (insert tab A into slot B) easily collided with the many land mines that could set either of us off. We marched through New York that day, only vaguely aware of the chemical reactions we could call up in one another.

Doug and I had been each other's war brides in 1983. Like drunken swirling lovers in a soldier's bar the night before shipping out, we had quickly made our deal. The early casualty lists from the plague front had made a lot of us think it was time to cut through some of the fears about relationships and finally try to find a nice man (who was not insane) with whom to weather the storm. As young-faggot-boys-on-the-go in Manhattan, we battened down each other's hatches right as AIDS hurricaned in. This had mostly worked for us. Doug and I had both been in other relationships, so we had already learned the necessary techniques to support or destroy each other. We engaged our repetitive battles over art, sex, and narcissism in a manner that often left us bloodied but always still standing.

Still smarting from my messy breakup with John, I had insisted that Doug and I nurture our relationship in privacy for close to a year. I would hop on the First Avenue bus and leave the Lower East Side so I could have an anonymous weekend at Doug's East 52nd Street apartment. After years of living below 14th Street, I felt that these trips uptown provided me crucial breathing room. My weekends with Doug allowed me to escape the small-town pressure cooker of the East Village. Slowly Doug and I began making forays out into the world — we decided to go to a friend's

faggot art-world party on Yom Kippur to mark our
coming-out as a couple.

Since I was more established in my chosen career,
Doug apprenticed himself to me and started to perform in my increasingly overblown multimedia spec-
tacles. This began what Doug would refer to as "the
years of slavery in Egypt under Pharaoh." We had
always battled over our clunky sex dynamic.
(Increasingly frustrated that Doug didn't like me to
fuck him, I would accuse, "You're castrating me,"
always ready to play dirty.) At the time it did not
occur to me that Doug's closed back-door policy might
be a way he could preserve power and manifest dis-
pleasure for his Egyptian exile.

Doug and I stepped off the edge of the cliff into the
free fall of two wounded, ego-driven men trying to
make a life together.

We grew up side by side.

Our experiment in living together had gone pretty
well. After a period of intense, almost medieval
domesticity during which we would stay home most
nights playing duets on our recorders, our structure
normalized and was ready to grow in new directions.
Now that our intertwined roots were strong enough to
stand a little wind, Doug and I began to explore new
ways of connecting with the world as a unit.

Thus, after two and a half years of boyfriend-dom,
Doug and I decided that it was time to procreate. We
had been thinking about it for a long time. It struck us
that it might just be the thing we needed to bond our
relationship at the sublet loft on Bond Street.

Finally, during an extended trip to Los Angeles to
avoid the hot New York summer, it seemed like the right

time for us. Though I have discovered ass fucking to be
the font of numerous gifts both physical and spiritual,
in my experience it has proved an inefficient manner of
producing a little bundle of joy. Condoms don't help
matters either. So Doug and I decided to adopt.

We looked at him as he slept, his baby fat sighing
up and down with each breath. Our hands crept
toward each other as we stared at this little creature
full of farts and needs.

"He looks like me," I whispered.

"Ridiculous," Doug countered. "Look at his nose.
He's definitely Jewish."

"But check out his long, lean torso. That certainly
comes from my side of the family."

"Right, Mr. 'Tomorrow Belongs to Me,' " Doug said,
aghast at my comment. "You have to make him an
Anglo-German track star, don't you?"

I sighed, tired of playing Jews and Christians. "It
just seems to me a striking resemblance."

Doug and I looked down at the black Labrador
retriever puppy sleeping at the foot of our bed. We had
finally made the classic gay men's move toward stability: We got a dog. In a world where two men in a
relationship are repeatedly denied a bundle of society's
goodies that are freely bestowed on straight folks, you
need to be ready to improvise. That's where the dog
comes in.

I had been raised my whole life with dog consciousness. But for Doug, dogs had always carried a scary
danger with them. Growing up in the high-rise projects
of the Bronx, he felt that a dog was a little too close to
the messy natural world for comfort. On the other paw,
I had always had dogs in my life. Growing up in
Southern California, I constantly had some creature

yapping in the backyard, terrorizing the mailman, and chewing up my favorite copy of *Charlotte's Web.* The dog was as essential for the smooth running of a home as was a station wagon or indoor plumbing. The dog could be hugged and kissed so we could demonstrate that our family was as warm as our Cuban in-laws. The dog could be yelled at. The dog could be fed delicious scraps under the table. The dog could be put outside when he was annoying. The dog could have his face rubbed in his own shit. These were all things my family would have liked to do more directly with each other but were too scared to try. So the love and the anger and all kinds of other juicy feelings would be projected to the dog (who would be named Sandy or Rags or Brindle).

Doug had been raised to see dogs as inappropriate creatures from another planet. They were at best dirty uncouth animals and at worst Jew-hating collaborators. Doug's mom would cross the street to avoid the gruesome possibilities of an encounter with a stranger's overweight dachshund: "See, it even has a German name!"

Doug had warmed up to the idea of getting a dog in much the same way he had realized he needed the companionship of a genuine WASP from the West. First there was skepticism. This was followed by a period of reflection on the pros and cons. Finally the full avalanche of desire and compulsion propelled him forward. We were spending the summer in L.A., and we decided this was the perfect moment to search for the dog for us.

"What kind of dog do you want?" I asked Doug as we drove to the pound. "Personally," I prompted without giving him time to answer, "I know I want a big dog. I want him to be big enough to be able to kill me if he wanted to, but, of course, he chooses not to." The moment I said this, I knew I shouldn't have mentioned killing.

"Well, whatever else he is, he should be sweet," Doug said, wavering.

" 'He!' So you're saying you want a boy dog?"

Doug couldn't resist the obvious politically incorrect joke. "Well, it could also be nice to have two bitches around the house."

"Keep our sex life out of this!" I added, ignoring his glib remark. "It makes a big difference whether we get a male or a female. Males are usually more aggressive and hyper. They tend to wander."

We were stopped at the corner of Santa Monica and Robertson boulevards. A cute man modeling cutoff sweats and no underwear was walking his Jack Russell terrier to Pavilions, the faggy West Hollywood super-market where you could get twenty-eight kinds of let-tuce. I couldn't decide who was cuter, man or dog. My head pivoted to follow his progress. You could see his balls loll left and right with each loping step. He knelt down to pet his Jack Russell, and one of his testicles fell out of the baggy cutoffs.

I continued. "Female dogs are calmer and smarter and don't chase after every piece of tail when they get a good hot whiff of pussy like a male dog will."

Doug considered this carefully. "What are some of the other good attributes of boy dogs?"

"Well," I free-associated, "they do have big beauti-ful balls that you can look at all the time."

"Let's get a female dog," Doug said, watching me eye Mr. Sweatpants as he disappeared around the cor-ner. "Would you mind keeping your eyeballs in your head and off that guy's butt?"

We arrived at the dog pound in Santa Monica. I thought there was a chance we might be able to find a higher quality of mutt in a Westside animal shelter. The moment we opened the front door of the utilitarian structure that looked like it was a dentist's office, there was a tremendous racket of barking and mewing. Zipping quickly past the floor-to-ceiling pens full of cats and kittens, Doug and I went straight for the dog kennel and began cruising the cages.

"This looks like Auschwitz," Doug said, tugging at my arm. "The ones that don't get picked are going to be destroyed. I can't take this."

"Don't be so dramatic," I stage-whispered, a little unnerved by the scene myself. "Just imagine, if we don't pick one of these dogs, he might be doomed."

This half-baked logic seemed to help Doug as he allowed a small dog that seemed to be an unlikely corgi–Great Dane mix to lick his fingers through the bars of the cage. I smiled at the sweet image, and then a flash flood of panic hit me. It was a gasket-blowing surge of 5,000 pounds per square inch of pure adrenaline hitting me in the middle of my chest. My head pounding in time with my accelerated heartbeat, I felt queasy by the enormity of this decision. This could be a fifteen-year commitment. Could I rise to this challenge?

Like most gay men, I had already had a lot of dogs in my life: purebreds, mongrels, show dogs — I'd done them all. I remember one encounter vividly.

I was cruising a dog pound in Provincetown one hot September night. I thought I would have just one more drink of water from the bowl when a handsome golden retriever caught my eye. His name was Sven. Our eyes met across the animal shelter, and I felt this spark. We moved toward each other, the dog and I, and touched through the kennel bars. There was an immediate and strong connection. I got him a bowl of water and a milk bone. I asked him to come home with me.

I know it's not the most important thing, but this dog and I shared a physical relationship that was passionate and deeply satisfying. We shared long walks on the beach at dusk in P-Town, quiet evenings in my hotel watching Lassie *reruns, and candlelit romantic dinners. So he wasn't an intellectual; that didn't matter because I knew I had met the dog for me. Mr. Right Dog.*

But after a few days that glow faded. The magic went out of it. Sven, my beautiful golden retriever, started to get on my nerves. The way he was always chewing on his tail disgusted me. His bland golden-retriever good looks seemed too vanilla.

Then, well, I did meet another dog that I was attracted to, a rottweiler named Rex who was into leather. I just wasn't ready for commitment at that point in my life. I panicked and started to plot my escape.

I had a talk with Sven as I squeezed his favorite tennis ball, soaked with his saliva, in my hand. "Sven, I like you very much. I do," I said. "I just feel like I'm not ready for a relationship at this point in my life. I really want to preserve the friendship that exists between us. That's the most important thing, I think. So maybe I should take you back to the animal shelter now, okay?"

A single tear slipped down Sven's furry face as he gathered his belongings — a chew toy and an ancient Boy Scout blanket — and mournfully made his way back to the pound.

I picked up the phone and made a date with the Rex the rottweiler.

The terrible memory of this relationship with a dog mixed with my equally checkered past with men haunted me as Doug and I browsed through the cages of the Santa Monica pound. I had gone to bed with more than one golden retriever who, through no fault of his own, seemed to me more like a basset hound the next morning.

I squashed down my impulse to flee the animal shelter. What if I made the wrong choice again? What if this new dog is too needy? What if he cries all night? What if he chews up my first edition of *Giovanni's Room*? What if he doesn't fulfill my expectations? What if we aren't a good match for each other's emotional needs? What if we don't click in bed? What if he loses his hair before he's thirty? What if he can't keep a job? What if he can't make dinner-table conversation? What if he won't let me fuck him? What if he's never read Marcus Aurelius? What if he talks to his mom too often on the telephone? What if I can't love him the way he needs to be loved? What if he has HIV? What if he...

"This one looks sweet," Doug called over to me, pointing out a short-haired blond dog.

"I want a black dog," I said, pulling myself back together. "They look cleaner. It's the same principle as when you buy a couch. If you spill some coffee on the dog, I don't want it to show."

"Good point. How about him?" Doug said, pointing out an entirely reasonable Airedale-shepherd mix that was licking his own asshole.

Not thrilled, I demurred. "Well, I don't know. He looks too much like he belongs at a Grateful Dead concert. The shedding problem alone would be a trial."

A loud bark grabbed our attention. Doug and I both wheeled around to check out the source. On the other side of the cage area, we saw the sweetest black Lab mutt smiling at us. His tongue was acid-trip pink and flicked almost to the floor while he ran in ever tighter circles, as if trying to draw our gaze. To undercut his almost purebred Lab profile, he had a white bib and paws that made him look like he was on his way to an opera opening. Doug and I exchanged a glance. This could be it.

"I like him," Doug said, intuitively moving in the direction of this new dog.

"Me too," I added, opening up the cage to let the Lab mutt run around a bit. The instant the door swung open, the dog leaped out and began an ecstatic dervish dance.

"You don't think he's too wild?" Doug asked as the dog began leaping joyfully at least three feet up in the air.

"He's a puppy," I reasoned. "Puppies are directly tapped in to the life force of the planet."

This dog danced around us, sniffing everything in sight. He squatted down to pee, still too young to lift his leg, then smelled the piss and looked at Doug and me like he expected the Nobel prize. We rubbed his flanks as he sniffed our crotches.

Then I did something that has haunted me ever since. At that moment *another dog caught my eye.* Sometimes at night as I gently stroke my dog's sides while his breath flows in and out as sure as the tide, I wonder whether he has ever really forgiven me.

"Well, I like this dog," I said, "but he does seem a tiny bit wild." The Lab mutt was levitating around me again. "There's another one over there that looks quite similar. Let's take him out of his cage for a look."

With that I grabbed the first dog by the collar and pulled him back into his pen. He looked at me like I had personally just killed Old Yeller. Maybe this was not the first time someone had taken him out of his cage, gotten his hopes up, and then stuffed him back into the ticking clock of doom.

"Dougie," I coaxed, "let's see how we like *this* sweet dog. He's a little smaller. The other dog's paws are so big. He might grow up to be bigger than we are. Do you want to have a dog that could eat you?"

"Please!"

I opened up the other kennel and lured a sweet, melancholy black dog out into the running area. He looked a lot like the first dog, but he carried himself in a more dignified manner. This second dog made a halfhearted attempt to do the expected canine activities — jumping, running, playing — but seemed to lack interest in his dog vocation, like an underpaid actor doing his thousandth performance in a road-show production of *Cats*. (Mustn't mix metaphors.)

"This dog has a contemplative quality that I like," I said, peeking over my shoulder toward the first dog, who was standing on his hind legs, making furious barks to catch our attention again. "But I must say, that first dog has something going for him."

We put dog number two back in his cage. He seemed to have known all along that this was too good to be true and resigned himself to the fact that we were not to be his masters. As I shut the door with a frosty metallic clang, the dog made a world-weary sigh and put his face underneath his paws.

Doug and I walked back to the first dog in the evening clothes. When he saw us approaching him again, he did a triple turn in the air and let out a yip that could set off a car alarm in Brentwood. We put our hands on the cage. The metal was alive with the energy of this animal. It sent a shiver up my back. The mixture of terror and excitement moved through me as I imagine it would if I ever have a wedding day. Doug and I looked at each other.

"Well, this is it," I said, nodding at the creature who was soon to be our dog.

"Are you sure you're ready for this?" Doug asked.

"As ready as I'm ever going to be."

"It's a big commitment, Tim," Doug said to me, only half joking. "To have and to hold. He's our dog in sickness and in health."

"I know. Are we ready for this?"

Doug thought about it for less than a second. "I think we are. What shall we call him?"

"Let's call him Buddy," I said, sure that this was a good name for him. Plus there was this performance I intended to make about the idea of the "buddy system," the ways we bond with others to make life work. I thought Buddy the dog might be able to help me with it.

Solemnly we opened the cage again, and our new dog Buddy, ecstatic at his reprieve, jumped all over us, almost knocking me off my feet. He squealed with pleasure at what the day had brought and celebrated the meals and pats to come. His appreciation of the universe was something he would patiently try to teach me for the next several years.

Doug, Buddy, and I made our way to the pound office. We paid our ten dollars and picked up some flea pamphlets, and the lesbian animal-regulation officer wished the gay boys well with their new dog.

Buddy, suddenly a little disoriented by all this excitement, was starting to crash. It was time to get all of us home. He was afraid to get in the car, though. We tried to tempt him in with a treat without success. We cajoled him with luring voices. Finally I picked him up and put him in the backseat, where he immediately fell asleep in a clump. We headed for our Venice Beach sublet.

Buddy would come to be the most tangible manifestation of our relationship. With unerring accuracy he would broadcast the feelings that slipped and burrowed their way through our lives. He shrieked delightedly when we were all happy to see each other at the end of the day. Tucking his sweet Lab head under his paws, Buddy pouted when Doug and I were not being attentive to each other. His deep sighs of contentment would tell the house it was okay for everyone to go to sleep. Most important, when the rage level would get too intense during a fight between Doug and me, Buddy would always leap up and bite whomever he perceived to be the aggressor.

On one occasion I pinned Doug to the wall with a half nelson while shouting a series of accusations about a perceived insult to my sexual prowess he had lobbed my way in front of our friends. As I lifted up a stereo speaker to toss in rage, Buddy flung himself on me and firmly chomped his teeth into my butt.

"Fuck! He bit me!" I screamed, feeling the blood start to seep through my boxer shorts covered with happy-face designs.

"It serves you right for getting so mad about nothing," Doug said as he knelt down and comforted Buddy. "Are you okay, Bud-Dog?"

"Is *he* okay?" I shrieked in pain. "What about *me*? My butt is bleeding!"

"Look how upset Buddy is!" Doug shouted at me over his shoulder. "Hold him and tell him you're sorry." The dog's eyes were rolling heavenward in agony for having bit one of his masters. Buddy was always stricken with shame and grief after these outbursts.

At first I made for the door, not ready for my rage to be mollified, even by Buddy. Then my dog made a cry from deep inside his chest that melted my crankiness. Where do they learn how to do this stuff? I got down on the floor, and Doug and I petted him.

"We love you, Bud-Dog!" we crooned again and again in his floppy black ear, slowly soothing his whimpers. This gave Doug and me a cooling-off period to detach from the demons of the fight. Of course, these episodes usually ended up with Doug and me petting one another. It took Buddy's teeth, sometimes, to help us find that "I love you" with each other again.

It was important for me to get Buddy because I deeply desired redemption. With an urgency I could barely understand, I wanted to discover if I was actually capable of being in a relationship with a dog. This concern spilled over into my noncanine love life as well. My string of aborted relationships (two years seemed to be the limit) had made me see myself as someone incapable of establishing a long-term connection to man or beast. I carried a deep guilt about one particular dog in my life, and this shame had hounded me (sorry) across time and other relationships.

It all started when I was thirteen. I suddenly decided that I desperately wanted a dog. This was probably some kind of obvious effort toward being a normal boy at a time I was aware my gender behavior was being called into question.

My friend Jim, of a Lithuanian immigrant family, had a Scottish terrier named Mactavish that was about to have puppies with a female Scottie named Bonnie. I had been hearing his family's lengthy discussions about bitches, sires, and whelps for months whenever I was at Jim's house. This had all started to seem impossibly sexy to me. Listening to Jim's parents talking politely over their Lithuanian stuffed cabbages and stewed beets about animals fucking each other, I thought I should become part of this world. I convinced my parents that we should get one of the Scottie puppies when they arrived.

"Please! Please! Please! Please, Mom and Dad!" I bleated plaintively. "Let's get a puppy! I promise to take care of him and give him walks three times a day, and I'll do everything, and you won't even know he's around because I will see to the dog's every need! Please! Please! Please!"

Bettie and George agreed. This gave me a new pretext to spend more time with Jim and his Lithuanian lips and sensual thighs. Now Jim and I could also talk about bitches and sires and whelps.

This quest for the Scottie puppy was merely the latest in an endless series of gestures I made growing up toward claiming the attention of boys I loved by aping their habits. Over the years there had been a string of such impassioned sudden interests in animal husbandry, surfing, and stamp collecting. I could become a devotee of anything if it would help me get my man.

The fascination with dog rearing seemed to do the trick with Jim. This Baltic beauty began to put a great deal more energy toward me. As the time grew nearer for the puppies to be born, our excitement grew as big as the pregnant Bonnie's belly. Jim and I put our

hands next to each other on her swelling stomach to
see if we could feel the puppies kick. It was almost as
if Jim and I were having them ourselves. We got to try
on the roles of bitch and sire, kick the tires of these
personae, and take them out for a test drive.

The litter came, and I got my puppy, the previously
agreed-on runt since I couldn't pay much from my
car-washing job. She was a tiny creature, delicate as a
soufflé, albeit a constantly moving soufflé. Her jowly
whiskers belied her age of eight weeks. I desperately
needed something weaker and smaller than myself to
look after. My puppy became the designated storage
bin for the fragile parts of me. I named her Brindle
Mactavish (after her father). I thought about naming
her Jim, but my mother tried to dissuade me.

"Jim!" my mom exhaled in shock as she folded
some sheets hot from the dryer. "What kind of name
is that for a little girl dog? She should have a pretty,
feminine Scottish name like Lassie or Fiona. I can't
imagine why you would want to name your dog after
some *boy*!" This last word was spat out as if it were a
cuss word scrawled in a public toilet.

The doggy came home, and I deluged her with
attention. Brindle had her Stuart tartan sweater with
a matching bed, her embossed leather leash, and the
best food that could be bought at our local supermarket. Brindle was one lucky dog. For about six months.

Once I entered high school, though, Brindle began
to seem a liability. Dogs were kid stuff, after all. I went
through a particularly hideous period of selfish behavior in ninth grade. Goofus would have smirked with
pride. Desperate not to be seen as a weirdo or faggot,
I quickly ditched all the odd friends I had known since
I was five and cruised for new ones from the expand-

ed gene pool at Lowell High School. This period of trying to assimilate into the new big pond lasted only a few months, but it left a lot of wreckage.

Brindle was one of the casualties of this purge. With my new life in high school, I had so many activities in drama and the Great Books Club that I no longer had time to comb her stiff coat to its full luster. I was too busy becoming a homosexual to acknowledge Brindle's existence anymore. No longer did I allow her to cuddle into my bed every night. Instead she slept outside the back door in a cardboard box that my new record player had come in. Why did I get such a faggy breed like a Scottie? Brindle started to seem like a wimpy little dog that made me look like an old queen in a caftan. She now had come to represent all my failings as a boy. I couldn't even pick out the right kind of dog. So I cast her out.

Deprived of the love that every dog drinks up like I drink the validation of sex in my late thirties, Brindle quickly withered. She lost weight and got a terrible mange all over her hindquarters. Her fur fell out by the handful as her health deteriorated.

At the last moment I panicked as I realized I had doomed Brindle, had betrayed her love. I was haunted by the skinny hairless shadow of her former Highlands splendor, so I tried to revive her with renewed attention. I lavished Brindle with presents and love. But it was too late.

I lost interest again when I was cast as the lead in *The Crucible* my senior year. My dad, in view of my inaction, finally took matters in hand and had Brindle put to sleep. When I found out after our final dress rehearsal for the play, I clutched at my Salem witch trial costume. What had I done? This little creature had depended on me, had relied on me! My adolescent emotional circuits started to smoke and fry with the overload of the guilt and sorrow that was blossoming inside me.

In the years that would follow, I always felt like I had fucked up big time with Brindle. I imagined she had revealed my fatal flaw, an inability to love properly when the game went into overtime. Some of my relationships with other men had compounded this suspicion. By the time Doug and I had firmly established that we were marriage material for each other (bring on the *huppah!*), I decided I was ready to have a new dog. I thought this could be a way to honor Brindle's memory. In one big swoop I could cement my relationship with Doug *and* erase my bad karma around dogs.

As Doug and I escaped humid New York and set up household with Buddy that summer in Venice Beach, our behavior had the frantic air of new parents trying to give their child all the things they never had. Buddy was treated like a little prince with his imported-from-Germany leash and expensive chew toys. I felt I was really ready for the commitment required to have a dog. This time I was going to do it right.

Life with Buddy made the domestic reality between Doug and me reach a brand-new potential. Suddenly there was another creature to nuzzle and fuss over. Buddy became a safe space of total love and acceptance. Of course, Doug and I had no idea what we were doing with Buddy, what we hoped he would give us. I imagine it was a little bit like the hit-or-miss efforts of twelfth-century alchemists who were willing to try *anything* to see if they could turn a rock into gold. They would boil the clumps of lead in blood or swing them over their heads. Since we didn't have the heterosexual-privileged rituals of family and marriage, Doug and I needed to find a way of marking our life together, and Buddy was the key.

We all went back to New York in the fall of 1985 to live in the eight-foot-wide apartment on Mulberry Street in relative bliss (with occasional nuclear blowups). It was our version of married life for young men in the mid eighties.

Someone wise once said, "He who forgets the past is condemned to see it on summer reruns." I should have tattooed this onto my forehead; maybe it would have prevented more mishaps.

By 1986 Doug and I had journeyed through three years of life together. We had been together when I received the shock of the sudden death of my father. My dad finished work one Friday and then suffered a massive heart attack as soon as he got home to Whittier. My brother woke me in the middle of the night with the news. Doug and I ate pancakes together at dawn after he had done his best angry New Yorker voice over a pay phone at the restaurant to get me the last available seat on a flight to Los Angeles.

During our time together I had bolstered and encouraged Doug as he made the choice to move toward an artist's life and away from the familial expectation of academia. I happily encouraged him to leave the predictable Ph.D. route and follow his desire to be a writer instead.

Doug returned the favor when he nursed me through the crash after my first big public performance debacle at the Brooklyn Academy of Music, just down the block from where I had cut off my finger years before. For weeks I didn't leave the house in humiliation over a string of terrible reviews. "I'm washed up!" I would cry, groping for my sleep mask and earplugs so I could stay unconscious. Doug slowly coaxed me back into the performing saddle.

We supported each other as we struggled with our careers: Doug had blossomed into a respected gay writer about town, and I had rebounded with a powerful new performance that I created with Doug's help. As we lived these first three years of life together, our relationship came under the full scrutiny of the press, family, and ex-boyfriends, *and* we had a wild animal living with us that most people mistook for a dog.

Most important, we held each other close as the merciless target practice of the early years of the AIDS crisis kept hitting closer to home. Barry had become sick. Martin was dead. John had not been doing very well, and it was now clear that he had full-blown AIDS. I was convinced, on account of the vast amount of unprotected sex John and I had shared, that it was only a matter of time before I got sick too. Doug was convinced, on account of the vast amount of unprotected sex he and I had had, that any minute he was going to drop dead. During a checkup with our mutual doctor, the physician had pulled Doug aside in the examining room and dramatically warned him that, judging by my T-cell count, I was probably in the early stages of AIDS. Doug would carry this encounter with the doctor inside himself without telling me for the next ten years.

How did we manage to live with such a relentless spin cycle of fear and despair? Our relationship was stalked by the feeling that we were both almost certainly infected. We had to always be looking over our shoulder to see if we had been followed home by the plague. Doug and I lived through the '80s *certain* that every bruise was a Kaposi's sarcoma lesion; every lingering flu, our death sentence.

One thing was for sure: The fear of imminent death had kept our libidos on a very short leash. Doug and I were completely monogamous for the first three years of our relationship. (Well, *I* was anyway. Years later Doug would let me in on his trysts with the legions of Puerto Ricans at the video arcades in Times Square.)

There came a point when my eyes started to wander, though. Doug and I had gone to our friends Beth and Greg's wedding shortly after Michel Foucault's death. As we bused back through Connecticut, I started to feel too married myself. All the stag-party jokes had taken their toll.

I'm not sure what chain reaction started to knock the monogamy dominoes down. Maybe the taming effect of our domestic life together had made some of the erotic fizz start to shift away from our relationship. Like an overflowing glass of Alka-Seltzer, it ran down the sides, across the table, and onto a new man's lap. It wasn't that I didn't still love Doug and want to have sex and a life together. I was just ready for some new adventures.

Quite simply, I knew I needed some nooky on the side. It had gotten to the point where I felt like the most exciting part of my day was eating a delicious Peppermint Pattie on my way home at night. I had begun to bristle under the premature lockdown on my young sex life that panic in the AIDS era had deemed necessary. I had barely gotten off the starting block when the rules of the race all changed. Now, armed with the new idea of "safe sex," I was ready to run.

Tim was about to stray.

My second-grade teacher, Mrs. Bishop, once wrote about me on my report card, "Tim is very bright and personable and succeeds at whatever he puts his mind to. I just wish he had a greater attention span."

I remembered these words as I set my eyes on a beautiful South American man who was dancing near me at Open Movement. It had been some time since I had made an appearance at this event. In village societies a person's social standing would be informed by how often they showed up in church. In East Village tribal dancer-performer culture, a similar monitoring went on, scoring how often one came to Open Movement. I was nervous that my long absence would be noted.

I quickly warmed up and began to launch my energy into the room. I had just flipped through several cartwheels and then made a curious little stamping rabbit movement that had been moving through my body of late when I laid eyes on this wildly dancing guy. His loose pants covered the long lean muscles of a body built for movement. His dark kinky hair moved faster than I could blink. I threw myself into a walking handstand and inserted myself into his peripheral vision. As we began to dance about together, I sensed his energy tightly coiled to his center. We flung our bodies through space, and I felt the heat of his skin begin to melt the accumulated savings account of fidelity with Doug that I hoped was going to keep me from getting AIDS.

"What's your name?" I whispered in his ear as I perched my hip on his shoulder in a bold contact improvisation move that I had learned in Seattle.

"I am called David," he replied, pronouncing his name "Da-veed," which gave me goose bumps.

"I'm Tim. I have a boyfriend. Maybe we should go to your house."

"Oh, I don't know," David frowned. "Why don't we just go have some tea."

"Okay. Can we dance a little more first?"

By way of reply David began to make a big backward running circle around me as I got pulled into his flow.

David was from Venezuela. He had come to New York to dance. Movement exploded from him with the unpredictability of weather. David's legs shot out from under him as he twirled balls over ego (not to be confused with "head over heels") on his strong hands across the floor. Like a gazelle on caffeine, his compact form shimmered through a neat series of contrasting rhythms with each change of direction.

I was a goner. I had to have him.

At moments like this my Scottie Brindle would often come visit me in my thoughts. Like Banquo's ghost, she would remind me of my dangerous ways and cheating heart. Her doomed visage would loom in my dreams to tell me, "Be careful!"

Of course, David and I began a very powerful and completely unsatisfying affair. I felt the structure of my life dissolve. I was racked with guilt as I got on the subway the next day to go to David's house in Brooklyn. After we had clunky, panic-filled ("Are you *sure* this is safe?") sex, I slunk back to Little Italy. Doug was making dinner.

"Doug," I said, sounding like Morticia Addams, "I need to tell you something. I met this guy at Open Movement. We've kind of been having a thing."

"A thing?" He pronounced the word carefully, as if this mysterious *thing* were radioactive, as he put the spatula next to the frying pan.

"Yes," I replied, my hands shaking. "A thing."

"What kind of thing?" Doug asked, his arms a force field over his heart.

"Well," I stammered, "a sex thing. It's nothing serious, but we're sort of having an affair. He's a nice guy. I know you'd like him."

"Great," Doug fumed. "We're just starting to establish ourselves in our relationship, and you have to go drag your dick around Open Movement. I can't believe it." He started to head for the door.

"No, wait," I said as I blocked his way. "I'll stop seeing him. There's no reason to get so upset. We're having safe sex."

"Oh, that makes me feel a lot better!" Doug shouted. "Well, if you want safe sex, I'll give you really safe sex. I'm moving out."

We fell into a sleep, lying as far apart as two people possibly can. Dinner was now burned, the charred marinara sending its mushroom cloud of angry smoke up the air shaft.

When I woke the next morning, Doug was already out of the house. I dropped myself from the loft bed to the cold cement floor of the apartment. I thought I was having a midlife crisis at the age of twenty-seven. I felt so guilty.

I walked around the East Village feeling like Michael Caine after his infidelity in *Hannah and Her Sisters*, a movie I had ironically seen with Doug the previous week. I kept looking for a *New York Post* truck to throw myself under.

I called Dona in her darkroom from a pay phone at the Staten Island Ferry. I was so upset, I had gone to Battery Park and taken the boat out onto New York harbor for some perspective, my twenty-five-cent version of therapy at that time.

"Dona," I whined, "what should I do? I've gotten myself into a big slippery pickle."

"I heard," Dona replied, her voice a little strange since she had the phone crooked between her cheek and shoulder as she processed her film. "News travels fast from the Open Movement gossip circle. I had two calls on my machine this morning. They're already circling like vultures."

"What should I do?" I asked again. I looked to Dona as my spiritual adviser in all matters of love and art. Her second marriage had just ended, and she had become a lesbian. I figured she had looked at life from both sides now.

"Well," Dona said, "it's a tough one. David's cute, but so is Doug. Tim, face it, Doug's the best thing going in this shitty city. He's such a mensch!"

Oh, that word again.

In agony I had lunch with David that afternoon in SoHo. Our urgent whispers volleyed across the table, which concealed our intertwined hands under the table.

"David," I said, afraid someone I knew might see me, "we have to stop this. It just seems hopeless. I still love Doug. This is driving me crazy."

"I knew this would happen," David said as he made a mess of the butter next to the bread. "Maybe we shouldn't be seeing each other for a while."

I paid the check and went home.

As I opened the door, I instantly knew something bad had happened. There were papers all over the floor. Buddy was huddled in a corner, afraid that it was all his fault.

Doug had moved all of his stuff out of our apartment. The house looked like it had been nuked. Doug had even taken the coffee filters. There was a note: "Tim," it said in tightly printed script, "I'll be staying with a friend on the Upper West Side until you figure out what you want to do. Doug."

Oh, shit, I said to myself as I paced the floor with Buddy following my every move. *This is getting out of hand. I'm all alone here. I'd better do something quick. Should I call Doug and beg him to come back? No, I'm too proud.*

Buddy came up and laid his Lab snout on my face and breathed his doggy insights into my ear. He reminded me that Doug and I had only barely begun our work together. Buddy told me that there were lots of journeys and adventures the three of us were going to have together in the next years. He shared his dog wisdom with me, channeling Brindle at this point, no doubt. He said that there are moments in life to blow up your house and there are moments to call your boyfriend who has moved out and beg him to come back. Then Buddy asked me if he could have another one of those delicious dog bones.

During the three hours it took for me to psychically crawl on my hands and knees to the phone to call 109th Street and beg Doug to come back, I had an opportunity for quiet reflection. I realized how desperately I needed Doug in my life. We had started to make a soup together that could probably feed us for a long time ahead.

Doug moved his things back in later that night.

In the years to come, Doug and I would often relive this time and chew it over like the way Civil War buffs deliberate about the second day of fighting at the battle of Gettysburg.

In our case the rehash over dinner would go something like this:

"Tim," Doug would say, wagging a finger in my face. "If I hadn't taken the strategic initiative and moved out at that moment, you might never have realized what a mess you were making of your life."

I won't share with you the gory details of the inevitable threesome Doug and I soon had with David as a way of socializing the affair into our relationship. I don't want to bring up the eventual clandestine romance that Doug had with David for the next several months without my knowledge. It would be unreasonable to remind Doug of his late nights at David's house when I thought he was on deadline at the *New York Native*. I won't share any of that with you. It would be tawdry and unfair to do such a thing at this point in time so many years later. After all, as Doug would remind me at the end of every debate about *l'affair David*, I had started it.

Doug moved back in. We shook up our household and realized we were going to have to allow the possibility for us to explore other men or we would huff and puff and blow each other down. Buddy would decide for us that we couldn't live in a tiny apartment in Little Italy anymore and that it was time to create a new life in Los Angeles. Our dog knew it was time to get out of New York long before Doug or I did. Buddy's wisdom for what we really needed helped us escape from that dark basement apartment and into a home in the hills above Hollywood where we could watch the sun go down over the Pacific Ocean, the ocean where the next time of life would occur.

I am grateful for the teachings the dogs in my life have given me. Today I still see those lessons in

Buddy's sighs as he lives and breathes, now a senior-citizen dog complaining about his arthritis. From his current wise-dog vantage point, Buddy always says to me, "I taught you everything you know!"

In 1986, as I packed my things to leave New York and move to Los Angeles, I saw another example of this dog wisdom in something I found in the back of a drawer at Mulberry Street. My fingers tried to identify this object as I fished it out from the catacombs of my desk. It was a small brown leather band with a metal tag on it. I turned the leather circle over and over again in my hands, sobered by this reminder of all the hurt we give and receive as we shove our way through life. I packed it in a box of special things destined for my bookshelf altar in my new home.

It was a dog collar that has a tag embossed with just one word:

BRINDLE.

A STRETCH MARK

DOUG AND I WERE LATE for a big ACT UP demo. We were supposed to be at County Hospital at 2 P.M., and our 1974 AMC Gremlin refused to turn over. The car's jaunty, though flaking, green racing stripe didn't seem to help the lifeless engine one bit. Each hopeful twist of the key coaxed only a sharp click followed by the anemic growl of a lazy, overweight cat.

"We're gonna be late, and I'm already on deadline!" Doug offered helpfully between turns of the key.

"Lemme try one more time, please!" I snipped back.

"Snippiness" had become one of the most provocative modes of speech between Doug and me. Getting snippy was often reason enough for a big row. In fact, the Gremlin had been the scene of some of our most thrilling fights. The added frisson of driving a large American car that could also serve as a deadly weapon was just the prop a couple of drama queens needed to transform a minor tiff into World War III.

During fights the car also offered itself for the game of Who Will Drive Away First? This challenge would often have Doug and me each diving for the keys so that one or the other of us could be the first to make the operatic exit followed by the roar of a Detroit Gremlin. Once our landlord came by for the typically late rent check only to catch a glimpse of me standing on the hood of the car with a cinder block raised over my head.

"If you drive away," I shouted, "I'll break the wind-shield!"

It would be a number of years before we entered couples counseling.

The Gremlin wasn't all Sturm und Drang. The silly yet soulful car had lubricated the process of making a life together in California, escaping from the grinding wheels of poverty, art, and inadequate living space in New York City. This AMC behemoth, a bargain at $200, symbolized the possibility for a second chance here in Los Angeles. We changed the Gremlin's oil, and it helped us change ours.

Doug and I lived beyond our means in Venice Beach, a mixture of the East Village and a seaside resort. The house was dwarfed by towering bamboo. It was wrapped thick with passion vines. Such greenery gave the place a *Swiss Family Robinson* quality that was the perfect antidote to gray, stony New York.

The Big Move launched Doug and me into a more gracious way of life for our relationship and helped ease our relative poverty. Though we were usually broke, often living off a series of credit cards our gay banker scammed for us, life was kinder here in California. Each dollar seemed to go further now that the dough was spent somewhere not pestered by snow and ice. My days included impulsive jumps in the Pacific Ocean and bike rides to Santa Monica. We found ourselves far from the Lower East Side.

Our improved quality of life more than made up for driving a Gremlin, perhaps the ugliest car Detroit ever created. That car, rusting out on Venice Boulevard, represented something else too: that there was some-thing wrong with this new picture. The bamboo and passion vines didn't make the "something wrong" go away, and maybe that's why we both loved and hated the Gremlin. The car was like a crazy uncle kept hidden from view in the attic that scarred the otherwise rosy picture of our new life in Los Angeles. But who had time to worry about that eccentric uncle when all that made sense was ACT UP? We focused our attention on trying to stop AIDS. We also saved quite a bit of energy for acting out.

"I'm gonna call a cab!"

"Give me one more chance," I replied, flush with Waspish self-reliance. Doug made an ancient Hebraic gesture over the steering column, and the engine — all eight cylinders — roared into life.

"Yes! ACT UP, here we come!" we cheered.

It was January 1989, and ACT UP was rattling the nation in a massive upheaval of gay energy not seen since the assassination of Harvey Milk. The kettles were all boiling as a generation of good queer boys and girls got gnarly.

ACT UP mobilization was exactly what I had been waiting for. At last all my lefty programming and queer erotics had a social movement to saddle up with. For years my body had felt so isolated in a paralyzing fear of AIDS. With the bathroom door locked, I would check the lymph nodes in my groin and armpits each morning to see how my immune system was doing. Suddenly those scary worries inside were not so alone. These feelings were able to come out, linked with other people who had also been crushed under the same fears. Elbow to elbow we shouted loud at politicians and cops in New York, Chicago, or Los Angeles. After many years of being so damn afraid, I felt great getting to be pissed off instead.

Doug and I drove down the Santa Monica Freeway, past rain-scoured downtown, and then made the short jog on the Golden State Freeway toward L.A. County/USC Medical Center, better known as "County." When we parked we pointed the car downhill in the hope that we could always coast to a gas station if the Gremlin wouldn't start again.

Doug and I walked briskly with our furled banners toward the demo. Silent and somber, the tall hospital glowered above us, its implacable surfaces unforgiving and judgmental. The towering vaulted cement walls always reminded me of a place in a horrible dream I had many times as a kid.

The dream first came to me after an incident during a family vacation when I was three years old. The snapshots show the Millers taking a day trip from Las Vegas to the Hoover Dam — the largest poured-concrete structure in the world, as the tourist brochures boast. My entire family stood along the perilous lip of this monster dam that held up a lake the size of Connecticut. I was too small to see over the protective barrier down the vast slide of cement to the Colorado River far below, so my mom reached down and lifted me up to have a look. Her hands holding me tight, Mom carefully raised my upper body out over the abyss. My toddler-self looked over the edge of the dam a thousand feet straight down in ultimate danger. Hearing my brothers' and sister's laughter, I imagined my little body thrown by my parents into the pit and tumbling down the slippery chute of cement into the Colorado River.

"Put me down! Put me down!" I shrieked crazily to my mom, attracting the attention of a nearby Nevada cop.

"You be quiet right now, young man," she whispered, checking to see if people were staring as she held my arm in her pincerlike grip.

I cried so loud that heads of nearby tourists turned to look at the family with the uncontrollable child. My mom and dad hustled me back to the car, and we returned to Whittier.

Tossing and turning that night in my bunk bed with the Beany and Cecil sheets, I had a terrible nightmare. I dreamed I was walking in a vast desert, like the desolate land surrounding the Hoover Dam. As I walked through this dreamscape, I knew that if I made even the tiniest misstep, my world would blow up. I knew it would all be my fault. The dream told me I was the worst boy on the planet. The dream gave me a sick, empty place in my stomach.

Again and again sleep would take me to this nightmare, its topography shipped directly from *The Outer Limits*. In the dream the narrative was always the same. There was a huge sloping shape, like the Hoover Dam, like the tall concrete sides of County Hospital. This enormous surface was very fragile, and if I disturbed it in the slightest, the world was going to end. Of course, in the dream it was urgent for me to get somewhere. Each footfall I took near this vast concave shape ran the risk of complete destruction.

I traveled through this dream thousands of times in my childhood. I would wake up screaming at the moment apocalypse loomed as my foot hit the wrong place. The dream pinned me against the wall and told me I was constantly being tested, that the possibility was always there for ultimate ruin if I took a false step.

The nightmare faded away when I was about ten and didn't visit me again until 1988. I had the dream one more time shortly after my ex-boyfriend John had died in New York. The long march through the plague in the '80s felt exactly like the plodding trek in my nightmare. Struggling for seven years with AIDS, John's battered body had had enough that summer. This loss piled up a force field of numbness all around me. Yelling at do-nothing politicians was the *only* thing that helped thaw that numbness out. That's why I was there that day at County Hospital with ACT UP.

John's death had hastened the feelings of fear I had for my own future but not enough to make me go and finally get an HIV antibody test. This was becoming a tender subject between Doug and me.

"Tim," Doug said tentatively, his feet slapping the wet pavement as we approached the demonstration, "I've been thinking about something."

"What?" I asked, trying to keep my defenses from showing.

"I think we should get tested sometime. We're here fighting for an AIDS ward, and you and I don't even know what's happening inside our own bodies."

To test or not to test. That was the question, and it was *not* a new subject. What sick Stephen King type came up with this testing concept? It would have fit right into the dark void of my recurrent dream. For gay boys, who had always felt ourselves "tested" by parents, priests, and our gender, to have to submit our blood to the big pass-or-fail seemed fit only for a soap opera, the Old Testament, or a little kid's nightmare.

So far Doug and I had carefully avoided entering the HIV-test sweepstakes. Periodically one or the other of us would propose we actually go get our blood taken. We would debate the pros and cons heatedly for a few days until the subject was beaten into submission, fading away into a comforting blur of inaction.

"I don't know if I could handle the news," I said, giving my standard reply. "I'm probably positive. It would stand to reason, considering the sex John and I had. I just don't know if I want to have that confirmed right now."

"If we knew," Doug the AIDS journalist spinned, "there are things we could be doing."

"There's so much I want from this time in my life," I said with the pained exhaling of a tire deflating. "If I knew I were positive, it'd make me crazy. I'm such a hypochondriac." At this point I changed the subject. "Look, there's Connie."

The arrival of Connie Norman, a wisecracking, stereotype-defying, Goddess-channeling transsexual with AIDS, put the testing discussion on ice for the time being.

"Hey, darlin'!" Connie drawled as she smacked a kiss onto my cheek that left a lipstick smudge the size of child's fist. "Well, look who else the cat dragged in."

Weaving into view were our friends Chuck and Luis, staggering under the weight of a huge ice chest. These boyfriends fought more than Doug and I did, so I always enjoyed their company since it gave me the illusion that Doug and I got along more harmoniously. Chuck, a 29-year-old Jewish muscle boy, and Luis, a Latino Radical Faerie, lived near us in Venice. The two of them worked for Tree People, an urban environmental group, and that day they both looked quite sexy in their ecological-anarchist drag. Admiring their nature-boy-meets-horny-earth-mother splendor, I tried to decide which one of them I would flirt with if I ran into them on the beach. Chuck? No, Luis. (Eventually it was both.)

"We have to feed the troops!" Chuck called over his shoulder. "Hurry up, things are about to start."

"Chuck!" Luis protested in his delightful Peruvian accent. "Hold up your side of the ice chest! It's dislocating my shoulder."

Even though we had just narrowly avoided a major confrontation ourselves, Doug and I exchanged a smug glance that said, "Aren't you glad we don't fight as much as they do?"

Connie looked back at us, perturbed. "Tim and Doug, move it! We're all waiting to kick some county supervisor butt!"

In Los Angeles ACT UP was focused right now on the dismal state of health care in the county for people with AIDS. Specifically, we were trying to pressure the people in charge, the county board of supervisors, to cough up the money and open an AIDS ward at County Hospital. For months we had been camping out on the supervisors' front lawns, disrupting meetings, and doing media zaps to embarrass the foot-dragging homophobic elected creeps into action.

Now, in our boldest maneuver yet, we had created a conceptual AIDS ward on the pavement in front of County Hospital with the hope that the spectacle of people with AIDS being forced out into the cold to receive treatment might shame the powers that be into doing something. Ancient hospital beds, IV poles, and doctor's coats had been commandeered from a theater prop shop to get our point across. We had been living in this shanty town for the better part of a week. The media was eating up the rage-filled theatrics like ice cream in August:

PEOPLE WITH AIDS SLEEP ON PAVEMENT TO PROTEST INADEQUATE HEALTH CARE!

These strategies seemed to be forcing the negligent county supervisors to get out of their country clubs, pull the nine iron out from where the sun don't shine, and allocate funding for the AIDS ward at the largest public hospital in the world.

"By our actions we will expose the hypocrisy of the supervisors," expounded Mark Kostopoulos, an ACT UP spokesperson who carried the whiff of a Molotov cocktail about him. Barking out his message, he cornered the cowering reporter from the ABC affiliate. "People with AIDS need this ward now!"

A gothic iron fence that surrounded the hospital would have complemented a haunted house just fine. Hung over its pointy, rusty bars, banners and signs, symbols of protest and manifestation, signaled ACT UP's fury:

SILENCE = DEATH

HEALTH CARE IS A RIGHT!

In one area a dozen or so tents sat pitched for the seven-day vigil, an ironically cheerful display of fluorescent colors amid our serious goal. The AIDS ward vigil had managed to create an alternative model of public space, half Radical Faerie gathering and half civil disobedience action. For a few days artists, activists, and health care workers lived communally, in gorgeous smelly proximity, as we demanded better health care for people with AIDS. All of this occurred under the watchful eyes of the Los Angeles County sheriffs.

"Hey, Dougie," I said, rubbing his always tense shoulders while I eyed the cops, "if my performance really gets me inspired and the police get cranky, I think I may need to get arrested tonight."

Doug was in an expansive mood. "Do you have your driver's license and the phone number for legal support?"

"Yeah. I have both in the zip pocket of my leather jacket."

"It's late already," Doug reminded me. "They might keep you in jail overnight."

"That's okay. There's so many cute boys, it might be fun in the holding cells," I said, checking out a number of gym boys who had taken these protests to heart. They were present and accounted for with their big biceps and sleeveless shirts in spite of the cold.

"They're our secret weapon!" Doug whispered to me. "It's like we've been developing them in research gyms all over the country for just this moment. The cops haven't got a chance against their low body fat."

This group of gym guys had cut their StairMaster program short at the Sports Connection and arrived for the ACT UP demo. I had always wondered if all this pumped-up muscle would ever be put to any use. Big pectorals suddenly seemed good for all kinds of new activities: overturning police barricades, for example, or flinging potted trees through the doors of the Ronald Reagan State Office Building.

Shifting my focus away from the buff fellows, I walked over to a huge piece of white fabric covering a wide swath of pavement. Scribbled all over its surface were the names of thousands of people who had died of AIDS. Was this memorial the terrain I walked across in my dream? I had written John's and Martin's names there in Magic Marker the first night of the vigil. As I carefully printed each letter, *J-O-H-N*, a trembling of loss shook through me. This knocked the pictures off the walls inside my head. Doug had watched this earthquake quietly and brought me a mug of tea.

The media, of course, couldn't care less about real sorrow. They saw, quite simply, a hot story for *News at Eleven*. Aware of the visual possibilities, TV crews and various print reporters surrounded the memorial on this final day of the AIDS vigil. They pointed the gaze of their cameras and wrote glib ironies down in long skinny books. Hundreds and hundreds of votive candles made their gentle glow in the cold-for-L.A. winter wind. As I surveyed the colorful swarm of activity, it struck me that we had everything we needed: protest signs, memorials, media, and votive candles. These are the four basic food groups for a successful demonstration.

Since I'd been living here on the pavement for much of the week, I had been asked to make a special performance for the final rally. At that time artists filled some of the ranks of ACT UP. We played a crucial role that mixed the responsibilities of chaplain and cheerleader.

"We need you to perform something inspiring," one of the rally coordinators, a fellow I had had a brief fling with, told me while we waited in line the previous morning for the one public toilet. "You know, the usual. Something that will bring forward the metaphors of what we have done this week as a means to coalesce our rage. Plus, it should be funny and sexy."

"Uh-huh," I replied sleepily. This kind of ordered-by-the-yard request felt familiar to me. "How long should it be?"

"Make it about ten minutes," he replied. "We've scheduled two ACT UP speeches, two poets, two politicians, and two performers."

"Okay," I said, looking toward the heavens as I hauled out my dick to pee. "I'll do my best."

Doug and I had gone home for a night to take care of Buddy and to give me a chance to prepare the performance. I had scribbled down some memories and impressions that had been provoked by the vigil. I tried to find a shape for the most idiosyncratic experiences that had come my way during the week.

Overnight ACT UP had created a performance
space for the rally, a circular area surrounded by a
crescent moon of hospital beds and tents. The space
was important to me. As Doug and I stepped over
reclining figures, I examined it the same way I imagine a stonemason looks at a hunk of rock. I wanted to
see where the cracks were, which way the performance
would fit, how I could fill the space and make it
breathe.

I carried with me two simple props: a sharp knife
and a plain brown bag full of Venice Beach sand. I had
walked by the ocean that morning to open up myself in
preparation for the performance. A cyclone of associa-
tions and images of loss weighed on me, but I hadn't a
clue how I should bring them into the piece.

Doug and I found our way back to our campsite.
Our sleeping bags were soaked through from the rain
in the early hours of the morning. We tried to make
ourselves comfortable as we listened to the demo. We
cheered boisterously the speeches by two ACT UP
members, two poets, but only one politician. (A second official had been scared off by the likelihood of
heckling.)

Performing in addition to me was my new pal
Michael Kearns, who did a piece in which he railed as
fierce as King Lear on the heath. Clapping for
Michael, I fidgeted nervously in agonizing excitement
about what I was preparing to do. I breathed deeply
and tried to allow myself the full spectrum of inner
psychic divadom. As I shifted my wet behind on the
sopping sleeping bag, I felt somewhere between
Barbra Streisand at the Central Park concert and an
Aztec youth about to get his heart cut out so that the
harvest would be fruitful.

Like most performers, I was intensely superstitious. During my walk along the ocean that morning, a seal had poked his head out of the surf and looked at me from the cold gray waves. I was certain this had been one of the same seals I had sung with years before at Land's End. A visitation like this augured well for the performance. Either that or I was totally fucked. I chose the first interpretation.

Doug nudged me, "It's your turn! They want you to get up there."

"Okay," I whispered back. "Wish me luck!" Doug gave me a kiss and sent me on my way.

I came out of the mass of bed frames and tents. Tripping on a recently burned effigy of President Bush, I walked to the center of the performance area. I looked out over the crowd of friends and ACT UP partners and saw Doug's face, as bright as a street-light, sending me vital support.

For a second, as it often happened, an electric surge of panic and worthlessness burrowed up my spine. Who the fuck did I think I was? That gave me the opening inside myself to try to make something happen. Filling my body with breath, I held my bag of sand up to the ominous cloud-filled sky and began:

"For ACT UP/L.A.'s weeklong vigil in front of County General Hospital, we're here to demand proper care, programs, and an AIDS ward at the biggest hospital in the world!"

I sang the last word like I was a comically pious priest in a mass. The arching sound moved from somewhere behind my frightened heart. I held the final note as long as I could, till my oxygen was so depleted that I thought I might pass out. This show-offy turn got a sprinkling of whoops and applause. A little voice inside told me this piece could take off in a good way if my big fat ego didn't get in its way. With a big gesture I peeked behind me as the applause quieted. I gave County Hospital a long quizzical Buster Keaton look before continuing.

"There is a big building behind me. On this building these words are written: 'Erected by the citizens of the County of Los Angeles to provide hospital care for the acutely ill and suffering to whom the doctors of the attending staff give their services without charge in order that no citizen of the county shall be deprived of health or life for lack of such care and services.'

"I looked up at these words this morning after waking up to the cold cement after pissing in the toilet next to the emergency room with the perpetually bloodstained walls.

"Why do those words sound so old and crinkly, like they just slithered off some asshole's Victrola? Have the county board of supervisors or the mayor or the governor or our brand-new fucking president, George Bush, ever read those words chiseled into this rock during the administration of Herbert Hoover, that tacky queen!

"Oops, sorry, Herb. I got you mixed up with your girlfriend, J. Edgar.

"Lots of us have been gathered here this week to try to make those words become true."

I stabbed my Swiss Army knife into the bag full of sand as I held it above my head, and a steady stream of gray specks passed in front of my face. The words moved through me, a free-fall improvisation of what I had prepared.

The sand flowed past my eyes, every grain seeming to stand for a person who had died of AIDS. How could I still be alive when John was dead? Had he ever really forgiven me for leaving him? I let the sad silence linger as the sand slipped between my fingers. I saw Doug sitting surrounded by our queer artist friends. My fight with Doug that morning felt as remote as the Norman Conquest. My voice hummed inside my chest. I let the sand carry me back to the shiny swimming seal I had seen on the beach that morning. I looked up at the sky and shouted.

"I sat on Venice Beach on Inauguration Day, the day before this vigil began. As I sat there on the beach near the homo zone, a.k.a. Speedo-Lido, three things happened:

"First, I saw the jet planes taking off from the near-by airport and thought of my recent and brutal fear of flying. I thought about my friend Elizabeth Marek, who died in the bombing of Flight 103 over Scotland. She was a spectacular lesbian and performer and activist who got blown up at 33,000 feet. I have no conclusions here.

"I watched the planes taking off from LAX and heading out over the Pacific Ocean, and then on the beach arrived a Midwestern tourist family, shooting lots of photos to be sent back to Hays, Kansas, with the exclamation, 'Here we are on the beach in January!' This group included a mother type, who snarled to the others very loud, 'I don't care what any of you want. I have no interest in going to Mexico!'

"Finally, I heard an announcement over the loud-speaker on the lifeguard's truck that said, 'Attention! All lifeguards! Begin checking all persons lying in the sun to see if any of them are a dead body!'

"This is the world I am living in, this day in front of County General Hospital."

I was lost for a moment as the frothy rapids of the images pummeled me. Everything got all mixed together in my head: the morning at the beach, the fight with Doug, John's death, the memory of that dream, and Herbert Fucking Hoover. I looked at the faces in the crowd, serious and beautiful in the gray light.

I saw Connie's face with her finely coiffed nimbus of teased orange hair. She made eye contact with me and nodded. "C'mon, baby. Say it!" she quietly whispered to me.

I remembered where we were, the indifferent hospital looming behind me. I suddenly remembered what we had been trying to do.

"Something has been happening here. Some people have passed seven days and seven nights in front of this building together. Soup has been made. Stories have been told. Performances have been done. TV cameras have been pointed. Wet, sloppy, noisy sex has been had by those two perseverant ACT UP dudes in that pup tent over there that is still wobbling and shaking.

"I say unto you now that if Boy Scouts had been like this, I might have made it past Tenderfoot.

"Powerful gestures have been made as we in ACT UP/L.A. have actually seen what each other looks like before coffee in the morning, and yet still we are here!"

The mention of the two ACT UP boys who had fucked each other noisily two nights before followed by the joke about coffee had won over some of the "I hate performance art" types. The humor set the tight WASP part of me loose too. A crazy place in my mind laughs to keep the world and my heart from breaking in two. I felt that laugh now. That laugh helped join separate parts of me: the trained circus animal that is ready to sing and dance at the drop of a hat and the frightened, hurt child that is scared to death I'm going to get sick any day. All I could think about was John, dead four months now, as I tried to keep my words moving.

"Now, what has actually happened here? Has all our ACTing UP made County General Hospital rise from its foundations and fly away? Do we see it levitate, trailing its rotten plumbing, sadnesses, and a thousand IV tubes doing a slow antiviral drip as it disappears over the barrio?"

I remembered going to Bellevue Hospital on a hot July afternoon to see John a month before he died. Dona's former girlfriend, Lori, met me on the street to accompany me upstairs and soften the blow. I had not been in New York for a year, and she knew I was afraid to see how sick John had gotten.

"Maybe — it will begin to seem to more of us that it is at least as important to get people who need it proper health care as it is to shop for a new leather jacket or to make yet another performance piece that obliquely deconstructs print advertising. Believe me, I've made my share of those."

After Lori met me on the street, I put an ugly, shapeless sweatshirt over my torso to cover my flesh and Venice Beach tan. Knowing John's skin was covered in painful sores, I was ashamed for the life in my own body. I felt embarrassingly healthy. I wanted to cover it up.

"Maybe — when we force the county to get its shit together, people who are dealing with AIDS stuff right now and don't have health insurance will have a place to go where they won't have to sit in a public hallway on a hard bench getting their chemo and throwing up from the side effects in view of all."

Lori pushed open the door of the hospital room. There was the wreckage of John. He was hooked up to

an IV feed and a respirator. How could he be so thin,
his hair so brittle? How can I reach him through the
machines and tubes? I kissed him on the forehead, a
nervous compromise to avoid his frighteningly blis-
tered lips.

"Maybe — we fags and dykes can become a model
for how Americans can stop forgetting and holding in
and avoiding and feeding off of a lot of suffering in
this world and off of the world herself as she strains to
deal with my 1974 Gremlin's carbon dioxide. It's time
for some lines to be drawn, some absolutes to be
acknowledged, some choices to be made. Because.
Because. Because."

Remembering John dying in that bed, I sang out
those "becauses" just like in *The Wizard of Oz*. A
motor spun inside me fast. I didn't have to know what
came next. I knew my voice, my faggot's voice, my
faggot's body could turn up the volume and shake the
hospital behind me. For a second I thought to myself
that I could die now except I had never wanted so
much to stay alive. I channeled the Cowardly Lion for
the final shouted-out "because."

"Because — silence actually does equal death.

"Because — action actually does equal life.

"These are not metaphors or gymwear.

"Because — there may not be all that much time left.

"Because — maybe it's time for a lot of art to be
quite useful."

I sat next to John's hospital bed and held his hand.
Lori made an excuse to leave the room so we could be
alone. John and I were silent for a long time. "Have
you been performing lately?" he asked me. I told him
about the pieces I was doing for ACT UP. "That's
good," he said. "Do that some more, okay?"

"Because — maybe it's not enough for us to be sad and pissed off for our boyfriends or our friends who are boys who have been lost to us. There are lots of different kinds of people there in that building behind me."

I stroked John's hand slowly. I just wanted us both to be on East Sixth Street again, alive in our bodies, eating bialys, in love with each other. How did we get here? I looked out the window of his hospital room, which a friend of John's had decorated with intricate cutout silhouettes of satyrs, dragons, and birds. I wanted to be anywhere with John except this hospital room with the insultingly beautiful view of Manhattan beyond the paper figures. Lori came back in. John was tired. It was time to go. I kissed him. "Bye," John said.

"Because — as I walked on Venice Beach this morning, I saw a seal. That seal is watching us to see if we can come together and make this world less fucked-up. We need all of us homos, people of color, the undocumented, feminist ecologists, crazed global performance artists...even all you cool straight white guys! Both of you!"

As I left John's room, I looked at him one more time. I saw him staring out the window past the paper satyrs at the New York summer day. I saw how powerfully John did not want to die. I saw that for my whole life, however long it would be, part of me would always be in this hospital room saying good-bye to John.

"Because — each of us writing, agitating, painting, kissing, performing, designing, activating, fellating, detailing, coiffing, public relating, primping, obsessing, committing, masturbating...might make a society not quite so stuck on itself and able to speak so fucking glibly about kindness and gentleness!"

I shouted "gentleness" so loud that I heard an echo ping-pong off the danger-filled cement surface of County Hospital. I held the silence as long as I could stand it and felt the gorgeousness of the demonstrators here in this hard time. I saw the ACT UP tribe lean in toward each other. I quietly spoke the last words of the piece.

"Because — there is no question that more lesbian peace activists from Venice will be blown out of the sky over Lockerbie or Burbank.

"There is no question that each of us, like that woman on vacation, is going to have to go to Mexico.

"There is no question that each of us is going to walk along the beach and find a body or two there in the sand."

Then it was over. I gathered my stuff, sweeping up the sand and wrapping the knife in a cloth, because you always want to leave your campsite cleaner than when you found it. People were silent for a moment, and then I heard the clapping. The sound of those hands helped cover me during my return to the spot where Doug was sitting.

As I stepped over sleeping bags and shivering candles, I saw my art friends and activist pals. I was scared for a second that maybe this moment was going to be the best that I would have in my whole life. *Will it be all downhill from here?* That thought felt too scary and more than I could handle on a rainy day in January. I weaved through the rally and sat down beside Doug, becoming part of the crowd again.

"That was beautiful," Doug whispered into my ear.

"Thanks. Did I go on too long?"

"No. It was just right."

"Are you sure? It felt like it dragged a bit in the middle," I asked, groping for more strokes.

"It was perfect!" Doug said, finding the right answer.

"Can we go home soon?"

"Sure."

Doug and I ended up waiting till the rally was over, the last TV camera talked to, and the final banner folded away. We drank burned coffee with our comrades as the afternoon began to turn to dusk. We helped clean up. I hugged and kissed a number of people. Many of them would be dead within a year.

We trudged back up the hill to the Gremlin. The car looked a little decrepit, but the heavy rusted doors creaked open and allowed us to climb in. Doug and I exchanged a look for good luck as he turned the key.

It started on the very first try.

BREATHING NAKED

I WALKED WITH A DARK-HAIRED MAN down East Sixth
Street in New York on a teeth-chattering December
night in 1992. The slippery footfall of our Doc
Martens on the newly iced pavement pulled us step by
step toward each other's human warmth. Avenue by
avenue we moved nearer. Our shoulders brushed
briefly at Second Avenue. At the corner of First
Avenue, we sneaked our arms around each other to
shield ourselves from the wind blowing unapologeti-
cally crosstown. I put my hands in his pockets while
crossing Avenue A. Would we be inside each other's
bodies by the time we got to Avenue B?

How many times in my life had I walked down East
Sixth Street in New York? How many times had I
walked down this street with blood on my clothes from
the cut-off end of a finger, with groceries in my arms
for a dinner with friends, with a new man at my side
for a night's work? How many times had I walked
down East Sixth Street looking for sex? Or Indian
food? Or both? Sometimes I would sit in an Indian
restaurant, beloved Kismoth or tasty Shagorika, snug-
gled into a booth with a man I was seeing. The come
would still be marking our bodies, crackly on my neck
or sticky between his legs. The Bengali waiter would
arrive with his freshly-starched-white-shirt smile.

*Waiter, I'll have the mango chutney and a large
Wash'n Dri, please.*

How many footsteps have walked here before me,
the memory of their soles wearing the East Village
concrete into sand and dust? How many footprints of
the dead who came before us are layered beneath our
striding feet? They ate their bagels, wept in their beds,
and read the newspaper with great interest long before
I had gulped in my first breath. Right now I might be
stepping on the tiny footprints of Doug's dead grand-
ma. As if I were crossing a river on a series of slippery
stones, I can follow her path as she walked up to 14th
Street from Delancey Street in 1912. She walked up to
buy a book or a piece of meat. Maybe she was win-
dow-shopping for a dress she'd never be able to afford
for the new year.

Our feet joined that throng.

(Am I being sentimental here? Well, I'm sorry, but I
listen to doomy and gloomy music frequently, and this
makes me remember the footfalls of the dead. I hear
that music loud in my head. I do what it takes to keep
the memory alive of each slaughtered queer poet on
each battlefield or immune-suppression ward. I spend
hours looking at the photos of my dead lovers on my
altar at home. I touch my first SILENCE = DEATH button
with a nostalgia I can't help feeling for 1988, my first
tour of duty with ACT UP. I jab the SILENCE = DEATH
pin into the palm of my hand, hoping for blood. If I
find it, I hope that the blood might actually mean
something.)

I had come to be with the man I was walking down
East Sixth with at PS 122 earlier that day during a
gay men's performance workshop I was leading. The
space was wall-to-wall ghosts for me. I heard my nineteen-year-old self laughing at me from one of the dark
corners. The faint echo of past lovers and past perfor-

mances almost made it impossible to stay in the room. I stood on the exact spot in the space where John and I had sucked each other off in front of the tall windows on Ninth Street until we saw a balding man across the street looking at us with binoculars.

Today the light poured in through those same tall windows as I opened the curtains and swabbed the deck to get the room ready for the workshop. I welcomed the grounding experiences these queer men's performance workshops provided me with. I needed it bad lately on account of some crazy events surrounding me.

Since the 1990 overturning of my solo performance grant from the National Endowment for the Arts because of the "content" of my work (meaning a gay man talking about life, sex, and politics), every move I made as an artist was now under the vengeful eyes of a phalanx of right-wing groups. I shared this honor with three other performers, and we were clumped together and named the NEA Four. Life as a freedom-of-expression poster boy was not a pleasant experience. During the peak of this particular controversy, one of the main battles of the culture wars of the '90s, I flipped on C-SPAN one morning just in time to hear an unpleasant politician describe me on the floor of Congress as a "porno slime jerk."

The workshops I led gave me a chance to forget all that nonsense and gather gay men for an adventure together. The queers would arrive, hold hands in a circle, and away we'd go. I saw my gay men's workshops as a kind of gymnasium for queer men's imagination and spirit. I had always loved make-believe play when I was a boy. It didn't matter whether it was a game of haunted house or knights of the round table as long as we got to thrill and scare each other. In these workshops we could move our bodies and raise our voices as we played war with our demons inside or created ritual performances about our feelings about unprotected sex.

I finished mopping the floor at PS 122. One by one the two dozen guys arrived, bundled up against the cold-even-for-December cold. Some of the men knew their way around 122, changed into their comfy warm-up clothes, and started stretching. Others came into the room and only by exerting the greatest will kept themselves from fleeing the building.

As the workshop convened I invited the men to breathe deeply as we walked among each other. We were in a room full of queer men who had chosen to overcome their inherent fears of other gay men so that we could spend some time discovering who we actually are. We gathered to tell some stories about our lives. I hoped the warm breath of our raised voices would keep us toasty.

The weak 4 P.M. sun spread long and low on the floor as it shone through the somber stained-glass window that had preached to generations of immigrants this inscribed poem:

"Every waking hour we weave,
whether we will or no —
Every trivial act or deed,
into the warp must go."

That "party on" message spread its soft glow on the group of huddled-together faggots eleven years into the plague. In our own way how much like immigrants we were too. We had left our families and our places of birth to come and be in the New World together. We, like them, had also discovered the terrible sadness that comes when you see the streets are not paved with gold.

Two dozen men of various ages and races placed their arms around each other's shoulders, sweaty and swaying. I forgot how hard it is for us to simply look other men in the eye. Today was no exception. Nervous laughter and wise-ass defensive comments made their usual appearance. We were close enough to smell the person nearest us, close enough to listen to one another as our stories now made our very own weave together, our sum definitely greater than our parts. To stay fully human, I need such gatherings in my life as much as I need coffee, sex, barking dogs, and science fiction.

"I'm Andrew," he had said as we went around sharing our names. This was the man I would walk down East Sixth Street with later that night. Andrew was broodingly dark and handsome, a Heathcliff on Houston kind of thing. He broadcast a sweet generosity that I wanted to know more about. On account of his trendy East Village haircut, buzzed on the sides and rock-and-roll jet-black on top, I guessed his age at twenty-eight, though he could easily pass as twenty-four. That octopus-ink hair made a dramatic curtain across his forehead while he swooped through the space. *I know you,* I thought to myself.

Andrew and I rose to our feet even as the workshop's tales of sissy boys and first loves swirled about us. I looked at him, and he met my gaze. The glance lasted only a second or so, but the daring look was enough to get the wheels turning. I noticed how we began to orbit each other as the men in the workshop improvised some movement together. A flurry of gestures containing the little boys, wild animals, and angry men that dwell inside us exploded from the workshop participants. I saw Andrew slip like a cobra through a tangle of men's arms and legs.

Andrew and I were wearing almost exactly the same outfits (how unusual). We were boldly duochrome in our beat-up black sweatpants and white sleeveless T-shirts with crosses and religious medals dangling from our necks, sort of a City Ballet–meets–St. Marks Place kind of look. It was as if we had spoken on the phone to decide what to wear to the first day of East Village High School!

"How long have you two known each other?" someone asked me, commenting on our similar getups.

Not long enough, I said to myself as I maneuvered my way nearer to him. The generous hula-hoop action in Andrew's hips showed me his Generation X cool exterior was balanced by a more than nodding acquaintance with his Big Queen Within. In fact, he *was* pretty big! Tall, I mean, a bit taller than me. I hated that. It meant that if we kissed later, I would have to twist my neck up and around to reach him. I would be sure to get a neck ache.

Andrew wore a religious medal I didn't immediately recognize. What was it? A petite St. Peter and Paul medal? Understated yet boner-producing.

Who was Andrew, anyway? I had taken in the signs and symbols he displayed of queer urban culture, but what does the presence (or absence) of a nipple piercing really tell you about someone? Can that Tom of Finland tattoo or Superman pompadour haircut let you in on the secret of what books a man reads or whether his father beat him when he was a kid? I knew one thing for sure: Andrew's dark eyes and black hair reeled me right in. I could fight that tight fish line, try to get that hook out of the soft flesh of my cheek, but I knew the story would end up with me flopping around on the deck.

We sneaked a look again, longer this time.

The workshop ended after three hours of creating performances about the secret powers we held as gay men. Andrew and I hung around the room till almost all the participants had already left. We stood by our shoes, which had ended up next to each other (oh, fate!) on a well-worn seating platform. Those black boots waited for us to get our act together. They engaged in Doc Martens gossip.

The size 10½ wide muttered, "I just wish they'd go talk to each other."

"I just wish they'd go fuck each other!" the 11 narrow complained through the sock that was suffocating him.

Finally, to shut the boots up before they said something really embarrassing, Andrew and I grabbed the Doc Martens and stuck our feet in their mouths and flattened their shoe tongues as we threaded every last eyelet. These were the eleven-hole and *not* the eight-hole variety, so this trying activity took a little while. Each diving swoop of the shoelaces drew Andrew and me nearer and nearer. Face-to-face while we waited for the last person to leave, we tugged the laces tight and made a knot.

Everyone was now gone. One of us had to do something quick. I crossed my fingers and stepped into the void.

"I'm glad you came to the workshop," I said with false confidence, sounding like my football coach uncle.

"It was great. I had a really good time," Andrew responded with a friendly look. "It's been a while since I've done this kind of thing."

"Are you a performer? You look like you've done a lot of movement."

"Yeah," Andrew replied as he hoisted his sweaty shirt over his head to change into something dry. I was treated to a quick glimpse of pale skin and erect nipples. "I studied dance in college."

"Well, I should probably get going." I dragged each word out to buy myself extra time. "Um, would you like to hang out for a while?"

"Sure," Andrew replied. "That would be great."

"What shall we do?"

"What would you like to do?" Andrew tossed it back to me.

"No, you decide," I countered.

"No, you," Andrew parried.

"It's up to you," I said almost shouting.

"You're the visitor in New York. It's definitely your decision," Andrew said, putting his Doc Martensed foot down. Checkmate.

I wanted to say something like "Let's just find a place that is quiet and sit and recognize the essential truth and spirit in each other." Because that is really what I hoped would happen. In lieu of that, I floated a more conventional proposal: "Why don't we go to Yaffa Café and eat something?"

Wrapping our Bob Cratchit scarves around our necks, we pushed our way out of the big oak doors of PS 122 and into the flow of the pre-Christmas jostle of First Avenue.

"It's fucking cold!" I complained, feeling like my lips were going to fall off with frostbite.

"Let's run," Andrew said and took off.

We quickly covered the short distance to the café, shoved through the crush in the narrow entry, and slipped into a cozy, warm corner table.

"I hate the winter," I, the typical Californian, complained. "I think it's why I left New York for California."

"Hey, I'm a Californian too," Andrew said, removing several layers of jackets and sweaters.

"You're kidding! Where are you from?" I was pleased to have discovered our common origin.

"Well," Andrew began, lavishing several vowels on this one word, as though it were a huge tale to tell, "I was born in Stockton in a manger. Then when I was six..."

We were off and running in the delicious orgy of two native Californians comparing their tan lines. As we shared nostalgic memories of hitchhiking in the San Joaquin Valley and which sex acts we had had on which rides at Disneyland, I began to get a picture of Andrew's journey to the big city. He was here to seek his fortune, not with a huge expectation of fame and glory but with a sigh of relief that he had managed to escape cheerless Stockton.

We had tea surrounded by the late-baroque punk splendor of Yaffa on St. Marks. For two hours we talked and traded and teased and tempted as we lunged our pita bread into the spicy hummus dip. Feeling daring, I licked the last bit up off the plate with my tongue and winked. This could have been the opening salvo of our intimacy, but Andrew glanced down at his watch.

"Oh, look at the time!" he said getting up. "I have to go to work. I'm late."

"Yikes!" I exclaimed, using a characteristic retro expression that made me sound like one of the Hardy Boys. "I have a show to do. I need to go too." Then I added nervously, "Would you like to meet later?"

"Sure," Andrew shouted through the pullover sweater that covered his face as he climbed into it. "This time I'll decide where to eat."

Later that night, at 10 P.M., I walked down First Avenue, feeling pretty good. I had wiped the sweat and metaphors of that night's performance off my brow. Now the thrill of the hunt was upon me. I was addicted to the feeling of excitement that came from having a rendezvous scheduled with God knows who to do God knows what with each other. I had the keen anticipatory look of an eager seven-year-old creeping down the stairs on Christmas morning. My breath a fog machine, I strolled past Holy Stromboli Lubricated Pizza. This had been the favorite place John and I would eat in the neighborhood. We had featured the greasy site in a number of our *Live Boys* performances.

Poking my head in the door of a beloved Eastern European restaurant, I sniffed the aroma of the sour-cream-filled pleasures of Poland.

"Dobry vyechoor!" I called out to Zenya, my favorite waitress, in one of the eight sentences I still remembered from my brief study of Polish in 1979 before a planned pilgrimage to work with theater director Jerzy Grotowski in Wroclaw. Zenya smiled, pleased that one of the East Village gay boys would talk to her in her own language. Feeling expansive, I made up words to bless all of First Avenue in every language that I would never study.

I ran across the street and almost got hit by a cab making my way to a Mexican restaurant at Sixth Street and Avenue A where Andrew and I were to meet. It was called Banditos or Caballeros or something like that. New York doing Southern California Mexican food.

"Buenos días!" I said to the glacially glamorous young Frenchwoman working the door of the crowded restaurant. She glared at me as if I had spoken to her in Swahili. "I'm meeting someone," I quickly

added, since it seemed like I owed her an explanation for my craven existence.

"Please, you will wait here," the mistress of attitude icily commanded as she checked her list.

I looked around the restaurant for Andrew. I couldn't see a sign of him. *I've been abandoned!* I thought to myself as I turned into a puddle of panic under the withering gaze of the Frenchwoman. Then I saw Andrew waving madly, trying to get my attention from the little table behind the pillar. Counting my breaths in an effort to calm my involuntary hyperventilating, I lugged my "abandonment issues" in their enormous mismatched steamer trunks across the restaurant and sat down across from him.

"Hi!" he said as he leaned across the table and gave me a matter-of-fact kiss.

"Hi," I replied. One breath. Two breaths. Three breaths. "Nice to see you. Have you been waiting long?"

"Nah. Long enough to order a margarita. Are you okay?"

"Oh, sure, I'm fine," I improvised nonchalance, kicking the panic-filled steamer trunks further under the table till they fit. "I just got a little nervous as I walked here."

"Relax." Andrew rubbed my forearm. "I won't bite."

Andrew was dressed in a thick-knit black fisherman's sweater and a motorcycle jacket. He could pass as a chorus boy from *Carousel* on his way to a leather bar. It was definitely a look. The margarita arrived: a frosty tureen the size of a bassinet. The salt chunks trembled in slow motion down the melting sides.

"Waiter," Andrew asked, "can we have two straws?"

Andrew shucked the straws slowly, the paper peeling away from the plastic tube like a molting snake.

He thrust one straw in the slushy corner of the margarita closest to me and placed the other between his lips, lowering it like a vacuum cleaner into the delicious cold cocktail. We sucked at either end of that margarita, a queer postmodern Norman Rockwell painting of homosexuals in a Mexican restaurant.

Nursing our beverage, Andrew and I swapped stories of love and families and school and coming out and hopes and fears. In other words, we had a conversation. The stories bounced back and forth like a first round of tennis between a couple of people getting to know each other's skill. Our game plan included the usual dinner-conversation topics: hustler boyfriends, drama queen–ism, international travel, and adolescent erotics.

"I had a boyfriend once who was a hustler on Santa Monica Boulevard," I started with an easy overhand serve. "He told me he did it so that he could buy a grand piano. But after all those blow jobs, once he got that grand piano, he found he could only play in E minor."

Andrew returned the lob with a free association: "Well, now that you mention blow jobs and the performing arts, I got my first blow job at the International Thespian Conference in Muncie, Indiana. It was with a boy from St. Cloud, Wisconsin, and happened backstage during a parochial girls school production of *You Can't Take It With You*."

Lunging to display my backhand, I sent the ball back with a difficult corner shot. "Oh, yes, travel brings out the best in us. My friend Doug and I once had a big fight in the Parc Royale in Brussels, so we split up for a couple of days and then met in the train station in Berlin Bahnhofzoo. We saw each other next

to the express train to Moscow. Doug and I were so
happy to see each other as we hugged and kissed our
way onto the U-Bahn that we almost missed our stop
at Karl Marx Platz."

Andrew was good, very good; he stretched long
and thwacked the ball into my court with a story that
psyched me out: "When I was seventeen I lived with
my mom in a house in the San Joaquin Valley next to
some alfalfa fields. Every night of my seventeenth
year, I walked far out into the fields. I would carefully take off all my clothes and then jerk off over the
green alfalfa leaves, dreaming of the Latino workers
of those fields."

I reached for the ball but missed. Game and match!

The edgy cultural politics of this alfalfa-field story
had given me an instant boner. "Waiter, can we have
the check, please? *Por favor?*"

Andrew and I quickly paid the bill. Accurate as
accountants, we divided it precisely down the middle.
As we left the restaurant, I grabbed a handful of mints
from the bowl by the cash register to quash the smell
of the anchovies from my Caesar salad. Finally, our
bodies brushed together as we walked down East
Sixth Street in the direction of his house on this cold
night in New York City.

We strolled past the mysterious fortlike walls of the
Con Edison electrical plant at Sixth Street and Avenue
A. It looked like a Wild West outpost for a minor John
Wayne movie. What did they actually do inside those
walls, anyway? No one knew. The sides of our bodies
moved closer yet as we wandered past the bright
facade of my favorite gay watering hole, the Wonder
Bar. The hopeful primary colors, freely borrowed from
Wonder Bread, were as brilliant as my third-grade

Jonny Quest lunch box. We walked on and on toward
Avenue B.

We got to Andrew's building. My memory was
nudged by the sight of the combination beauty shop
and botanica that made up half of the ground floor.
Was this the building in which I built a loft bed for
that New York University film student who then
bounced his Citibank check on me?

Andrew asked me, "Do you want to come in?"

I wish life were that simple, that tidy. This wasn't
how it happened at all. Andrew didn't ask me. I had
to ask *him*. Such a request — "Can I come in?" — is
not an easy thing to make at someone else's front stoop
at 2 in the morning.

"Gee," I said enthusiastically, channeling Joe Hardy
this time, "here we are at your house. Can I come in?"
What a cad! But I dared to take a chance.

"Oh, sure," Andrew said, pleased but a little surprised. Maybe mentioning Doug the Boyfriend had
thrown him off-track. "Come on up."

We went up the narrow stairs. Up, up, up into his
apartment. Andrew struggled heroically with the
police lock, the dead bolt, and door-handle lock (part
of the nonstop glamour of New York living), and he
heaved his shoulder against the door. We tumbled into
the dark apartment. His fingers reading the wall
braille, Andrew at last found the switch and flipped on
a light. I saw a billowing white prom dress being used
as a lampshade. There was a row of big-hair wigs on
styrofoam heads above the hat rack.

"My housemate is a drag deejay," Andrew
explained. "He's playing tonight."

No one else seemed to be home. That was good, I
remember thinking. The solitude would make the pre-

liminary moves toward grabbing each other's bodies more smooth. No distracting conversations *à trois* in the kitchen. In an attempt to take off our coats in the narrow hallway, Andrew and I managed to bonk heads as if we were in a queer Marx Brothers movie.

"Hey, I hope you won't sue me," I joked, softly rubbing his forehead, which had no visible dents.

"I won't if you won't."

I extended my hand. "It's a deal."

We shook hands like two farmers at the state fair in front of a prize heifer. Then we tried it again. This time we shook hands like who we *actually* were, two nervous gay men in a dark hallway on the Lower East Side who were wondering what was going to happen next.

We stopped shaking hands, but the touch held on. For an instant, as I looked at Andrew, I remembered when I was a little boy and how tempted I always was to look with my naked eye at a solar eclipse. My mom tried the usual scare tactic: that I would be instantly blinded. Somehow her warning just didn't wash. How could the light of day hurt me? The sun was there, and I had to see. I tried to look at Andrew, but he was too bright, and I had to cover my eyes. Maybe I should get some smoked glass.

Andrew pulled me by my hand into the apartment, and he began to show me his sacred things, the apartment relics and icons. He had his extracted wisdom teeth placed on the altar next to the TV. His barbells were stacked next to the radiator by the shelves with the hand-painted ceramic dinosaur collection ordered from the Franklin Mint. The Virgin Marys on the toilet tank fixed the flat firmly in the post–*Nuevo Wavo* junk-shop tradition of East Village decor. How the neighborhood had changed in ten years!

Finally, Andrew tugged me into his whitewashed bedroom to see a sixth-grade class photo. I was dismayed to notice his bed, a beat-up old futon, in one corner on the floor. I couldn't stop myself from beginning to redesign Andrew's bedroom. I had a vision of how this room would benefit from one of my loft beds. I saw where I would put it on the wall, bolting the bed frame to the wall halfway up on the window, keeping the light above and below. Drawing the plans in my head, I imagined how this would open up an area underneath for a desk or a love seat.

For now, we flopped down on his futon on the floor, and I admired his black, black, black hair against the bed's white, white, white sheet. With a studied casualness I flopped one of my legs over one of his as we stared up at the ceiling in an uncomfortable what-will-happen-next? silence. Andrew and I now faced that most challenging of existential situations: Who is going to make the first move?

Before we mere humans could answer, Andrew's pet feline, Hamster the Miracle Cat, poked into the room. Hamster the Miracle Cat probably was really on the lookout for some extra wet food from that morning's still-open cat-food can on the roach-friendly kitchen counter. But meanwhile, Hamster proceeded to perform the "cat head thing," when a cat drops all pretense of aloofness and caresses you with its entire face. I suppose the animal kingdom was daring us to be more spontaneous and find our touch together. By example, Hamster tried to teach us how to rub the head into the crotch and drag our body's side against another body's side.

Taking Hamster's lead, Andrew and I began to rub our faces together. The tip of my nose caressed

Andrew's cheek as his lips grazed over my stubble closer to my open mouth. We kissed. It was tentative at first. The tongues slowly rose to the occasion, like dipping yourself into still-chilly Lake Tahoe early in the season and asking yourself, "Is this really what I want to do?" Then we dived in and braved the rush.

Oh, I liked Andrew. I had started to trust his sweetness when I had seen the sixth-grade photo. He was kind and smart and hot. He knew how to stand next to me and slowly reach his little finger toward mine. Most of all he was a Californian like me, yet he wore even more black clothes than I did! We savored taking those black clothes off — hands reaching into the 501s, tugging down the thick sweat socks, yawning out of our shirts with a sigh. The thrill of each touch given and received made my thoughts tumble in my head like clothes in a dryer.

Wow! I thought to myself as my hands searched Andrew's skin. *His leg goes into his hip right there. Unheard-of! He has a little hair here on his belly but not here on his shoulders. Fantastic! His recently shaved balls are attached to his dick in a bouncy saclike structure. Wonder of wonders! The skin is so soft. His mouth tastes good. This all feels good.*

I sensed Andrew's ceramic dinosaur collection begin to stir from the shelf above. The prehistoric creatures slowly levitated above us as we licked each other's cocks. It was as if the dinosaurs who had been sucked down at the tar pits had found their way into the room, wanting to get in on the action. I recognized one or two of them. A woolly mammoth settled on Andrew's butt as the Virgin Mary floated in just to bless us as we got closer. All of Andrew's childhood snapshots sneaked out of the drawer where they had been stashed. The photos set up a camp around the bed, the past witnessing this present moment. Even his barbells started to move a little nearer to one another and, at last, began to clang together as well.

Well, to make a long story short, I came on his chest. He came on my leg. Andrew and I felt our breath race and then quiet. Then we suddenly realized we were sprawled on a bed covered in come with someone we had just met. This realization hit me like a shock, but just for a minute. I smelled the hint of the free fall of postorgasm depression about to strike me, the dreaded after-the-squirting deflated-balloon syndrome. But that little despair receded, and I settled into a new place, as if Andrew and I had hiked up a steep cliff and hauled ourselves at last to a plateau. At first it seemed strange and a little primordial and scary up there, like *The Lost World,* but then we saw that we could inhabit a new terrain. We could forage for food and build civilizations. Stroking each other gently for a long time, our touch freed for a while from the bass-drum sex call, Andrew and I talked into the late hours.

I was glad I was there. I was glad I was alive. I loved New York. But then a kind of weird paranoia attacked me. This was too good. Something bad was bound to happen. With that doom-laden thought, I fell into a deep sleep full of dreams of exploding buildings and machine-gunned nuns.

The next morning we woke up early in the flash-bulb-bright sunshine coming in from the East River. I was covered in the sticky-come closeness of waking up with someone for the first time. For a moment I backed away nervously from the splurge of ambiva-lent feelings that comes as you wake up in bed with another human being. One or two of my masks came down: scary, even though there were still lots held in reserve. Turning tentatively onto my side, I looked to Andrew to see if he was awake. His eyes were open but still sleepy.

"Hi, handsome," he tossed my way.

"Good morning." I yawned out the words as I stretched. "Do you mind morning mouth?"

Andrew kissed by way of reply. We were tentative about opening our mouths to each other, like checking with a sniff the milk after you've been away from home for a few days. But then we slowly opened our clamshell lips, let our tongues slip and slide, saw it wasn't so bad after all, saw that our mouths smelled of our lives and our sleep and our dreams too. The morning kiss floated on the grace of trusting that we liked each other and that neither one of us was going to make a hasty exit.

"So," Andrew said, beginning the cross-examination as he abruptly broke off the kiss, "you probably have a boyfriend, right?"

"Yeah." I opted for a matter-of-fact tone. "We've been together ten years this month. His name is Doug. We have an open relationship."

"If I were him," Andrew said, rubbing his knuckles playfully, though a little roughly, on my forehead, "I wouldn't let you wander around without a chaperon."

"Doug and I believe that our connections with other men are an important part of our relationship," I replied, immediately going into my stump speech. "We aren't trying to emulate the straight fucked-up marriage model that never worked for our parents anyway..."

Blah, blah, blah. The truth was that for two years I had been quite extravagantly conducting a complex series of love affairs around the country. I had a fuck buddy in Philadelphia, a lover in Minneapolis, a boyfriend in San Antonio. Since testing negative (surprise) in 1990, I had started to live out the sexual adolescence that I didn't get to have on account of AIDS bringing the curtain down on my personal sexual revolution when I was twenty-two.

For a while this rather conventional wild-oats sowing had been a nice vitamin pill for Doug and me. Our extracurricular activities had enlivened our connection. We would swap stories and tips about other guys like a couple of jocks after the game. Our older gay friends had modeled this recipe for romance.

But there was a price to pay for this "freedom." As these relationships got more involving, they leaked a lot of energy out of our — for lack of a better word — marriage. Like a frog that is put into water that is slowly boiled so he never notices the heat turning up, Doug and I didn't see the trouble that was looming. For now, when the topic of open relationships came up, I did my best liberationist spin doctoring.

"…somehow Doug and I have turned the old open-relationship axiom upside down." I was still spouting off like someone trying to sell a used car as I explained my life to Andrew. "We feel that the rule 'You can have other affairs as long as you don't fall in love' is totally fucked-up. For Doug and me, the proper rule is more 'You can have affairs as long as you *do* love these other men and invest some psychic energy in the connection.' If there isn't a strong feeling, then we probably shouldn't bother."

I stopped myself before I could make any promises about lowering taxes (or falling in love). This confessional had gotten a little too dicey so early in the morning; too many of my trade secrets were being revealed. There are limits to how much relationship talk one should sustain before coffee is made.

"What about you, Andrew?" I asked, hoping the focus would shift away from me. "How do you figure all these relationship questions out?"

"Well," he began, "I moved to New York with my lover, but now we pretty much function as best friends."

Pleased that the conversation had shifted away from me, I began asking a series of increasingly nosy questions. Andrew and I lounged as we talked shop about boyfriends, present and past. I could slowly see that our conversation was inevitably going to come around to *the* subject, the AIDS tune-in. "Health concerns" began to present themselves from a distance, like the music on the stereo of your downstairs neighbor gradually getting louder and more vexing. But it was coming regardless.

Now, at that time in my life, I usually didn't engage in this conversation on the first date. Being a good ACT UP boy, I assumed all my partners were positive and behaved accordingly. Normally, I would wait and have the HIV talk after I had sex with a fellow a couple of times. I believed that as long as I was having safe sex, it was okay to allow this waiting period.

I had a clutching-at-straws faith in safe sex, and I convinced myself that I could trust its principles. I structured my understanding of the world around its precepts. It behooved me to have that faith because I was having sex with a *lot* of people in the early '90s. I had to believe in safe sex just like I had to believe in other forces essential for life: gravity, photosynthesis, friction. I felt compelled to be a party-liner about safe sex because this system helped me to keep my fears at bay. That faith allowed me to get up in the morning, make my breakfast, and not have a nervous breakdown.

Since Andrew and I had been careful in our sex, according to the accepted mores of the time, this was a perfectly responsible time to have the discussion, if indeed we even needed to have it. The subject came up on its own, as it so often does.

I said, "Andrew, it's intense to be here, lying in a bed on East Sixth Street, talking about all this relationship material. My boyfriend John, the guy I told you about who died of AIDS, he used to live on East Sixth, just down the block."

"Ouch," Andrew said, hugging his arms around me. We breathed together for a bit. "It sucks, I know. My ex-boyfriend back in California is pretty sick right now. I worry about him a lot."

We held this close between us as we circled the subject like hunters tracking a wild animal. The about-to-stampede elephant was in bed with us now.

"So, Andrew…um…" I hemmed and hawed, trying to spit out the obvious question. "Where are you in all of this AIDS stuff?"

"I'm positive," Andrew said, looking directly at me. "I just found out a little while ago. What about you?"

"I'm negative," I replied after an exhale whistled between my front teeth. "The one time I checked, anyway. I could hardly believe it, considering my history. You know…John and all."

Well, the cards were on the table: It was a full house. The cameras zoomed in for the close-up. Everything was going real slow, spooky and sci-fi. At this point there was a hydrogen bomb blast over the East River. This explosion blared through the windows onto our bodies, burning away the bullshit between Andrew and me. I witnessed a powerful moment between two human faggots at the end of the twentieth century.

I felt as if a strange bird, strange as the subject at hand, had flown into Andrew's bedroom. This creature was a little clumsy, like Big Bird, as it broke through the glass and flapped around Andrew's room, knocking his high school graduation pictures off the wall. This bird landed at the end of Andrew's futon and looked at us. This bird, like this moment between us, could be fierce or friendly. It was *totally* up to us.

I looked Andrew in the eye. I had nothing useful to say, nothing that wouldn't collapse under the weight of its own structure of obvious verbs and insufficient adjectives. I felt our fates float around us for a moment. There was a hurt that hovered over Andrew's face for an even tinier instant.

"I hope you're not freaked out that I didn't tell you earlier," Andrew said quietly, looking down toward our feet.

"No." I said the right thing, though I knew no single word could describe the snarl of feelings that were revving up inside me. Without thinking, I quickly toured the inside of my mouth with my tongue to see if I had any canker sores there. Everything seemed okay. "I'm a big boy. I know how to take care of myself."

Then I put my lips on Andrew's. Our tongues touched, and it was like a promise, eyes open, hearts too. Andrew and I started to make love again. We moved our hands over the hills and valleys of our bodies just as we had a few hours before. Our fingers sketched across the details and limits of our skin and shape, and I felt a powerful mix of excitement and fear. What was different now? There was an honest thrill in knowing who we really are.

I knew something special had happened. I didn't want to make it into a big deal. In a way it was just how things were, our lives as we need to live them. I wasn't even sure what any of this positive/negative information meant anymore. But if I tried to say it meant *nothing* to me at that moment, that would have been a lie, a whopper of a lie. I was so tired of lying.

I had been in this situation before, of course, with other men who were positive. There was a guy from Cedar Rapids. And a fellow from Spokane. One man was white. Another man was black. I confess they were all cute. All dear. All very hot. I am weak.

One of these men used to lead workshops in Texas for ex-gay born-again Christians. That didn't last too long before he met a nice boy at a gay bar in Tulsa. They moved to San Francisco, and he now works in a card shop in the Castro.

Another man won a scholarship to Princeton, where he pored over medieval texts while eyeing the water polo players with his feet propped up on the back of the swimming-arena bleachers.

One man escaped the death squads in San Salvador and walked all the way through Guatemala and Mexico to make a new life in Los Angeles. He sent money each week to his family.

Another man went home with Jeffrey Dahmer yet managed to live and tell the tale. (If that's not a fucking success story, I don't know what is.)

I put my skin next to the skin of each of these men. I needed their touch, maybe more than they needed mine. I loved one man's crazy Brillo hair, his crooked smile, his deeply dimpled ass. I loved another man's

wild courage at his job, his scary family story, his dick
that veered to the left like a stretch of road.

All of these men were positive. They told me this.
They knew. I'm negative. I was pretty surprised that
the coin flipped that way. It always scares me to tell
people this. I worry that they'll think I'm a lightweight
know-nothing who-said-you-could-talk-about-AIDS-
from-your-position-of-negative-privilege? queen.

I worry that mentioning being negative is a kind of
a social faux pas, a breach in etiquette. I should probably just keep quiet about my status since I don't get
tested very often anyway. Some experts suggest a person should be tested every six months. For me, it's
more like every six years, 1990 and 1996. I worry that
talking too much about being negative might jinx it,
make it somehow not true, make it somehow pop like
a dreamy soap bubble when the alarm rings at 6 A.M.
All it takes is a snap of the fingers, and suddenly I
become a superstitious old Italian woman in Bari worried about the evil eye. It's best to shut up.

Andrew and I made love that morning in the light
of day in the eleventh year of the plague. I heard his
housemates stirring in the other room and their
raised-eyebrow comments about the two pairs of Doc
Martens in a pile outside of Andrew's wedged-shut
bedroom door. As usual my thoughts while we fucked
were honking their horns like a traffic jam at the psychic corner of Hollywood Boulevard and 42nd Street:

*Oh, that feels nice. His kisses, so sweet. Those kiss-
es, so wet. Well, they're not really that wet, not in the
big scheme of wetness. I can't be bothered worrying
about saliva anyway. I can't live in a world where we
can't kiss. Does he feel me holding back? No, I think
it's okay. He knows I'm a little nervous, I think.*

Hey, now Andrew's sucking my dick. Ooh, that's nice. He can do the thing with his throat with such ease, the thing that always makes me gag when I try it. Wait, if Andrew's sucking my dick, does that mean I have to suck his dick? No, I'm an adult. I took that workshop about boundary drawing. I can own that I won't be comfortable with that. I can say yes and no in my life. Well, maybe I'll just lick his balls some. That would be a friendly gesture. Well, maybe up the shaft for a bit. It couldn't hurt to just lick across the head of his dick for a bit, could it? No, better not. If I do, I'll have an anxiety attack tomorrow.

Fuck, this is why so many HIV-positive men I know don't want to be bothered dealing with fucked-up negative dudes' panic attacks like mine. Oh, but his asshole feels so nice on my fingertip. Does he have condoms beside the bed? If we're gonna fuck, I have to fuck him. The man who's negative becomes insta-top, right? Well, that's cool; I've really gotten more into my top energy lately anyhow. It's really who I am, my deepest self, right?

But what if tomorrow it's been a long day and I'm tired and I don't have the yang savings account to smack his butt and lift those legs and huff and puff and blow my load up the boy-pussy-man-cunt-hot-hole of my desire? What will I do then? One finger, two fingers, three fingers. It's like a song on Sesame Street.

I gotta fuck him. It feels too nice. Where's a rubber? Wait, maybe I can fuck him without a rubber. Shoot my HIV-negative come up him? The man who fucks isn't at risk, right? Well, it depends what country you're in, doesn't it? No, better use a condom. Gotta stay safe, right? Right?

But what about that big Wuthering Heights mansion inside me that wants to put my come in my lover's mouth and asshole? I want to get him pregnant. That's biological, right? What about that part of me that wants to eat up that come and stuff it up my butt and feel that skin-to-skin contact?

What's safe, anyway? You can never be totally safe. You would have to never get out of bed. That might be safe. You should never cross the street against the signal. Never climb on slippery rocks just for the seashore thrill. It would be much safer never to get close to anybody ever again, not close enough to touch.

Put the damn condom on!

My cock is slipping into Andrew's asshole. That feels so nice. He's kissing me now, telling me he likes my dick inside him. C'mon, this kiss, I gotta have it. It's that simple. It's that necessary. I gotta have it if this nice man Andrew lets me.

Where am I on my map now? Where did I put my compass? Here I am, right here by this winding river! I can't stand on one side of the water and only wave a clumsy oar. I can't let this kiss not happen. And I want to know its whole story.

Hey, my brain is quieting down! I'm actually in the experience of fucking another man! I'm not looking over my shoulder, waiting for the police siren! Andrew turns over, and I see his beautiful back and skin and ass as we fuck. I feel his hipbones inside his body in the palms of my hands. He's slapping my chest as we fuck. This is great! Wow, look at me, Mom! Here's your HIV-negative son confronting his fears and having hot sex with a man who's positive! Aren't you proud of me, Mom? Mom?

My mom appears inside my head with gobs of left-over filling from Taco Night dripping through her fingers. "Didn't you read all those Los Angeles Times

*articles I've been sending you for years? Aren't you
scared, you dirty faggot son o' mine who will never
give me grandchildren?"*

*(Oh, God, I'm going to lose my hard-on, I know!
This always happens when I think of my mom while
I'm having sex. Quick, Tim, think of smooth-skinned
English boys in wet underwear, splashing in the foun-
tains of Trafalgar Square. That always helps.)*

"Scared, Mom? Oh, I guess once in a while I worry
sometimes for a second or two. Okay, I go mad with
crazy worry, wildfire fear. All the fear you gave me. All
the fear you had in your life. Sometimes I fear everything. I fear getting on airplanes. I fear that I left the
stove on. I fear that I said the wrong thing. But in this
Museum of Fear, I have a special wing, about the size
of the Louvre, dedicated to all the things that I might
get from the men I get close to. Have sex with.

"Clap! Warts! Hepatitis! Crabs! Amoebas! HIV!

"Okay, Mom, this fear sometimes chews me up for
breakfast. This terror is a tidal wave hovering above
me. It whirls, and I feel like I'm going to scream. This
crazy fear is a virus too. It's a fierce enemy, completely merciless. It takes no prisoners.

"This fear can haunt my dreams when I have sex
that is not so safe, like that time in London. It kept me
sleepless and tortured an entire night in a crummy
hotel in South Kensington, London. I replayed my
judgment lapse a thousand times, watched it in slow
motion. I had to feel my body swell up with dead bodies, then a horrible beast pulled them out of my asshole. Spinning in my bed, I was spitting distance from
the gloriously tacky memorial to Prince Albert, who
long before he was a dick piercing was the beloved of
Victoria. When he died Victoria (that queen) took

whatever was good and hot in her woman's body and entombed it with Albert, her dead husband, and worshiped it all as a dead thing! Mom, she gave that fear to you and to me, okay? Fuck all that! I'm pretty busy right now, so, Mom, get out of my head!"

Andrew spits in my mouth. Pulls my dick hard into him. Does he want me to shoot inside him? *I wonder. Andrew's about to come. I can see his dick getting bigger. The head of his cock looks like the face of someone about to sneeze. I'm getting close too. Maybe I should pull out? We can shoot together. He wants me to come inside him, in the rubber, I know it. Should I ask him? Maybe I'll just tell him. Then the ball is in his court.*

We turn the fuck upside down. He moves onto his back, his legs up where I can lick them. Top to bottom, I want to turn this fear in my life around too. I want to flip the scary meaning of that word get upside down like a fried egg. Over. Easy. I need to understand what I get in a different way. Oh, fuck, I have to remember both sides of the things I get from the men in my life: We get close. We get hurt. We get touched. We get left. We get laid. We get scared. We get held. We get Dad. We get love. We...

At last Andrew came on his belly and chest. I poured my body into his as I shot inside the condom in his asshole. My body fell onto his. As careful as if I were handling nitroglycerin, I grabbed the condom and pulled out of him. I dangled the Trojan Extra Sensitive in front of my eyes. I saw the liquid heavy at the bottom. I wanted to fill it with water and throw it out onto Sixth Street. I loved water-balloon fights as a kid. I loved the wet possibilities.

I carefully dripped the splooge from the condom, like I was decorating an anniversary cake, onto

Andrew's chest, which was already covered with his own come. I mixed the substances all up together, and I dragged my cross through it. Like a proper nasty boy, I covered the cross with the different stories of these fluids. No chemistry class had ever taught me this experiment.

In the last moments before we came, all the competing voices in my head had suddenly simmered down, as if I had hit the mute button on my TV remote. For once, I was just in my body inside another man's body, doing the thing that our bodies know how to do. Could anybody really see the positive and negative signs buzzing like insistent neon over our heads? I couldn't. But I could feel the electrical current we had generated between us.

Dropping my torso onto his as if from a great height, I rubbed my body from side to side. We got really sticky and smelly as my weight made Andrew let a breath out. I was drenched in sweat by the time Andrew and I had finished. I let our bodies get glued together.

"Whew," I breathed a sigh. "That felt great."

"Yeah," Andrew whispered, his breath returning.

"How ya doing?" I sang the question softly in his ear.

"Good," Andrew purred. Hamster was still on the bed. "This all feels new. It's the first time I've told someone I was having sex with that I was positive. It was pretty scary. I'm glad you didn't do anything weird when I told you."

"I'm glad you told me," I said truthfully.

"Me too. What a world we live in." We lay there quietly for a moment, then Andrew sat up suddenly as if he had realized something important. "Want some coffee?"

"I need some," I replied, shifting my feet off the low-slung bed onto the floor.

"My housemates have gone out. We've got the run of the place."

"Do you want to do something today?" I asked, ever the organizer. "Want to take the Staten Island Ferry, see the Caravaggio show or something?"

Andrew was ready to negotiate. "Maybe we can just rest for a while? Maybe make some pancakes?"

"Okay," I said.

We walked naked to his dark kitchen. The sounds of the neighbors above floated down the air shaft. He opened the fridge, and there, by the soft light of Amana, we drank some orange juice from the bottle.

SHIRTS & SKIN

I HAVE TWO BOYFRIENDS. The instant you look in my laundry baskets and scrounge through the decade-old jockstraps and now barely legible ACT UP shirts (READ MY what?), you can deduce that I live by myself in a house where two other men also sleep over.

You could learn more if you dig a little deeper in each laundry basket beyond my clothing. There is a younger man's sassy recycled-for-queer-use soccer T-shirt: blue, rayon, and chock-full of spunk and rage. There is also another man's Gold's Gym sweatshirt: stark in its serious black-and-white purpose of disciplining the body and mind, workout clothes for someone older, a bit wiser, and a real Jewish pain in the ass.

These shirts tell a whole life story about how one man sometimes isn't enough and two are too many. Remember Birkin at the end of *Women in Love*, having the last word (what a surprise) as he claims his need for two kinds of love in his life? I wonder who did *his* laundry? Well, I suppose I need two different boyfriends.

What a strange word to sum up my complicated ties with another man: *boyfriend*. I know that mystics, theologians, and gossip columnists have battled for centuries about just exactly how we should define the word *boyfriend*. These pundits have struggled mightily in the effort to determine the most appropriate single word for two men in intimate relation.

My mom weighed in with her opinion when I was
seven years old with a simple maxim: "A boyfriend is
just a friend who is a boy." I suppose she probably
would have offered the same homily for the explanation of *girlfriend* on those occasions when I protested
wildly that Gail Gardener was *not* my girlfriend.

To some people, the word *boyfriend* is far too casu-
al; to others, too intimate. There are other words, of
course.

Lover. Too illicit.

Partner. Too businesslike.

Significant other. Too long.

Husband. Too bourgeois.

I've always liked the word *boyfriend* for its sense of
possibilities. There is a bounce and a wide vista to the
word. It's a chance to rewrite the high school yearbook
and fulfill a wet dream of comradely love. I'm not sure
that the word *boyfriend* is exactly the right word to
use for someone you are seeing. What does it really
mean to "see" someone? Does it mean that you are
seeing his face at the end of the day? Seeing his asshole up close? Seeing the come squirt out of his dick?
Seeing his scared little kid inside? Seeing his mouth
open while he sleeps? Boyfriends do all of that kind of
"seeing," for sure. And is there a statute of limitations
on the term? Can you really still use the word
boyfriend for someone with whom you have been intimate for fourteen years?

My mom got the *friend* part of the equation right, I
think. But let's face it, that is just the beginning. A
boyfriend is much more than a friend who is a boy. A
boyfriend can also be your business-partner, ego-
booster, man-pussy, coffee-maker, cock-slurper, poet-
weaver, bed-fellow, heart-ripper, vengeful-daddy, lit-

tle-brother, shaming-mother, weeping-midwife, butt hole–plunging soul figure! All this plus someone you might go to Palm Springs with for the weekend! Whatever the fuck a boyfriend is, I am pretty sure I've got two different kinds of them.

I know many people would say you can never really have two boyfriends. There's probably truth in that. But inside myself I know I've almost always had two distinct lovers. One real, the other imagined and secretly desired.

Since I was little, I've always been worried that there would not be enough love to go around. This anxiety sprang from being the youngest child and having to move fast or there wouldn't be any bacon left at breakfast. When I was seven, after watching the movie *Ben-Hur* at Easter, I worried that my parents would sell me into slavery because there were too many mouths to feed. This bizarre panic transformed, after watching a television program about the Lindbergh kidnapping the following year, into a constant fear that kidnappers had their eye on *me*. I was compelled to double-lock all the doors and windows before bed.

At ten I became terrified that my parents might die and leave me an orphan like Oliver Twist. (I had the sound-track album of the musical *Oliver!* and feared I would suffer his fate.) I wanted to have *two* sets of parents. This would be like having a spare tire. In case anything horrible happened, like my parents' getting divorced or burned up in a hotel fire, it seemed wise to have their stunt doubles in reserve as an insurance policy. I could just wheel out the new pair of parents, change the tires, and off we'd go.

This ever-lurking feeling of scarcity, of never having enough love or parental attention, probably explains how I have gotten into this situation (one is too little; two, too much) with both of these men. But the polygamy isn't all bad. The persistent sorrow of working out so much hurt and rage on all three of our parts has jump-started a new conversation between my life and me. I can't just point at Doug and my marriage certificate (which gay people never get anyhow) to know who I am. Not depending on this certificate for my identity has gotten the latter part of my mid-thirties midlife crisis going in high gear. It has not always been pleasant.

One morning recently Doug was over at my house, snoozing happily in my bedroom after a sleep-over date. While I slurped my coffee, read my newspaper, and enjoyed my early-morning solitude, I heard Doug's quiet, sleep-blessed sounds coming from the other room. This moment felt like thousands of other mornings over the past decade.

It was different, though. After eleven years of cohabiting, Doug and I had stopped living together the previous year. I can put whatever spin you might want on this "breakup"; I vary it myself from day to day. The spiel can go from "high-drama divorce scenario that ruined our lives and has been the talk of arcane queer circles" to "New Age metamorphosis that allowed Doug and me to finally start communicating like grown-ups and shake up our worlds." It's definitely been a lot more the latter than the former, but these things dwell on a continuum. Depending on how the emotional weather has been, I can pitch the situation either way as eagerly as a Hollywood screenwriter up to bat for the big sell.

This change had been coming for a long time. You could see it on the horizon like a purple-and-green–clouded summer thunderstorm coming toward shore.

For a dozen years Doug and I had groomed each other and fought together and fucked together and ACTed UP together and made art together and had a dog together. We had grown up together. During all this time it had become increasingly even more routine for Doug and me to each have other lovers of varying degrees of intensity. Because of my extensive travels, such a habit had become especially typical for me. This behavior amused our friends; it became normalized over time, and a code of behavior was established. The cardinal rule over the years and travels was "Thou shalt not sleep with your boyfriend's boyfriend!"

Increasingly these other men were afforded special acknowledgment. Our outside-the-relationship lovers became honored supporting players, almost as if they were important representatives of neighboring duchies or principalities of love. This system of checks and balances had made someone like Andrew in New York or Billy from Philly a part of the family, a respected individual with rights and responsibilities. It had also continued to dilute the intimacy between Doug and me.

That unsuspecting frog on the stove top had finally just about gotten himself boiled.

Doug and I had become so woven together, we didn't know where one of us stopped and the other began. As I looked through the laundry, I couldn't honestly answer the question "Whose shirt is this really?" At what moment did we become "Doug & Tim"? Was there a precise instant of merging when that sneaky ampersand sent its tendrils out and enmeshed both our individual names into one? Was it when we moved into the loft on Bond Street together? Was it when we got Buddy? Was it when we went and got

tested for HIV together? Was it when our fights began
to echo those of our parents?

We had been dividing up the jobs for such a long
time. Column A and column B: You, the Jew, have the
feelings, and I, the WASP, will pay the bills. You cook
the lasagna and set the table, and I'll dig in the earth
and grow the tomatoes. You go to therapy, and I'll go
to Australia. It started to seem to both of us, I think,
that we would have to dynamite our house to see what
was still there. So after a particularly ruinous series of
fights, in 1995 Doug moved out.

Now, Doug might say that I didn't stop him, and I,
reflecting sadly, would acknowledge more than a cup-
ful of truth in that. But, really, I think there was some
intelligence afoot that told both of us that this needed
to happen to keep stirring the soup of our love.

So that morning, while Doug was still in bed after
our sleep-over date of the previous night, I thought
how odd to be dating a man you have been in a relationship with since Reagan's first presidential term! I
wondered why it felt so oddly awkward to see Doug. It
seemed that we had to relearn how we performed the
simplest activities together, like discovering how to
walk again after an especially severe broken leg. We
realized we hardly knew each other anymore. Yet we
still felt attached or — dare I even say it? — in love.

So we courted each other again, now almost as
strangers, with new emotional rules. We settled on a
routine that only sometimes included sleeping together. Sex together had become quite tender, not to be
taken for granted but certainly not entirely necessary.
We negotiated this new world of intimacy from different apartments, with Doug's being a few blocks away.
The new situation no longer made me feel like Anna

Karenina, everyone's favorite home wrecker. Indeed, this morning as I folded the laundry and drank my coffee, I felt relieved that Doug slept nearby.

Doug had brought his laundry over. All right, I'll be more accurate: Doug had brought his *dirty* laundry over. In one of the few gestures of bourgeois stability in our marriage, Doug and I had gone to Sears to buy a washer and dryer after we tested negative in 1990. Deciding it was reasonable to assume that we would probably not die before the warranty ran out, Doug and I made the big, almost yuppieish move of washing clothes at home. When we stopped living together, I got to keep the washer and dryer in the new arrangement (I had the hookups, after all), so when Doug and I were going to spend time together, it only made sense that he would bring his dirty clothes over to wash while we ate, fumbled like new friends in bed, and watched a movie on the VCR. (I had kept the VCR too.)

Some people might say that, under the circumstances, it wasn't the healthiest behavior for Doug to bring his dirty laundry over. They might suggest that we should mark our new boundaries a little more appropriately, not continue the rituals of our merged life together, try to consecrate how we spend time together separate from the banalities of daily life. I can see these people's points, but the laundry has still got to be done. If they're that concerned about it, these kvetches can go to the gross Laundromat in Venice Beach and wash both our dirty gym clothes. The people who say these things would also probably not be thrilled that Doug and I had also had hot sex the night before. This worked for us.

I finished my second cup of coffee and glanced toward the piles of laundry by the French doors lead-

ing to one of the many overgrown garden areas of my
yard. I padded over there and sat down on a swivel
desk chair that used to be in Doug's office. Opening the
laminated white dryer door, I pulled Doug's warm
clothes out of the still-swirling dryer and tumbled them
like a waterfall into a bright red plastic basket. I began
to fold Doug's clothes. I folded the aforementioned
Gold's Gym sweatshirt and the jockstrap. I folded the
Calvin Klein underwear that used to be mine before
Doug had "liberated" them. The nice tie-dyed shirt
Doug had just bought got neatly flattened and placed
on top of Doug's trademark deep violet sweatpants and
the University of Iowa Athletic Department shirt that
had belonged to Michael Callen, our great friend the
singer who had died in 1993. I folded the beat-up jeans
and the brand-new socks. Finally, I reached the bottom
of the basket and picked up Doug's favorite shirt, a
splendid dark purple sleeveless shirt that I had bought
for him on a tour to Australia in 1993.

My journey to perform at Mardi Gras in Sydney had
been problematic from the get-go. When I was a child,
my father had always filled me with glossy World War
II memories of his experiences in the world down
under. I was tremendously keyed up about the trip.
The huge and unrealizable expectations I had for a tri-
umphant experience in Oz (packed houses, great
weather, a cute Aussie romance) had made me a knot
of nerves the night before my flight. This had erupted
into a huge fight with Doug during which I shoved a
table so hard that I thought I had broken my hand.
("Now look what you've made me do! I've broken my
hand, and I won't be able to go to Australia!")

At the airport Doug and I sat for hours in the
Northwest Airlines terminal and floated the thought

that maybe we should live apart. I got onto the plane feeling as if I had no bones left in my body. I poured myself into my tiny seat on the 747. The too-cheerful flight attendant quickly gave me a screwdriver.

Flying to 33,000 feet can do wonders for easing the pressure cooker of feelings built up before a big trip. When I changed planes in Honolulu, I called Doug and we placed another Band-Aid on the troubles we were facing in our life together. We agreed to a peace treaty during my trip to the southern hemisphere, and we began a very tender communication with each other.

On account of our terrible fight before my departure, it was absolutely essential that I return to Los Angeles laden down with thoughtful and surprising presents for Doug. I had searched all over for the T-shirt that I was now folding. I had gotten a glimpse of it on a cute Aussie faggot on Oxford Street in Sydney one day. I thought to myself, *Doug would like that!* The T-shirt, I meant, not the boy.

I looked all over for this shirt. Clearly, it was a magical thing, covered all over in medieval cabalistic markings. It was kind of a Faustian batik pattern that would punch both Doug's New Age and Jewish mystical buttons. It would look good at the gym too. I had to find one.

I combed the trendy stores of Paddington and Darlinghurst. I madly shuffled through the racks of the T-shirt shops on the Circular Quay as tourists loaded themselves onto the ferry for Manly Beach.

I had given up hope, when, one day as I walked down Goulburn Street, I popped into the Wilderness Society of Australia gift shop. This place could fulfill all your needs for a stuffed duck-billed platypus or

Aborigine-styled kangaroo stationery. (I got one of each. Well, actually I got *two* platypuses. Platypi? Platypussies?)

I saw the T-shirt rack, and I approached nervously. There was a blur of purple at the very end. I tried not to get too excited. I even went and checked out the "authentic" boomerangs on the wall and then coolly approached the T-shirt from the other side. Special garments can be quite skittish, and I didn't want the shirt to catch my scent, bolt the store, and head for the bush. It was crucial to approach the shirt quietly, without any sudden movement. Pretending to admire the tea towels decorated with favorite tourist traps in New South Wales, I reached an arm behind me to scratch my back and then struck cobralike and grabbed the T-shirt from the rack one second before a stringy-haired German with a backpack could drag it back to Hamburg.

It was perfect: a gorgeous sleeveless affair detailed in every possible overlapping shade of purple, covered with a medieval Roman Catholic rendering of the cosmologies of the cabala. The Latin text described each level of that elegant and passionate Jewish universe. It was a mystical mandala design for living found on a T-shirt in an Australian crunchy-granola tourist shop! I checked the price tag: thirty Australian dollars! Expensive, but the item was definitely worth every Australian cent.

The next day I got on the plane to go home, secure in the feeling that I had found a good present for Doug, nestled safely next to the stuffed duck-billed platypuses in my suitcase. Good thing I didn't come home empty-handed. Without my knowledge I was also bringing Doug home a nice smoldering case of intestinal amebiasis from the Antipodes. In the last few days of my trip, I had hurriedly downed a massive dose of Flagyl, the hideous poison pills prescribed to seek out and destroy the parasites. I would soon discover that the Flagyl had not done the trick. This souvenir of a wild night of partying during Mardi Gras would make its presence felt in a few short weeks. However, that is another story from down under.

When I got back to the States, I gave Doug his various presents: the platypus, the kangaroo stationery, the Vegemite toast spread, and the amoebas. He liked all these things — well, almost all — but when I gave him his T-shirt, he flipped.

"It's the most magical T-shirt I have ever seen," he kwelled (oops, not that trip. The crabs episode was my two-week run in Provincetown) — I mean *kvelled.*

The Australian medieval cabala T-shirt became Doug's main look. He would wear it to teach his writing workshops and to do public appearances in; he even wore it on the book jacket of his first novel. I, who have never thought of myself as a good present finder, had hit the big time.

Now, two years and one divorce later, I folded up this special shirt and put it on top of the neatly stacked and comfortably clean laundry. More than any other, this shirt represented things honest and brave about this man I love. I felt like Lois Lane ironing Superman's tights as I smoothed the mysterious folds of the cabala. Placing my hand on this still-warm shirt, I could also sense Doug's frightening complexities, the way he needed to be more separate from me, the way he screamed at me, the way he couldn't stand my inability to talk in a vulnerable way, a screaming that only made me afraid to be more open.

Hoisting the basket full of folded clothes, I heard Doug shift a few feet away in the bedroom, his familiar soft footfalls heading toward the bathroom, the sound of piss on water, and then the return walk to more sleep. I put his laundry by his briefcase and returned to the buzzing dryer.

There was a second basket of laundry to be folded there by the washer and another familiar shirt. It looked a lot like Doug's cabala shirt. In fact, it was the same design, just rendered in different shades of brown and gold. This one didn't belong to Doug. It didn't belong to me. This shirt belonged to my other boyfriend, an Australian man named Alistair.

I had met Alistair in London when I was performing at the Institute of Contemporary Art in 1994. The ICA occupies a building that was built as the Royal Stables, then served as the German embassy, and today cradles galleries and a performance space. The end product of this ascending (some would disagree) trajectory from horses to Germans to artists occupies a building that looks like an extravagant wedding cake hunkering at the edge of the Mall. My fellow Los Angeles art criminals and I were doing a panel about multiculturalism and new performance in our troubled city. There were half a dozen of us, and we all had paid extra-baggage charges for the weighty set of opinionated ideas we had brought over from the States. We sat on the stage of the ICA and proceeded to hold forth about art practice in the diverse cultural reality of urban life.

I was jet-lagged and distracted, so I thought it would be good form to be quiet for a while. I knew my pals' rap pretty well already, so I half listened and started to scan the audience.

There was only one person I knew there, my friend Richard, with whom I was staying. Richard and I had enjoyed a sweet romance when I was in Sydney a year earlier. Compellingly sexy with his saucy swagger, Richard was certainly a likely candidate for the source of my case of Australian amoebas. He had been voted Person Most Likely to Get Rimmed when he graduated from Oxford. It's all a big circle, I "reckon," as the Aussies would say.

In London, Richard and I had reconfigured as friends, though my first night in the United Kingdom, we had gone back to his flat in Ladbroke Grove. I fucked him in his big loft bed, which had slatted sides, making it feel like an enormous crib. Even with my vast experience of loft-bed building, this one in Richard's flat was remarkable, the Westminster Abbey of loft beds. Richard had the wild look of a Dionysian toddler as he gripped the sides of the bed and threw his head far back into space.

Aside from Richard, the panel was attended by the usual ICA hipsters and smart folk who had paid their two pounds to hear American artists talk about "radical performances straight out of the diverse communities that make up the disintegrating urban mass of Los Angeles today — sex and survival in a city *in extremis*," as the glossy brochure promised. Lois, the no-nonsense and quite brilliant moderator, had staked out an interesting terrain for us to explore.

While I let my eyes float over the crowd, they suddenly locked target on the fourth row. Sitting there in the comfy chairs of the ICA was a gorgeous neo-Celtic grunge boy. That there would be a cute guy at the panel taking notes was not in itself an unusual event. Happily, it's an event that occurs frequently in my line of work. But there was an aura about him that made me rub my eyes with my balled-up fists for a second, because *he was wearing Doug's shirt!* Well, it wasn't Doug's exact shirt. But it was definitely its twin.

I saw that he was looking at me, and we made eye contact for a moment. Richard, in row two, noticed me staring at someone behind him, and he glanced over his shoulder with his usual sly so-what-else-is-new? grin.

The boy in row four was so pretty. He had that wonderful, slightly shocked Scots-Irish nineteenth-century look, like those old daguerreotype photos of the fresh-faced Civil War soldiers of both sides, so optimistic about their big adventure before they got slaughtered at Antietam or Chickamauga. This look on the alternative-styled queer boy in row four made him exactly the kind of young man Walt Whitman would favor on his shifts as a nurse back at the Civil War hospital. Old Walt would have given many lingering thigh massages to such a youth.

Row Four and I kept looking at each other. I felt both foolish and daring to be flirting in so public an arena. Remembering that I was on a public panel, I thought I'd better say something intelligent and earn my keep. I suppose I needed to show off for Row Four. Fortunately, I hadn't been talking too much, so I wouldn't be a panel hog if I spoke up now. I couldn't have this young man in Doug's shirt thinking I'm a dumb faggot.

I saw my opening. I leafed through my mental Rolodex of recently sharpened panel points and found a good one filed under "Urban History Narratives." As fate would have it, on the way to the panel, I had noticed right outside the ICA a bloated statue honoring some colonial general in India who had massacred hundreds of Indians during the Sepoy Rebellion in the

1850s. With this pinch of paprika-like local color, I could now tailor my urban-culture theories for London consumption by talking about the monument.

"There's a not-so-funny statue just outside the door of the ICA honoring a man who publicly mutilated hundreds of Indians," I said. "My brother's wife is Indian, with lots of family in New Delhi. I have two fabulous Indo-Euro completely cute nephews. What do I say to them if someday we should walk past that statue together? What do I say every day when I drive across town in L.A. on the Santa Monica Freeway, which was designed as a cement curtain to separate white Los Angeles from black Los Angeles? The complex layering of such contradictions and challenges, whether it's that fucking freeway or that statue just outside the ICA, is why I feel I need to live and do my creative work in the urban environment."

There were general good vibes for a point well-made. Now I could keep quiet for the rest of the panel. I was hoping my comments would have impressed the Celtic beauty. He kept looking up shyly at me under his beach-umbrella–size eyelashes.

I tried to pay attention to what was happening onstage, but I felt weirdly drawn to this man in the audience. I had a fateful feeling of a pressure cooker building up steam. It wasn't just the shirt, though the shirt was a big tip-off. There was a feeling inside me of a camera lens focusing for a close-up shot of my heart. With the flair of a computer graphic, the eye of the camera went right through skin and bone to gaze on the rhythm of my bellowing aorta. Everything else in the room started to recede, and I was left in the theater at the ICA, where I had performed many times in my life, with just a spotlight on me and this guy in row four.

I had a premonition that this man in the special shirt was going to change me and hold me and blow me up a bit too. I started to eyeball the exits in case I needed to escape. The talking around me got quieter, and this guy and I started to exchange a look between us more openly.

I was jolted back to my awareness when someone asked me a somewhat aggressive question. Fortunately, my automatic pilot had just gotten a tune-up.

"No, I don't think the 'body as text,' as you say, has been done to death," I improvised freely. "Until the book *Anal Pleasure and Health* is taught in junior high, I don't think we've done our job as artists interested in social change." The discussion shifted back to the Los Angeles riots at this point, the subject of choice from the English perspective. At least we didn't have to talk about freeway shootings.

I noticed that Richard, in row two, was starting to get a trifle annoyed with me for my obvious flirting in public and looked over his shoulder again, glaring at this guy with his best faux East End Kray brother I'm-going-to-kill-you look, which covered up his middle-class origins and Oxford degree. I tried to keep focused on the panel for the last few minutes of the Q&A. I invited all the queer men in the audience to the Gay Men's Performance Workshop I would be leading at the ICA in a few days.

Lois from the ICA thanked everyone for coming, and the audience began to disperse. I watched Row Four carefully and saw him look up at me one more time before his friends took him away up the stairs and out. I thought he might come to the party upstairs, but no. Richard smiled at me jokingly as he waved a mock scolding finger and said, "Naughty, naughty boy!"

I went upstairs to the reception and enjoyed the hos-
pitality of the ICA's free beer. I kept an eye on the door,
hoping the boy from below would make an appearance.
The room filled up with a bubbling energy of artists
talking about their work, cruising each other, and getting pissed, a slightly nicer word for drunk. A good time
was had by all, except for those, of course, who had a
soul-killing experience during the party because the
person they asked to go home with them said no.

The following Monday I arrived at the ICA early for
my workshop. Gliding up the ornate stairway to the
meeting rooms, I realized how nervous and excited I often
was before these gatherings in which I am supposed to
help a group of gay men explore their lives. I knew full
well how clumsy, how still unformed my efforts in this
area were. I was usually afraid someone would stand up
and accuse me of being a fraud from California.

I opened up the big French doors onto the Mall. My
heart broke the legal speed limit as I waited for the
first of the men to arrive. From far below I heard the
clip-clop of feet coming up the stairs. First some men
entered that I knew from other workshops I had done
in London. I greeted every guy as he came in, began
to connect the specific name with the specific nose
piercing (there were six Simons and two septum
rings). One man told me he had just come out two
months before. Another said his lover had died of
AIDS the previous week.

Just before it was time to begin, I slid down the ban-
ister to the bathroom on the floor beneath to take a
pee. I heard a new set of footsteps coming up the
stairs. I peeked down. There he was, walking up the
stairs, the guy from row four.

"Hi," I said.

"Oh, hello," he replied, seeming to look around for a possible route of escape.

"I saw you in the audience at the panel," I said as I tried to see if he had the cabala shirt on under his sweatshirt. He looked nervous for a second. It was a look I would come to recognize later as that of a man who is close enough to his actual feelings to find it difficult to be anything but honest. He had the alertness and the terror of a sleek animal during hunting season. It seemed like he didn't know what to say next.

"Well, thanks for coming," I said. "I'm Tim."

"I'm Alistair."

He pronounced the last syllable of his name so that it rhymed with *hair*. Speaking of hair, his had been cut recently, approximating the standard London faggot short do. He was tall and skinny in his grunge-rock splendor. It seemed like he was still learning to occupy the man's body he had suddenly found himself in. His chest and arms bore vivid hints of the grown-up strength that was going to arrive as soon as he shook off the final terrors of adolescence.

We shook hands. A buzz moved through me, like sticking a fork in a light socket. Our hands held each other and saw the future. I saw a kiss in a bus station in Scotland. I saw his asshole squeezing my dick dry a thousand times. I saw a tearful parting in Pittsburgh International Airport. I saw hours of long-distance phone calls. I saw hearts that might open to each other. I saw the impossibility of the situation becoming possible. Then the room came back into view.

Sensing an unusual accent even for England, I asked him, "Where are you from?"

"I've just arrived here to live," Alistair said. He shifted his overloaded shoulder pack from one side to the other. "I'm from Western Australia. I grew up in Perth, the world's most isolated industrialized city."

Uh-oh. Down Under. This may be the beginning of a little journey to the underworld. A journey that I had been postponing for some time.

"I saw you in the audience at our panel the other day," I said slowly, walking backward up the stairs so I could keep my eye on him. I just *had* to ask the big question. "Where did you get that unusual shirt you were wearing?"

"Oh, I love that shirt," he said, pleased the conversation had shifted to a manageable subject. "A friend gave it to me before I left Australia."

We looked at each other for a while. Our encounter should have been uncomfortable, but it wasn't. One of us should have been looking away and shuffling his feet, examining invisible marks on the scrubbed clean floors.

"Shall we go up?" I asked.

"Oh, right. Yes."

We walked up the same steps that the German diplomats used before their exile from the Mall in World War I — too close to Buckingham Palace and Whitehall, I suppose.

I jumped right into the workshop with this group of English, Scottish, Australian, and French faggots. I led them on a discovery: locating a story a part of their body would tell. I had them mark that place by having another man draw an appropriate sign or symbol for that story on their bodies. All at once the room was full of men drawing broken hearts or flames rising from pubic hair with pens of many colors. A sense of serious play filled the room as one man carefully drew angel's wings on the butt cheeks of another. The men in the group did honest and metaphor-rich pieces

about the feelings and energies that dwelt in their ass-
holes, love handles, and palms. Alistair, who I was
watching very carefully throughout the workshop, did
a haunting chanting piece about his throat as a place
of power and expression.

After the last drawing had been made and the final
body history shared, we held hands in a circle and
exhaled with a wild yawp that disturbed Prince
Charles just down the road. The workshop ended. In a
loud mob we retreated down the stairs to the ICA bar
for everyone to have a proper chance to, well, get
acquainted.

I had stood in this bar in London so many times
since I was twenty-three. It felt more familiar to me
than any bar in New York City. Long before I had ever
really gone out and picked up men in the States or
gone to clubs much, I had always seen London as the
place where I could do such things. My own personal
Tangier, in a way. London was the first city where I
had ever brought a man home to a hotel, the first city
where I had gone to a place like the gay club Heaven
to dance the night away. The first city where, when I
was twenty-three, I had drunk pint after pint with a
man in the bar at the ICA before he fucked me above
a tandoori restaurant in Hackney. Looking back, I
sometimes feel like I grew up as a faggot in London in
a way I never did in scary Los Angeles or New York.
And the bar at the ICA had been an important ground
zero in my queer life.

Our group made quite a splash at this late hour.
Lagers were quickly bought, and the socializing
began. Chatting with several small groupings of men
who had taken part in the workshop I had led, I
moved my way around the tables to touch base with

the workshop participants. Finally, I approached Alistair, who was talking to Kevin, a performer friend of mine. They were both leaning against the heavy wood of the bar. I tried not to be too proprietary as I slipped into their tête-à-tête, pretending to order a drink.

"What do you want to be doing in London, Alistair?" I asked, futilely signaling to the barman, who seemed to have much better things to be doing than serving us.

"I needed to get out of Western Australia," he answered. "It seemed like the time to get away from my Scottish Catholic family. I want to write and maybe work on some performances."

"Did you enjoy the workshop?" I asked, genuinely not looking for strokes, but I wouldn't turn them down if they came.

"Oh, yeah," he said, very enthusiastically. "That's a really interesting exercise. I feel like it's hard for me to inhabit my body, like my body is a big car that I'm sitting in, trying to learn how to drive."

Nonchalantly I sipped my pint of lager, which the barman had begrudgingly slid down the bar to me. "How old are you, anyway?" I thought I should find this out. The longer you wait, the more difficult it gets.

"I'm twenty-two," he replied, taking a big gulp of his bitters. "I just finished university. How old are you?"

"I'm thirty-five." Another sip. That was out. I have never yet lied about my age. That's something I'll save for later on, I suppose.

"Wow, really?" Alistair sputtered as he coughed up some beer. "Full on! You don't look that old. That's the same age as my oldest brother, Rory."

"What did you study at college in W.A.?" I quickly changed the subject to more neutral territory.

"Queer theory and gender studies, mostly." Alistair nodded deeply to underline his point.

I felt quite a bit more panicky at this point, now that he was actually becoming a real person, someone with a specific religion, a brother named Rory, and a college degree. Some kind of action would need to happen pretty soon.

I made a big yawn and said, "Well, I'm going to get going."

Alistair didn't miss a beat, "Yeah, I should go too — before the tube closes."

My friend Kevin, who had been talking to Alistair, said, "Oh, I'll walk out with you guys."

The three of us — oh, inconvenient number — walked out onto the Mall and crunched over the crackly gravel through Admiralty Arch. I checked my watch and saw that we had just missed the last tube for the night, so I knew it would be the night bus on Trafalgar Square for Alistair to get home. I thought maybe Kevin might have his eye on Alistair too.

"Shall we walk for a bit since we missed our train?" I suggested.

Alistair brightened at the thought of the night not being quite over. "Oh, yeah. That would be good."

We walked past the night bus stand and then up Charing Cross Road in the direction of Kevin's Islington digs. There is an awkwardness to these moments of three-needing-to-be-two. It raises the trauma of playground antics when I would ditch or be ditched amid the restless tangle of kids' power struggles. I felt a compulsion this particular night to find some time with this young man from Perth. What had catapulted him out of the Australian desert into hot summer London and a gay men's performance workshop? What would it take to lure him into my bed? What would happen to me if he said yes?

Once we had reached a point of no return on Kevin's walk toward Islington, I announced, "Well, I think I'll head back to Piccadilly and get a cab."

Now, if Alistair wanted to get home that night, he would need to head back to the night bus stand for the hourly departures. Thus, he would have to walk in that direction with me. We paused underneath the gated entrance of a tube station.

"I think I'll walk back with you for my bus," Alistair quietly offered.

General good-byes. I thought I saw a tiny little look from Kevin, a smart cookie who clearly observed this maneuver. He would give me high marks a few days later. Alistair and I slowly turned on our heel and headed back through the West End.

"When did you arrive in London?" I asked as we strolled by the souvenir shops crammed with Tower of London dishware.

"I got here about a week ago."

"How long are you going to stay?" I probed further.

"I'm going to live here. I'm staying with my exboyfriend Phil and some people in a flat in Kentish Town."

"How is it feeling so far?" I asked, herding him down Shaftsbury Avenue a little away from our previous route.

"London is so great," he replied. "I'm just glad to have left Perth. Australians always want to escape for a while. It felt like I couldn't make my life happen there. There's hardly any queer culture. Certainly nothing like the workshop we did tonight. I suppose I could have gone to Sydney, but my dad's Scottish, so I have a British passport. It all feels very new."

I looked at him. He was glowing from the thrill of these first few days of a big life adventure. Changing his hemispheres like other people change their shoes, Alistair had gotten himself into the life that he really needed to be in. I thought of my first few days in New York during another steamy July sixteen years before. His was a different story than mine, of course. Only the weather was the same.

We got to Piccadilly Circus and managed to cross over to the *Eros* statue without getting killed by the boomeranging taxicabs. (The Australianisms are already creeping in!)

Alistair and I marked a careful circumnavigation of the *Eros* statue. As always, I looked at that perfect ass on *Eros* and wanted to climb up and feel the smooth muscle of his polished bronze butt.

Alistair and I began to wear a shallow path into the pavement as we strolled around Piccadilly amid the guitar-strumming Eurotrash. We beat around the bush as we repeatedly circled the statue. It was getting late. I was staying for two nights at a hotel the ICA put me in in South Kensington while I was doing the workshop, so I knew we had somewhere to go.

"Would you like to come back to South Kensington, and we could hang out at my hotel room?" I asked, much more nervous than I let on.

"Yeah. That'd be quite nice," Alistair said. Then, so he could be sure I had heard his soft-spoken voice, he said more loudly, "Yes."

Within minutes Alistair and I were in a cab heading down the Mall. We leaned into each other a little bit as the cab swung wide around the queen's palace. Speaking little as our bodies' heat basted each other, I tried to figure out this man in the confines of the roomy black cab. Alistair was smart — not just book-smart, though he could out-Derrida the best of them — and had a quick and intuitive mind that he was learning how to wield. His sweet body had FUTURE written all over it.

We got to the Gloucester Road tube station and hauled ourselves out of the taxi. Alistair put up a valiant fight, but I insisted on paying the fare. We bought some yogurt and cookies at the all-night yuppieish market, a real improvement on late-night London shopping, and strolled down Cromwell Road to the Adelphi Hotel. I am tempted now to start using U.K.-ish words like *lorry* and *singlet* and *gym boots* in a sentence such as *"The lorry laden with milk for morning shook the ground of Cromwell Road under our plodding gym boots as Alistair and I walked toward Hotel Fate, our sweaty summer singlets sticking to our expectant skin."*

But I will resist that temptation.

At last we walked into the lobby of the Adelphi Hotel. The Indian night clerk gave me a dirty look that seemed to say, *I have to stay up all night to make money for my family in South London and let in poofters with their trade to fuck on the sheets that my cousin will rip off their bed tomorrow and have to scrub the come out of.* I thought he was almost going to protest my bringing a young man back to this fine establishment — in spite of the water damage in every room — but he seemed to decide Alistair was harmless and handed me my key.

We went up the once-plush stairs and into my tiny room, which did have a toilet, at least. We sat on the bed and ate some sweets. Chatting about Australia and what it was like to be foreigners in London, we lounged closely. While talking about Protestant and Catholic stuff, Alistair told me that he had chosen Saint Sebastian as his patron saint during his catechism. This truly bizarre piece of autobiography told me it was time to make a move.

I rolled my head against Alistair's chest. Up and over his collarbone went my lips until we began to kiss.

I felt quite peaceful. I was sitting down to a meal that would go on for years, a meal with a loaves-and-fishes feeling to it. In that spark of desire was a renewable resource that would keep feeding us for some time. We didn't need to have "great sex" right then. What was clear to me at that moment was that the raw materials were there, the frame of a building that might one day be able to provide some shelter. Alistair and I felt one another's skin through our clothes. I saw his body, so long and skinny and full of life.

I loosened his hanging-by-a-thread worn-out leather belt and let his pants fall to the floor. I was nervous. I felt some performance anxiety, thinking I should immediately have a throbbing tire iron in my pants the moment I begin to make out. I rubbed Alistair's belly and grabbed his dick and quickly noticed *he* didn't have an erection either. This gave me a surge of confidence. It also gave me an instant hard-on. The sizzling heat in the hotel room blew out the top of the thermometer at this point.

I reached into his pants and untucked that Australian shirt, the cabala accordioned up under his shoulders. I slowly pulled it from his body and then dropped it into my laundry basket back in Venice Beach, California.

I folded Alistair's shirt carefully and put it in the pile of his clothes on the magenta butterfly chair. Doug was still sleeping in my bedroom. Alistair had come to live in Los Angeles a few months after Doug and I had stopped living together. So which came first, the fiction or the real life, the chicken or the man? Don't ask me.

After our meeting in London that summer, Alistair and I had immediately launched on a high-drama high-wire high-stakes romance. The excitement started before we had even woken up the next day. As we slept that early morning at the Adelphi Hotel, a bomb went off at the Israeli consulate a few blocks away.

"What was that?" I groggily asked, groping my way up from a sweaty summer sleep.

Alistair didn't stir. Instead he made an enormous sound as he ground his teeth and then shifted over onto his stomach. This maneuver took particular effort, almost as if he were lifting a great weight in his dream. I peeked at him lying there in his naked skin, the single sheet tossed away during our fitful night's rest. The flimsy curtains didn't block out much of the sun that avalanched into the room on the hottest day of the brief English summer. Looking at the sleeping Alistair, I saw his man's torso just starting to peek out from his alternative-queer-boy–Dickensian-work-house-waif chest. Years later this would be something I would tease him about after he discovered the gym and acquired his set of muscles. ("When I met you, you looked like this..." I would say, making my shoulders and chest go all concave and Little Nell–ish.)

In the oddly hot sun on that first morning, I let my
fingers slip down the long slalom from his slender
shoulders down to the hollow of his lower back, a little
hair sprouting there in that wild-animal spot. I rubbed
him at the base of his spine in wider and wider circles.
I felt the steep ascent up Alistair's ass, which, along
with his heart, was the most developed part of his
body. It was full and muscular under my hand as the
cheeks rose and fell a tiny bit with each breath. I could
sense that the energy inside his body was closest to the
surface there, ready to burst out. My hand kept circling
his butt, as if I were a penny-arcade fortune-teller rubbing a crystal ball, hoping for a sneak preview of the
future. My hand rested there on his sweet behind. I fell
back to sleep as the second bomb exploded.

Unbeknownst to us, while we slept together that
first night in my hotel in South Kensington, some
strange events were already taking place. Alistair's ex-
boyfriend Phil, who, as is so often the case, was not
quite so ex as Alistair had led me to believe, had gone
to the police and reported Alistair missing. The ICA
received calls from the authorities about a young
Australian who had been kidnapped from a gay men's
performance workshop. Phil had given the police a
photograph, and they were walking the sex beats of
Hampstead Heath, asking if anyone had seen this
man, Alistair McCartney. Fortunately, they had not
yet begun dredging the Men's Pond when Alistair
finally returned home to Kentish Town. Phil's fury was
immediately unleashed, and Alistair had to endure an
inquisition of shame. After a confession had been
forced from him, Alistair and I spoke on the phone.

"Wow," I said upon hearing the terrible tale. "No one
has ever called the police because I took someone home."

"It's pretty grim around here," he said in a barely audible voice so that Phil couldn't hear. "You'll probably be too busy with your show to spend any more time, I reckon."

"Are you nuts?" I replied, wanting to dispel any thought Alistair had that I might not want to see him again. "Of course I want to hang out. I have to move out of the hotel today and back into my friend Richard's house. What are you doing tomorrow?"

Owing to the, perhaps, righteous rage of Alistair's *not* ex-boyfriend and my return to Richard's flat now that my free hotel days were used up, Alistair and I had nowhere private to get naked. We spent the rest of the time I was in London in chaste walks around the *Eros* statue. Like teenagers without anywhere to go, we courted each other and felt the accumulation of desire build up. While we talked about everything we needed to cover in just a few days, we used these monastic walks around *Eros* as a way of containing the energy between us without immediate squander. The time at the statue was a good way to see what existed between Alistair and me.

The night before I left London, Alistair walked me to the Piccadilly tube to say good-bye. Dodging the usual wandering herds of drunken football hooligans as we walked up Regent Street, we fell into a sharpened awkward silence.

"I feel pretty bummed that we didn't get to have more time together this week," I said, strangely troubled by the terms of this farewell. "I don't just mean that we didn't get to have sex again. I just wish we could have gotten to know each other more."

"Well," Alistair replied, trying out his new wise-beyond-his-years voice, "you never know. The world is a small place."

"Alistair," I said, deciding I was ready to launch a possibility, like a frail paper boat into a stiff current, "I'm going to be doing a queer men's project up in Scotland in a couple of months. Maybe you could come up and visit me in Glasgow."

"Yeah," he replied with a careful suppression of enthusiasm, a lesson he had probably learned well as a child as a means of avoiding disappointment. "I would like that. My dad was born in Glasgow."

"Oh, really?" I said. The thirteen-year age difference between us made any mention of his father an unwelcome association. I was much happier being equated with big brother Rory. "Well, let's plan on it. I'd better catch the last tube. We'll write and figure it all out."

We quickly kissed, and I lunged into the underground entrance, hoping I could make the final departure from Piccadilly.

Those days together in London were followed by days in Glasgow a few months later. The Scottish sojourn together in the city of Alistair's father seemed like a successful science project. Alistair and I had already deduced that there was a strong likelihood that our sexual energies could ignite. It also seemed there was a powerfully tender place of feeling between us. Let's just add the mists of Scotland and a nice Glaswegian flat and see if the atoms divide!

Well, they did.

In the middle of my life, when I was thirty-five, I walked through a weird forest in damp-as-a-dishrag Glasgow, and a young man from Australia leaped out and cast a spell on me with a magic potion as potent as anything Tristan ever swigged down on a dare.

Alistair had been raised by kangaroos in the bush. They had rescued him from his unappreciative parents when he was a baby. The kangaroo commandos had swept down into the suburbs of Perth during a barbecue. One big kangaroo punch knocked out Alistair's dad, and the rest of the family fled. The kangaroos hopped to the cradle and peered in. They lifted out the youngest queer-boy child and spirited him out to the desert.

He was still small enough to fit in one kangaroo's pouch, so they raised him as the joey they never had. The kangaroos fed him only Patti Smith songs, creamed Rimbaud, and evaporated metaphor milk. Alistair grew strong but didn't talk much. He felt alone and hungered for a friend. Finally, the kangaroos knew they had to let him go, so they hopped with him to a major international airport and got him a ticket to London on Royal Jordanian Air (one of the kangaroos had enough frequent-flier miles). I met him fresh from the pouch.

As we walked in that murky Scottish forest, Alistair double-dared me to live more honestly. After years of my being a married man with a shifting merry-go-round of guys on the side, this man walked up to me and said, "I want some more." (Sorry, but if you knew Alistair, you would know it's appropriate to keep working the Dickens references.) As wags would note to me over coffee, "Well the chicken has certainly come home to roost!"

The time in Scotland was followed three months later by journeys together in the United States to such homo hot spots as Davis, California, and Hartford, Connecticut. During this time Alistair and I discovered a charged feeling and sex connection that ping-ponged both of us around the not-so-padded rooms of our lives. In spite of the obvious impossibility of our situation, we kept upping the ante. Everything but the kitchen sink and the taboo words "I love you" were thrown at each other. After lots of discussion, heaps of sex, and a bathtub full of tears, I told Alistair that there was no practical future for us, and he went back to London with his heart in two pieces on a rainy day.

Meanwhile, back on the Venice Beach farm, Doug and I were struggling with a few weeks of torturous couples counseling. It seemed like we needed some space from each other, so Doug and I finally agreed that we should stop living together. He found a nice little bungalow on a quiet street three blocks away, and we settled into a trial separation. We began to get acquainted all over again as we started to date after many years of living together.

As I tried to create my own life in a house Doug and I had shared for six years, I remembered that Alistair was miserable in London. It took a couple of thousand dollars in transatlantic calls for it to become clear that Alistair was completely pissed off and unsatisfied by the "abort mission" approach to our relationship. He sent me a ranting love manifesto–poem:

I will harness the energy from all our love and fucking to my heart like a horse. It will carry me through this confusion to a state of grace. I will fly to your house in the dead of night, drug the boyfriend, the dog, and
*   fuck you*
sweetly like the devil in Rosemary's Baby. *You will*
*   wake up*
with something coiled in your stomach, a serpent, an
*   ache.*
Things will taste weird, different. The aftertaste of me.
This will give birth to something.

What else could I do? Four months after Doug and I had stopped living together, Alistair flew to Los Angeles to begin his life there. The understanding, expensively negotiated on the phone, was as follows: Alistair and I would explore our relationship with each other. We would *not* be living together. I was still in a relationship with Doug, so Alistair and I would need to create lives that were independent and not "merged," the word of the day provided by Doug.

Now, I imagine that lots of other people have shared similar delusions about how certain situations might work out just fine. I'm sure Nixon, for example, thought no one would really be upset by an eensy-weensy little break-in at a Washington hotel. Alistair was so busy bailing water with a teacup off the decks of his emotional *Titanic* that he was ready to agree to anything. I was suffering from alternating bouts of abject neediness and numb isolation as I wandered helpless on my own sinking ship like Captain Ahab. Doug was getting bored with all these shenanigans and wanted to torpedo all these listing vessels. He had sensibly begun the process of returning to school to become a therapist.

Alistair's arrival in Los Angeles set off World War III. Every possible feeling of betrayal and panic and boundaries and abandonment and sexual hurt exploded over our heads. I was both delighted and freaked out to have this young man I loved here in Los Angeles with me. Doug was hurt and disappointed that I had invited this Australian into our very fragile and complicated situation. Alistair found himself in the middle of a huge tug-of-war between two men who had been boyfriends since the signing of the Declaration of Independence. A difficult period ensued.

Doug sensibly distanced himself from this shitty situation. His pulling away from me totally unhinged me. The reality of Alistair's presence began to cause a reactor core meltdown inside me. I felt the many years of my relationship with Doug slipping away. Suddenly Alistair was actually in my bed with real needs that I felt unable to satisfy. I felt my boundaries start to disintegrate.

"Alistair," I said as we lay catatonic in bed together after receiving an angry fax from Doug, "I'm losing it. I need both of you. It's like I'm being ripped in two. I'm so fucked-up. I feel everything falling apart. I'm..."

I couldn't talk anymore. My face shook, and all my energy was being used to stop myself from letting loose. Alistair stroked me, midwifing my tears almost the way we helped each other come. I finally broke down and cried. I fought it off as long as I could, and at the same time I wanted it so bad. At last I felt the glacier crack and start to move. A sound came from inside my body like a scared animal that sees the knife on his way to being slaughtered. I bawled as loud as I could for the tears I couldn't cry with Doug, feeling the sorrow for the world we had lost, all the joy of a more honest life ahead.

Alistair held his body to mine as he coaxed the earthquake to happen. We both had hard-ons as I wept. A new kind of turn-on: two men allowing life and sadness to wash over them, the energy that comes when we let go. He licked my eyes and drank my tears as he had eaten my come earlier that day. I felt my eyes watered by these tears, like a thirsty crop after a long drought.

I faxed Doug that I was breaking down. He could hear the WASP veneer shredding. Somehow those tears helped Doug and me find a new ground with each other. We cobbled together a loose agreement to continue seeing how our relationship unfolded. Part of that unfolding included Alistair's being part of my life.

Tim goes into therapy.

Alistair goes into therapy.

Doug becomes a gay-centered activist-therapist.

This was not going to be easy, but a new kind of living put itself together. The future would include many difficult times. A late-night pileup in the supermarket had all three of us meeting together for the first time (my shopping cart full of Weight Watchers lasagna). I felt like crawling under the frozen turkeys.

Then there was the day Alistair would go straight from a romantic weekend in Palm Springs with me to Doug's Gay Men's Writing Workshop. Alistair read a long piece in the workshop detailing the most intimate sex acts he and I had had all weekend by the pool. Doug, in his reaction to this, started out pedagogical but ended up homicidal.

Eventually Doug and Alistair became *close,* their common core drawing them near. Naturally, they started to flirt while I was in San Francisco for two weeks. As the inevitable erotics began to boil over between them, Doug and Alistair tried to find a way to handle the craziness of the arrangement. Being more sensible than I, they didn't have sex. It's lucky I wasn't gone *three* weeks.

Strangely, new ways of communicating and being honest with one another started to present themselves. Alistair got his own apartment, started making performances, and slowly began to trust me more in this bizarre arrangement. I tried to stop covering up and avoiding difficult feelings, a full-time job for me. Doug

realized that I loved him for life, and we began to discover new ways of being partners.

Doug gives Alistair a red sweatshirt.

Alistair gives Tim a green shirt.

Tim has a pair of Doug's underwear.

It all comes out in the wash. That's why I was folding the laundry. I like doing this for men I love. It's one
of the few places where my Susie Homemaker tenden-
cies shine. They certainly don't show up in the cooking and cleaning department. I also don't think my
instinct for hacking with a machete at the bamboo
that surrounds my house makes much of an impression on a man with whom I'm intimate. But when I
face off with the washer and dryer, I can sit there and
fold the clothes of the men in my life. There is an order
and a sweetness to the gesture. These are clothes that
go over bodies, cupping the balls. They trace the leg,
are removed during sex, warm the heart, and get
crumpled into sweaty balls and put in the hamper.

In these times with Doug and Alistair, I felt my
heart ripped out of my body and tied up with
kerosene-soaked rope and dragged down the dusty
streets of Dodge City. I've felt my balls get pulled west
while my dick floors it for NYC. I've seen my head
float like a balloon so far from my body that it has no
idea how to get back. There's just a scary feeling that
a nasty child is nearby with a big pin, hunting for me.

Like a silent-film heroine, I've been tied up to the
saw, my head moving closer and closer to the whizzing
blade, while Simon Legree carefully marks a line
down the middle of my forehead, nose, chin, chest,
belly, dick, one ball to one side, one to the other, in
order to cut me in two, as precise as a slice of lox. I've
felt the blade start to cut me in half, head to toe — the

only solution that makes any sense. I've felt an earthquake pull the fault lines along the breaking point of the past and the future.

I see that I need both these men in different ways. I've known what it is to need the history of one, the newness of the other; the strength of one, the tenderness of the other. Part of me wants to be a respectable married man; the other part wants to eat my young lover's asshole till I find my way to China. I need the wisdom of one, the intuition of the other. I want to be daddied and Daddy, held and holder, fucked and fucker.

There are two laundry baskets in front of me. There are two men before me. I have been on a journey these past few years with these men that has cracked me open, accelerated the gray in my hair, stretched me, and made me a less immature man.

I went Down Under. I made my beds, and I had to lie in them. (Lay in them?) I realize now that I created a hell for myself so I could fall into it — a hell that would be so hot and terrible that it would cook me and help me change and crack through the calcium deposits that have taken half of my life to build up. I feel lucky to have found my way into hell.

As I folded the laundry, I looked at the concentric circles of the cabala shirt. How human to think we can chart and diagram our journey through life. The overlapping parabolas made a little design like the rings of hell in Dante's *Inferno*. I sat and traced my fingers over the faint lines pressed deep into the weave of the shirt. As I looked at Doug's (or was it Alistair's?) shirt, I tried to imagine what *my* underworld would look like. If my hell were a theme park, would there be a ride in which all the men I lured into loving me before retreating into the walled fortress of my marriage get to stone me with bronze-plated copies of the love letters I wrote them? Maybe there would be a spook house where my feet are locked in ice for a millennium or two as penance for all the tears I froze, the ones I shut off like a big faucet at Niagara when my fifth-grade teacher told my parents I had cried hysterically because I couldn't check out *Charlotte's Web* from the library. I carefully folded the shirt, not wanting to mix up those discrete rings of hell, and placed it on the top of the laundry basket.

It seemed like it was time to wake up Doug. Over the years I've arrived at an intuitive sense of this, knowing when it's time to wake up the men in my bed. With Doug the usual recipe is find the balance between my needs for some solitude in the morning with his need to find as much sleep as he can. The time by myself allows me to fold the laundry.

I went into the dark purple-walled bedroom and peeked at Doug's sleeping face. He looked so still and angelic, the little boy inside him hovering there in sleep. I climbed back into bed and let the heat and nearness of my body register a gentle wake-up call.

"Wanna get up now, Dougie?"

"What time is it?"

"Ten thirty. Should I get you some coffee?"

"I'll get up."

I went into the kitchen and poured a cup of really strong coffee into the chipped Veselka mug, purchased from my Ukranian restaurant of choice in the East Village.

Doug dragged himself slowly from his particular dream terrain back into the familiar Venice Beach morning. As he stretched his fingers and toes, he took the time he needed to slowly return to the world. From years of training, I knew better than to speak to Doug for at least twenty minutes into his second cup of coffee. We read the paper, quietly taking in the news of babies being found in New Jersey Dumpsters and of all the promising AIDS treatments. I had heard from Andrew in New York that he was on the new drug cocktail and doing quite well.

Figuring we had left the No-Speak Zone, I said to Doug, "Good morning. How are you feeling today?"

"I'm okay," he said. "Have you thought more about what we should do for Thanksgiving?"

"I've been trying not to think about it," I answered truthfully. "It freaks me out how to make these holidays work now, with you and Alistair. It feels like a big bomb waiting to go off."

"It's tricky," Doug said, putting his cup of coffee down. "I have a fantasy that you and Alistair and my friend Mike and I could maybe have the meal together."

Doug had been seeing Mike pretty seriously for a few months. Our common challenges with our individual boyfriends had become a frequent point of discussion on our sleep-over dates.

"Well, that could be good," I said, meaning it but also a little scared at the prospect.

"It might be a little soon for that, though," Doug added on the other hand. "Maybe we should think about that for Christmas."

"Okay. Hey, Dougie, is this your underwear or mine?" I asked, holding up a pair of standard homo issue Calvins.

"If they have the buttons, they're mine."

"Are you sure?" I, ever the lawyer, asked.

"Yup. Hey, you folded all my laundry. Thanks. You didn't need to do that. Thanks!"

"It's okay."

"I'm glad we talked a little about the holiday stuff," Doug said. "That's probably more important than what we actually do on Thanksgiving."

Doug and I hugged each other, a good long one. Many feelings lived inside of our embrace. There was more than a little sadness between the two of us for the loss of the world we had once known, a world where it was certain that Doug and I would make a turkey together. In that hug was a reach for the honesty to live as we really are now, not as the young men who met in Manhattan before the war.

As we held each other, I felt surrounded by a promise to continue to love and know each other for the rest of our lives, lives that now included other loves and sorrows. Doug and I no longer had to *be* each other.

The dryer made its annoying buzz. I needed to get back to the laundry. Doug's black jeans were still a bit damp: That mysterious tiny pocket on the Levi's just never seemed to get dry. I balled up a pair of Alistair's blue socks that I had given him last Christmas. There was a small hole in the heel of one of them, the fabric worn through by the reaching stride of his 25-year-old bounce down Main Street in Venice.

I noticed a forgotten basket of laundry stashed behind the chair by the washer. Inside were many shirts that I hadn't seen for a long time, shirts that had whispered across the skin of my chest over many years.

Here was the cutoff Patti Smith T-shirt I wore all through my senior year of high school, the ragged arm holes now trailing their threads.

Underneath it was the denim shirt that David got stabbed in twenty years ago, right before he was the first man to ever make love with me. I put my finger through the hole on the collar where the ice pick went into his neck.

I folded the Harvey Milk T-shirt I got in San Francisco during my hitchhiking adventure. The colors were thin, and the fabric was even thinner where the SUPER in SUPERVISOR was underlined in a graphic gesture.

I saw the burned lapel of the pajama top I wore when John was still alive. The ashes were in a plastic bag inside the pocket of the safety-pin–cuffed red shirt I wore, in my interpretation of holiday spirit, to the Christmas party where I met Doug.

SILENCIO = MUERTE, read the crumpled-up ACT UP T-shirt I wore at too many demonstrations. I pressed flat the stretched-out neck where the cop grabbed me around my throat, dragging me down the hallway of the Federal Building in Los Angeles.

I found a sleeveless once-white shirt (obviously I didn't wash it separate from the colors), like something the lounging Vinnie would have worn in front of Oki-Dog in Hollywood. I was wearing this one when Andrew and I were pulled toward each other. The shirt had a big come stain on it, down by the left nipple.

Finally, there at the bottom of the laundry basket, was Doug's cabala T-shirt, right next to Alistair's.

I sat there with my dirty laundry, these shirts that I've worn close to my body, that have taught me. These shirts that remind me of the men who have made me who I am. Could these clothes ever *really* get clean? All the advertisements and all our moms told us it was so. They promised that if we scrubbed and soaked just right, we could make anything its whitest white again.

  But these shirts were covered in the blood, the come, and the sweaty salts of my whole life. I don't want to wash those things away. I want to remember their fierce and faded colors every day I'm lucky enough to breathe. I want to believe that in this memory, I can find a path right now through the messy tumble of my life. I want to discover the ways I will clothe my heart and belly and shoulders when I am the man I hope to become.

  I'll have to wait to find out. That shirt still isn't dry.